Advanced Language Practice

MICHAEL VINCE

Heinemann English Language Teaching
A division of Reed Educational and Professional Publishing Limited
Halley Court, Jordan Hill, Oxford OX2 8EJ

OXFORD   MADRID   FLORENCE   ATHENS   PRAGUE
SAO PAULO   MEXICO CITY   CHICAGO   PORTSMOUTH (NH)
TOKYO   SINGAPORE   KUALA LUMPUR   MELBOURNE
AUCKLAND   JOHANNESBURG   IBADAN   GABORONE

ISBN 0 435 24124 9 with key
      0 435 24125 7 without key

© Michael Vince 1994

First published 1994

The author would like to thank everyone who has
made comments on this book, and in particular my
editors Xanthe Sturt Taylor and Sue Jones. Many
thanks also to colleagues and students in Athens at
The British Council Teaching Centre, at CELT
Athens, and at Profile, Athens.

The publishers would like to thank Tony Triggs

Original design by Mike Brain

Illustrated by:
Rowan Barnes-Murphy (p18, 127, 129, 133)
Ed McLachlan (p 5, 11, 16, 22, 52, 68, 70, 99, 103, 112, 134)
David Parkins (p3, 10, 12, 37, 45, 51, 73, 123, 140, 145)
Bill Stott (p 40, 46, 75, 83, 98, 110)

Printed and bound in Egypt by Sahara Printing Co.
96 97 98 10 9 8 7 6

Contents

Vocabulary

Words and Phrases

Index

Introduction

THIS BOOK is designed to revise and consolidate grammar points at the level of the CAE and Proficiency examinations. As many advanced learners find the use of vocabulary the most challenging feature of advanced study, the book includes practice with many important lexical features, as well as with topic vocabulary, and with the organization of texts.

The grammar section includes both basic revision and more advanced points. There are also sections on spelling and punctuation. Units on phrasal verbs, prepositions and text features are also included. The grammatical information provided can be used for reference when needed, or worked through systematically.

The vocabulary section includes focus on topic vocabulary, on collocations and on idiomatic phrases. This section also recycles work on prepositions, particles and phrasal verbs.

This book can be used as a self-study reference grammar and practice book or as supplementary material in classes preparing for either the CAE or Proficiency examinations. If used for classwork, activities can be done individually or co-operatively in pairs or small groups.

There are regular progress tests which include forms of testing commonly used in both CAE and Proficiency. The materials cover a range of difficulty appropriate to both examinations.

Unit 1 Tense consolidation: present time

Explanations

Basic contrasts: present simple and present continuous

1 Present simple generally refers to:
   Facts that are always true
   *Water **boils** at 100 degrees Celsius.*
   Habits
   *British people **drink** a lot of tea.*
   States
   *I **don't like** gangster films.*

2 Present continuous (progressive) generally refers to actions which are in progress at the moment. These can be temporary:
   *I**'m staying** in a hotel until I find a flat.*
   They can be actually in progress:
   *The dog **is sleeping** on our bed!*
   Or they can be generally in progress but not actually happening at the moment:
   *I**'m learning** to drive.*

State verbs and event (action or dynamic) verbs

1 State verbs describe a continuing state, so do not usually have a continuous form. Typical examples are:
   believe, belong, consist, contain, doubt, fit, have, know, like, love, matter, mean, own, prefer, understand, seem, suppose, suspect, want, wish

2 Some verbs have a stative meaning and a different active meaning. Typical examples are:
   be, depend, feel, have, measure, see, taste, think, weigh
   Compare these uses:

State	Event
*Jack **is** noisy.*	*Jill **is being** noisy.*
*Deirdre **has** a Porsche.*	*We **are having** an interesting conversation!*
*I **think** I like you!*	*David **is thinking** about getting a new job.*
*This fish **tastes** awful!*	*I **am** just **tasting** the soup.*
*I **feel** that you are wrong.*	*I **am feeling** terrible.*
*This bag **weighs** a ton!*	*We **are weighing** the baby.*
*It **depends** what you mean.*	*I **am depending** on you.*

   The differences in 2 apply to all tenses, not just to present tenses.

1

Other uses of present continuous	**1**	Temporary or repeated actions

1 Temporary or repeated actions
This use emphasises a temporary or repeated habitual action.
> *My car has broken down, so I **am walking** to work these days.*
> *Are you **enjoying** your stay here?*

2 Complaints about bad habits
> *You **are always complaining** about my cooking!*
Other possible adverbs are: *constantly, continually, forever*

3 With verbs describing change and development
> *Things **are getting** worse!*
> *More and more people **are giving up** smoking.*

Other uses of present simple

1 Making declarations
Verbs describing opinions and feelings tend to be state verbs.
> *I **hope** you'll come to my party.*
> *I **bet** you don't know the answer!*

2 Headlines
These are written in a 'telegram' style, and references to the past are usually simplified to present simple.
> *Ship **sinks** in midnight collision.*

3 Instructions and itineraries
Instructions and recipes can be written in present simple instead of in imperative forms. This style is more personal.
> *First you **roll out** the pastry.*
Itineraries are descriptions of travel arrangements.
> *On day three we **visit** Stratford-upon-Avon.*

4 Summaries of events
Plots of stories, films etc, and summaries of historical events use present (and present perfect) tenses.
> *May 1945: The war in Europe **comes** to an end.*
> *... At the end of the play both families **realise** that their hatred had caused the deaths of the lovers ...*

5 Historic present in narrative and 'funny stories'
In informal speech, it is possible to use the 'historic present' to describe past events, especially to make the narration seem more immediate and dramatic.
> *... So then the second man **asks** the first one why he **has** a banana in his ear and the first one **says** ...*

Activities

1

Choose the most appropriate words underlined.

a) I haven't decided yet about whether to buy a new car or a second-hand one. But I think about it/I'm thinking about it.

b) All right, you try to fix the television! But I hope/I'm hoping you know what you're doing!

c) Every year I visit/I'm visiting Britain to improve my English.

d) It's time we turned on the central heating. It gets/It is getting colder every day.

e) Of course, you're Mary, aren't you! I recognise/I am recognising you now.

f) What's the matter? Why do you look/are you looking at me like that?

g) The film of *War and Peace* is very long. It lasts/It is lasting over four hours.

h) I can see from what you say that your mornings are very busy! But what do you do/are you doing in the afternoons?

i) I'm going to buy a new swimming costume. My old one doesn't fit/isn't fitting any more.

j) That must be the end of the first part of the performance. What happens now/is happening now?

2

Choose the most suitable word or phrase to complete each sentence.

a) What exactly ....B....?
   A) is this job involving   B) does this job involve

b) Who exactly ....?
   A) does own this car   B) does this car belong to

c) .... that we have been here for six months already!
   A) Do you realise   B) Are you realising

d) I'd like to stay longer. But .... just for the weekend.
   A) I come   B) I've come

e) Terry is in bed. He .... flu.
   A) has   B) is having

f) This new teaching job is really difficult, but ....
   A) I survive   B) I'm surviving

g) What .... on that notice?
   A) does it write   B) does it say

h) Ladies and gentlemen, I .... this ship *HMS Highlight*.
   A) name   B) am naming

i) Absolutely! I .... with you completely.
   A) agree   B) am agreeing

j) .... this car. Do you want to buy it?
   A) I sell   B) I'm selling

3

Put each verb in brackets into the most suitable present tense.

a) I *hear* (hear) that you have been promoted. Congratulations!
b) British people .... (drink) more and more wine, apparently.
c) I hope Sarah will be here soon. I .... (depend) on her.
d) Please be quiet! You .... (continually interrupt).
e) Hey, you! What .... (you think) you're doing?
f) Could you come here please? I .... (want) to talk to you now.
g) Jane is away on holiday so Linda .... (handle) her work.
h) To be honest, I .... (doubt) whether Jim will be here next week.
i) You've only just started the job, haven't you? How .... (you get on)?
j) Pay no attention to Graham. He .... (just be) sarcastic again.

4

Rewrite each sentence, beginning as shown, so that the meaning stays the same.

a) What's your opinion of Ted's new book?
What do *you think of Ted's new book*?
b) Nigel keeps interrupting me.
Nigel is..
c) What is the meaning of this word?
What does..
d) The number of people who own bicycles is increasing.
More and more people..
e) What about going to that new film at the Rex tonight?
How do ....
f) What is the weight of that piece of meat?
How much ....
g) Never mind about the price, just buy it!
The price..
h) There's a smell of onions in this room.
This room...
i) What is inside the box?
What does...
j) Paul has flu.
Paul is...

5

Put each verb in brackets into the most suitable present tense.

I work in a large office with about thirty other people, most of whom I (1) *know* (know) quite well. We (2) .... (spend) most of the day together, so we have all become friends. In fact, most of my colleagues are so interesting, that I (3) .... (think) of writing a book about them! (4) .... (take) Helen Watson, for example. Helen (5) .... (run) the accounts department. At the moment she (6) .... (go out) with Keith Ballantine, one of the sales representatives, and they (7) .... (seem) very happy together. But everyone (except Helen apparently) (8) .... (know) that Keith (9) .... (always make) eyes at Susan Porter. But I (10) .... (happen) to know that Susan (11) .... (dislike) Keith. 'I can't stand people who (12) .... (apologise) all the time!' she told me. 'And besides, I know he (13) .... (deceive) poor Helen. He (14) .... (see) Betty Wills from the overseas department.' And plenty of other interesting things (15) ....

(go on) For instance, every week money (16) .... (disappear) from the petty cash box. When you (17) .... (realise) that someone in your office is a thief, it (18) .... (upset) you at first. But I (19) .... (also try) to catch whoever it is before the police are called in. I'm not going to tell you who I (20) .... (suspect). Well, not yet anyway!

6

Rewrite each sentence so that it contains the word in capitals, and so the meaning stays the same.

a) Charles and his father are exactly alike. LOOKS
   Charles looks just like his father.

b) The cost of excursions is part of the price of the holiday. INCLUDES

....

c) I find working here really enjoyable. ENJOYING

....

d) I study hard, so I spend a lot of time in the library. MEANS

....

e) What's your opinion of Wendy's new painting? THINK

....

f) Sunrise is at 4.30 tomorrow morning. THE SUN

....

g) What's on your mind at the moment? ABOUT

....

h) Neil has the bad habit of getting in people's way. ALWAYS

....

i) I am losing my voice. GOING

....

j) How long is that wall? DOES

....

7

Choose the most suitable word or phrase underlined.

a) I work in this office all this year/all the time.
b) Are you studying French for long/at the moment?
c) I am not making much money these days/so far this year.
d) The food tastes worse now/usually. You've put too much salt in.
e) We normally/forever get in touch with customers by post.
f) Pete was ill but he is getting over his illness currently/now.
g) I'm feeling rather run down lately/at present, doctor.
h) I always stay on duty since/until six o'clock.
i) People continually/traditionally prepare coloured eggs at Easter.
j) Fortunately the baby now /recently sleeps all night.

8
Identify any possible errors in these sentences, and correct them *if necessary*.

a) I'm depending on you, so don't make any mistakes!
   (*no errors*)

b) Is this total including the new students?
   Does this total include the new students?
   ....

c) Excuse me, but do you wait for someone?
   ....

d) These potatoes are tasting a bit funny.
   ....

e) How are you feeling today?
   ....

f) I look forward to hearing from you.
   ....

g) I have a feeling that something goes wrong.
   ....

h) What's that you're eating?
   ....

i) Are you hearing anything from Wendy these days?
   ....

j) I think you're being rather mean about this.
   ....

Unit 2 Tense consolidation: future time

Explanations

Basic contrasts: *will*, *going to*, present continuous

1 *Will* is normally known as the predictive future, and describes known facts, or what we suppose is true.
> *I'll be late home this evening.*
> *The company **will** make a profit next year.*

This can also take the form of an assumption:
> *That'll be Jim at the door.*

This means that I suppose it is Jim.

2 *Will* is also used to express an immediate decision:
> *I'll take this one.*

Decisions expressed with *going to* refer to a more distant point in the future. Other uses of *will* and *shall* are in Units 11 and 12.

3 *Be going to* describes intentions or plans. At the moment of speaking the plans have already been made.
> *I'm **going to** wait here until Carol gets back.*

Going to is also used to describe an event whose cause is present or evident.
> *Look at that tree! It's **going to** fall.*

Decisions expressed with *going to* refer to a more distant point in the future. Other uses of *will* and *shall* are in Units 11 and 12.

4 Present continuous describes fixed arrangements, especially social and travel arrangements. A time reference is usually included.

5 Contrasts between *going to* and *will* may be a matter of speaker preference. The first two examples in 1 would not seem inappropriate if *going to* was used, possibly because the sense of the cause is present in the speaker's mind.

Future continuous

1 This describes an event which will be happening at a future point.
> *Come round in the morning. I'll **be painting** the kitchen.*

2 It can also describe events which are going to happen anyway, rather than events which we choose to make happen.
> *I won't bother to fix a time to see you, because I'll **be calling** into the office anyway several times next week.*

3 In some contexts future continuous also sounds more polite than *will*.
> ***Will** you **be going** to the shops later? If you go, could you get me some potatoes?*

4 It can also be used to refer to fixed arrangements and plans.
> *The band **will be performing** live in Paris this summer.*

Future perfect

1 This has both simple and continuous forms, and refers to time which we look back at from a future point.
> *In two years' time I'**ll have finished** this book.*
> *By the end of the month, I'**ll have been working** for this firm for a year.*

2 It can also be used to express an assumption on the part of the speaker.
> *You **won't have heard** the news, of course.*

This means that I assume you have not heard the news.

Other ways of referring to the future

1 *Is /are to be*
This is used to describe formal arrangements.
> *All students **are to** assemble in the hall at 9.00.*

See also Units 11 and 12 for uses expressing obligation.

2 *Be about to, be on the point of, be due to*
Be about to and *be on the point of* both refer to the next moment.
> *I think the play **is about to** start now.*
> *Mary **is on the point of** resigning.*

Be due to refers to scheduled times.
> *The play **is due to** start in five minutes.*
> *Ann's flight **is due** at 6.20.*

3 Present simple and present perfect
Present simple is used to refer to future time in future time clauses.
> *When we **get** there, we'll have dinner.*

Present perfect can also be used instead of present simple when the completion of the event is emphasised.
> *When we'**ve had** a rest, we'll go out.*

4 Present simple is also used to describe fixed events which are not simply the wishes of the speaker.
> *Tom **retires** in three years.*

Similarly, calendar references use the present simple.
> *Christmas **is** on a Tuesday next year.*
> *It's all go – next week I **have** my operation; then the week after that I **go** on holiday …*

Other future
references

1 *Hope*
This can be followed by either present or future tenses.
    *I hope it **doesn't** rain.*
    *I hope it **won't** rain.*

2 Other verbs followed by *will*.
Most verbs of thinking can be followed by *will* if there is future reference.
These include: *think, believe, expect, doubt*.
    *I **expect** the train will be late.*
    *I **doubt** whether United will win.*

3 *Just/just about to*
Just can be used to describe something on the point of happening.
    *Hurry up! The train **is just leaving/just about to leave**.*

4 *Shall*
The use of *shall* for first person in future reference is generally considered to
be restricted in British English and possibly declining in use. See Units 11
and 12 for uses in expressing obligation. For some speakers, *shall* is used in
formal speech and in written language.

Activities

This section also includes time phrases used in expressing future time.

1
Choose the most
appropriate
words
underlined.

a) Jack is/is going to be sixty-five next month so he retires/will be retiring.
b) Quick, here comes a police car! What will we say/are we going to say about
the broken window?
c) Helen and Andrew are due to separate/are on the point of separating.
d) Don't be so impatient! I'll just come/I'm just coming.
e) I have to be back at 3.30 so I'm leaving/I leave before lunch.
f) What do you think you'll be doing/you'll do in five years' time?
g) Come on, get a move on, or we'll miss/we'll have missed the plane!
h) Will you be working/Will you work the week after Christmas? I was
thinking of visiting you.
i) By the time Jean gets back, it'll be/it will have been too late.
j) Don't phone after 11.00. I'll be/I'll have been asleep.

2
Put the verb in
brackets into a
suitable tense.

a) In twenty four hours' time *I'll be relaxing* (I relax) on my yacht.
b) 'There's someone at the door.'
    'That .... (be) the postman.'
c) By the time you get back Harry .... (leave).
d) It's only a short trip. I .... (be) back in an hour.
e) What .... (you do) this Saturday evening? Would you like to go out?
f) By the end of the week we .... (decide) what to do.

g) It .... (not be) long before Doctor Smith is here.

h) I've pressed the red button. Now what .... (I do)?

i) It's very hot in here. I think I .... (faint).

j) What .... (you give) Ann for her birthday? Have you decided yet?

3

Choose the most appropriate continuation for each sentence.

a) Paula's flight is bound to be late although
   A) it arrives at 6.00. B) it's due at 6.00. C) it's arriving at six.

b) It's no use phoning Bob at the office, he
   A) will be leaving. B) is leaving. C) will have left.

c) Everyone says that this year City
   A) are going to win the Cup. B) are winning the Cup. C) win the Cup.

d) I don't feel like visiting my relatives this year so
   A) I won't go. B) I'm not going. C) I don't go.

e) According to the latest forecast, the tunnel
   A) will be finished next year.   B) will have been finished next year.
   C) is finishing next year.

f) You can borrow this calculator, I
   A) am not going to need it. B) won't have been needing it. C) am not needing it.

g) I'm sorry dinner isn't ready yet, but it
   A) is going to be ready in a minute. B) will have been ready in a minute. C) will be ready in a minute.

h) Can you send me the results as soon as you
   A) hear anything? B) are hearing anything? C) will have heard anything?

i) You can try asking Martin for help but
   A) it won't do you any good. B) it's not doing you any good. C) it won't be doing you any good.

j) Don't worry about the mistake you made, nobody
   A) will notice. B) is noticing. C) will be noticing.

4

Complete each sentence with a suitable word or phrase referring to future time.

a) By this time next year, the government *will have* resigned.

b) Wait for me here until .... back.

c) We are on .... clinching the deal.

d) No one can predict what Carol is .... next.

e) This time next week I .... on the beach!

f) Are .... on Wednesday evening? I've got tickets for the match.

g) I've lost the key! How .... get in now?

h) I won't be long. I .... just .... my hair.

i) We only posted the invitations yesterday so you .... received yours yet.

j) Goodbye for now. I .... in touch with you later in the week.

5

Rewrite each
sentence,
beginning as
shown, so that
the meaning stays
the same.

a) I don't suppose you have heard the news.
    You won't *have heard the news.*

b) The Prime Minister expects a victory for his party.
    The Prime Minister believes that ....

c) A new manager will take Mr Brown's place in the new year.
    Mr Brown is ....

d) I've been in this company for three years, come the end of the month.
    By the end of the month I ....

e) Why don't you come to see us during lunch?
    Why don't you come to see us when we ....

f) What exactly do you intend to do?
    What exactly are you ....

g) The arrival of the train has been delayed, I'm afraid.
    The train will ....

h) Let's leave at the end of the next lecture.
    As soon as ....

i) There will be a team members' meeting tomorrow.
    The team members ....

j) This book will take me two years to write.
    In two years' time ....

6

Choose the most
appropriate word
or phrase
underlined.

a) I'll be back <u>after a few minutes/in a few minutes.</u>

b) I'm sure that everything will be all right <u>at the end/in the end</u>.

c) Please call me <u>the moment/exactly when</u> you hear any news.

d) I should be back <u>by the time/at the time</u> the film begins.

e) I'm sure Fiona will be here <u>before long/after a while</u>.

f) I can't leave on Tuesday. I won't be ready <u>until then/by then</u>.

g) <u>By twenty four hours/this time tomorrow</u> I'll be in Bangkok.

h) Diana will be retiring <u>soon/already</u>.

i) There will be no official announcements <u>forthwith/from now on</u>.

j) Bye for now. I'll see you <u>in two weeks' time/two weeks later</u>.

7
Rewrite each sentence so that it contains the word in capitals. Do not change the word in any way.

a) What time is the train for Nottingham?   LEAVE
    What time does the train for Nottingham leave?
    ....

b) What do you intend to do now?   GOING
    ....

c) You'll find me waiting outside the station.   BE
    ....

d) Who will be your assistant on this project?   WORKING
    ....

e) Scientists are on the point of making a vital breakthrough.   ABOUT
    ....

f) Maria is pregnant again.   HAVE
    ....

g) I'll be home late.   UNTIL
    ....

h) No one knows who is going to win the match.   WHAT
    ....

i) David is bound to be here on time.   WON'T
    ....

j) Mary and Alan's wedding is next weekend.   MARRIED
    ....

8
Decide whether the pairs of sentences a) and b) could be equally acceptable in the context given, or whether one is more appropriate.

a) You can't leave early,
    A) we're having a meeting.
    B) we're going to have a meeting.
    (both acceptable, but A more appropriate)

b) We've run out of fuel.
    A) What are we doing now?
    B) What are we going to do now?

c) Oh dear, I've broken the vase.
    A) What will your mother say?
    B) What is your mother going to say?

d) According to the weather forecast,
    A) it'll rain tomorrow.
    B) it's going to rain tomorrow.

e) I'd like to call round and see you.
    A) What'll you be doing in the morning?
    B) What are you doing in the morning?

f) I've got nothing to do tomorrow so
    A) I'll get up late.
    B) I'm going to get up late.

g) It's my eighteenth birthday next month so
    A) I'm having a party.
    B) I'll be having a party.

h) Why don't you come with us?
    A) It'll be a great trip.
    B) It's going to be a great trip.

i) When you get to the airport
    A) someone will wait for you.
    B) someone will be waiting for you.

j) Shut up, will you!
    A) I'm getting angry in a minute.
    B) I'm going to get angry in a minute.

Unit 3 Tense consolidation: past time

Explanations

Basic contrasts: past simple and past continuous

1 Past simple generally refers to:
Completed actions
*I **got** up, **switched** off the radio, and **sat** down again.*
Habits
*Every day I **went** to the park.*
States
*In those days, I **didn't like** reading.*

2 Past continuous (progressive) generally refers to:
Actions in progress (often interrupted by events)
*I **was drinking** my coffee at the time.*
*While I **was opening** the letter, the phone **rang**.*
Background description in narrative
*I entered the office and looked around. Most people **were working** at their desks, but Jane **was staring** out the window and **pretending** to write something at the same time.*
Changing states
*The car **was getting** worse all the time. One of the headlights **was** gradually **falling off**, and the engine **was making** more and more funny noises.*
Repeated actions – criticism
With a frequency adverb, this use is similar to the use of present continuous to express annoyance.
*When Jane was at school, she **was** always **losing** things.*

3 Past continuous is not used to describe general habitual actions, without the sense of criticism mentioned above. Past simple is used for this meaning.
*When I lived in London, I **walked** through the park every day.*

Past perfect simple and continuous

1 Past perfect tenses in general refer to:
An event in the past which happens before another event in the past, where there is no time expression to make this clear.
*By the time I got to the station, the train **had left**.*
Compare this with:
The train left five minutes before I got to the station.
In this example, the sequence of events is made clear by *before*.

14

2   Past perfect continuous (progressive).
    The contrasts between past simple and past continuous can be made in past
    perfect tenses for events further back in the past.
    *I **had been living** in a bed-sitter up to then.*
    *While **I had been talking** on the phone, Jimmy **had escaped**.*
    *The whole place was deserted, but it was obvious that someone **had been***
    *living there. **They'd been cooking** in the kitchen for a start, and they*
    ***hadn't bothered** to clear up the mess.*

3   Past perfect is also common in indirect speech. See Unit 16.

4   Past perfect is not used simply to describe an event in the distant past.
    There must be another past event, less far away in the past, with which it
    contrasts.

Used to and   1   *Used to*
would   This often contrasts with the present. The contrast may be stated or
                           understood.
                           *I **used to go** swimming a lot (but I don't now).*
                           The negative form is either:
                           I didn't use to or *I used not to (rare for some speakers)*
                           The form *I didn't used to* may also be found. This is usually considered
                           incorrect, unless we consider *used to* as an unchanging semi-modal form.
                           There is no present time reference possible.

                       2   *Would*
                           This is used to describe repeated actions, not states. It describes a habitual
                           activity which was typical of a person.
                           Every week he'd buy his mother a bunch of flowers.
                           Used to would also be possible here. Compare:
                           I used to like cowboy films.
                           Would is not possible here.
                           Would is more common in written language and often occurs in
                           reminiscences.

Unfulfilled past   1   These describe events intended to take place, but which did not happen.
events   *I **was going to phone** you, but I forgot.*
                           *I **was thinking of going** to Italy this year, but I haven't decided.*
                           *I **was about to do** it, but I started doing something else.*
                           *Jack **was to have taken part**, but he fell ill.*

                       2   The contrasting past event is often understood.
                           *How are you? **I was going to phone** you … (but I didn't).*

3 Polite forms
  These are common with *wonder*.
      *I **was wondering** if you wanted to come to the cinema.*
  See Units 11 and 12 for comment on this.

4 Contrasts with present perfect tenses
  See Unit 4 for contrasts between past simple and present perfect tenses.

  Past tenses are also used to express unreal time. See Units 8 and 9.

Activities

1

Choose the most suitable words underlined.

a) When you passed the town hall clock, <u>did you notice/were you noticing</u> what time it was?
b) Last night my neighbours <u>were shouting/would shout</u> for hours and I couldn't get to sleep.
c) When you lived in London, <u>did you use to travel/were you travelling</u> by bus?
d) Everyone was having a good time, although not many people <u>danced/were dancing</u>.

e) – Excuse me, but this seat is mine.
   – I'm sorry, I <u>didn't realise/hadn't realised</u> that you were sitting here.
f) Jill <u>didn't eat/hadn't eaten</u> all day, so she was really hungry at this point.
g) – Paul has forgotten to book the tickets I'm afraid.
   – He <u>was always doing/would do</u> something like that!
h) It took a while for me to notice, but then I did. Everyone <u>stared/was staring</u> at me. What had I done wrong?
i) Nobody bothered to tell me that the school <u>decided/had decided</u> to have a special holiday that Friday.
j) I <u>was trying/tried</u> to get in touch with you all day yesterday. Where were you?

2

Put each verb in brackets into a suitable tense. All sentences refer to past time.

Suggest alternative tenses if necessary where the past perfect or another tense might be possible.

a) I realised that someone *was stealing* (steal) my wallet when I *felt* (feel) their hand in my jacket pocket.
b) When I .... (phone) Helen last night she .... (wash) her hair and she .... (not finish) when I finally .... (get to) her house.
c) Peter .... (offer) me another drink but I decided I .... (drink) enough.

d) Nobody .... (watch), so the little boy .... (take) the packet of sweets from the shelf and .... (put) it in his pocket.

e) I .... (not realise) that I .... (leave) my umbrella on the bus until it .... (start) to rain.

f) At school I .... (dislike) the maths teacher because he .... (always pick) on me.

g) Wherever Marion .... (find) a job, there was someone who .... (know) that she .... (go) to prison.

h) It was only much later I .... (find out) that during all the time I .... (write) to my penfriend, my mother .... (open) and reading the replies!

i) I .... (not understand) what .... (go on). Several people .... (shout) at me, and one .... (wave) a newspaper in front of my face.

j) I .... (know) I .... (do) well in my exams even before I .... (receive) the official results.

3
Decide whether the tense underlined is suitable or not in the context given.If you decide it is unsuitable, write a correction.

a) The train (1) <u>ground</u> to a halt at a small station miles from London, and it (2) <u>became</u> apparent that the engine (3) <u>had broken down.</u> Everyone (4) <u>was getting</u> their cases down from the luggage racks, and we (5) <u>were waiting</u> on the platform in the freezing wind for hours until the next train (6) <u>had turned up</u>.

1) *(suitable)*.....   4) ....
2) ....   5) ....
3) ....   6) ....

b) The other strange thing about our neighbour Mrs Black was that she (1) <u>would never go out</u> if it was raining. She (2) <u>used to look</u> up at the sky whenever (3) <u>it was getting</u> cloudy, and as soon as even the smallest drop of rain (4) <u>was falling</u> she (5) <u>had scuttled</u> back into her house and (6) <u>was locking</u> herself in her bedroom!

1) *(suitable)*.....   4) ....
2) ....   5) ....
3) ....   6) ....

c) Inspector Gorse (1) <u>was</u> in touch with Thames Valley Police six months before Professor Dowson (2) <u>was disappearing</u>, because the Professor's wife Jean (3) <u>would write</u> to him, accusing her husband of plotting to murder her. And now it was the Professor who (4) <u>disappeared</u>. Gorse (5) <u>considered</u> what his next step should be when the phone rang. It was Sergeant Adams from Thames Valley. A fisherman (6) <u>discovered</u> a body in the Thames near Reading, and it fitted the description of the Professor.

1) *(had been)*.....   4) ....
2) ....   5) ....
3) ....   6) ....

17

4

Put each verb in brackets into a suitable past tense. Only use the past perfect where this is absolutely necessary.

This time last year I (1) *was cycling* (cycle) in the rain along a country road in France with a friend of mine. We (2) .... (decide) to go on a cycling holiday in Normandy. Neither of us (3) .... (go) to France before, but we (4) .... (know) some French from our time at school and we (5) .... (manage) to brush up on the basics. Now we (6) .... (wonder) if we (7) .... (make) the right decision. We (8) .... (plan) our route carefully in advance, but we (9) .... (forget) one important thing, the weather. It (10) .... (rain) solidly since our arrival and that night we (11) .... (end up) sleeping in the waiting room at a railway station. Then the next morning as we (12) .... (ride) down a steep hill my bike (13) .... (skid) on the wet road and I (14) .... (fall off). I (15) .... (realise) immediately that I (16) .... (break) my arm, and after a visit to the local hospital I (17) .... (catch) the next train to Calais for the ferry home. Unfortunately my parents (18) .... (not expect) me home for a fortnight, and (19) .... (go) away on holiday. So I (20) .... (spend) a miserable couple of weeks alone, reading *Teach Yourself French*.

5

In each sentence decide whether one or both of the alternative tenses given are appropriate.

a) In those days, I always <u>used to get up/got up</u> early in the morning. *(both appropriate)*
b) When I got to the cinema Jack <u>had been waiting/was waiting</u> for me.
c) We <u>would always have/were always having</u> breakfast in bed on Sundays.
d) Mary <u>was always falling/always fell</u> ill before important examinations.
e) My sister <u>used to own/would own</u> a motorcycle and sidecar.
f) Pay no attention to Dave's remarks. He <u>wasn't meaning/didn't mean</u> it.
g) I felt awful after lunch. I <u>ate/had eaten</u> too much.
h) Brenda <u>left/had left</u> before I had time to talk to her.
i) The explanation was simple. In 1781 HMS Sovereign on her way back from India <u>had sighted/sighted</u> an empty boat drifting off the African coast.

j) Pauline has changed a lot. She <u>didn't always use to look/wasn't always looking</u> like that.

6

Rewrite each sentence so that it contains the word or words in capitals. Do not change the words in any way.

a) I intended to call you yesterday, but I forgot. GOING
   I was going to call you yesterday, but I forgot.
   ....
b) We used to spend Sunday afternoons working in the garden. WOULD
   ....
c) Paul had the irritating habit of making trouble. ALWAYS
   ....

d) Diana wasn't always as rude as that.   BE

....

e) I felt happy about the improvement in Jean's condition.   BETTER

....

f) I wasn't very keen on sport in those days.   USE

....

g) I might possibly go to the theatre tonight.   WAS

....

h) I had to go past your house so I decided to drop in.   PASSING

....

i) Susan booked out before we got to her hotel.   BY THE TIME

....

j) What did you do at the moment of the explosion?   WHEN

....

7

Choose the most appropriate time expression underlined.

a) ⟨Once⟩/Afterwards I'd read the manual, I found I could use the computer quite well.
b) It was more than a month <u>before/until</u> I realised what had happened.
c) I managed to talk to Carol just <u>as/while</u> she was leaving.
d) It wasn't <u>until/up to</u> 1983 that Nigel could afford to take holidays abroad.
e) George always let me know <u>by the time/whenever</u> he was going to be late.
f) I was having a bath <u>at the time/that time</u>, so I didn't hear the doorbell.
g) We bought our tickets and five minutes <u>after/later</u> the train arrived.
h) According to Grandpa, people used to dress formally <u>those days/in his day</u>.
i) Everyone was talking but stopped <u>at the time/the moment</u> Mr Smith entered the room.
j) The letter still hadn't arrived <u>by/until</u> the end of the week.

8

Put each verb in brackets into a suitable past tense. Only use the past perfect where this is absolutely necessary.

Harry went back to the camp the following morning, but it was in some confusion. Soldiers (1) *were wandering* (wander) around carrying equipment from one place to another, but there (2) .... (not seem) to be any purpose to what they (3) .... (do). Harry (4) .... (never be) in an army camp before, but it (5) .... (not take) a genius to realise that most of the officers (6) .... (take) the first opportunity to abandon the men and head for safety. He (7) .... (try) to phone the newspaper, but something (8) .... (happen) to the telephone lines. He (9) .... (try) to find out what exactly (10) .... (go on), when the first plane (11) .... (fly) low over the camp. A wooden building a few hundred yards away suddenly (12) .... (disappear) in an explosion of flame. Before long bombs (13) .... (explode) all around him, and then everything (14) .... (go) quiet. The planes (15) .... (vanish) as suddenly as they (16) .... (appear). Smoke (17) .... (rise) from burning buildings. A dead man (18) .... (lie) next to Harry, the first dead person he (19) .... (ever see). And suddenly it (20) .... (begin) to rain.

Unit 4 Tense consolidation: present perfect

Explanations

Present perfect simple

1 Present perfect simple refers to:
Recent events, without a definite time given. The recentness may be indicated by *just*.
> *We've **missed** the turning.*
> *I've **just seen** a ghost!*

Indefinite events, which happened at an unknown time in the past. No definite time is given.
> *Jim **has had** three car accidents. (up to the present)*

Indefinite events which may have an obvious result in the present
> *I've **twisted** my ankle. (that's why I'm limping)*

With state verbs, a state which lasts up to the present.
> *I've **lived** here for the past ten years.*

A habitual action in a period of time up to the present
> *I've **been** jogging every morning for the last month.*

2 Contrasts with past simple
Past simple is used with time expressions which refer to definite times. The time may be stated or understood. Compare:
> *I've **bought** a new car. (indefinite)*
> *I **bought** a new car **last week**. (definite)*
> *I **bought** the car after all. (implied definite: the car we talked about)*

Choice between past simple and present perfect for recent events may depend on the mental attitude of the speaker. This in turn may depend on whether the speaker feels distant in time or place from the event.
> *I've **left** my wallet in the car. I'm going back to get it.*

Here the speaker may be about to return, and feels that the event is connected with the present.
> *I **left** my wallet in the car. I'm going back to get it.*

Here the speaker may feel separated in time from the event, or be further away.

Present perfect continuous

1 Present perfect continuous (progressive) can refer to a range of meanings, depending on the time expression used and the context.
A state which lasts up to the present moment
> *I've **been waiting** for you for three hours!*

An incomplete activity
> *I've **been cleaning** the house but I still haven't finished.*

To emphasise duration
> *I've **been writing** letters all morning.*

A recently finished activity
*I've **been running**. That's why I look hot.*
A repeated activity
*I've **been taking** French lessons this year.*

2 Contrasts with present perfect simple
There may be little contrast when some state verbs are used.
*How long have you **lived** here?*
*How long have you **been living** here?*
Some verbs (especially *sit, lie, wait* and *stay*) prefer the continuous form.
There may be a contrast between completion and incompletion, especially if
the number of items completed is mentioned.
Completed: emphasis on achievement
*I've **ironed** five shirts this morning.*
Incomplete, or recently completed : emphasis on duration
*I've **been ironing** my shirts this morning.*

Time expressions with present perfect

Meaning with present perfect tenses is associated with certain time expressions.
Contrast with past simple may depend on the choice of time expression.
Past simple: referring to a specific time
yesterday, last week, on Sunday
Present perfect simple:
since 1968 (the beginning of a period of time)
already (indefinite past)
Many time expressions are not associated with a specific tense.
*I haven't seen Helen **recently**.*
*I saw Jim **recently**.*

Activities

1
Choose the most
appropriate tense
underlined.

a) I can't believe it, inspector. You mean that Smith stole/has stolen/has been
stealing money from the till all this time!

b) You three boys look very guilty! What did you do/have you done/have you
been doing since I left/have left the room?

c) Why on earth didn't you tell/haven't you told me about that loose
floorboard? I tripped/have tripped over it just now and hurt myself.

d) It's a long time since I saw/have seen/have been seeing your brother Paul.
What did he do/has he done/has he been doing lately?

e) I can't believe that you ate/have eaten/have been eating three pizzas already!
I only brought/have only brought them in fifteen minutes ago!

f) Don't forget that you didn't see/haven't seen Mrs Dawson. She has
waited/has been waiting outside since 10.30.

g) What did you think/have you thought of Brighton? Did you stay/Have you
stayed there long?

h) I feel really tired. I weeded/have weeded/have been weeding the garden for
the last three hours and I didn't rest/haven't rested for a single moment.

i) I'm having problems with David. He <u>has called/has been calling</u> me up in the middle of the night and <u>told/telling</u> me his troubles.

j) How long <u>did you have/have you had/have you been having</u> driving lessons? And <u>did you take/have you taken/have you been taking</u> your test yet?

2
Put each verb in brackets into the most appropriate perfect or past tense.

a) I'm sorry I *haven't come/haven't been coming* (not come) to class lately. I .... (work) late in the evenings for the past fortnight.

b) So far we .... (not notice) anything unusual, but we .... (not pay) very close attention.

c) I wonder if Mary .... (reach) home yet? She .... (leave) too late to catch the bus.

d) Here is the news. The Home Office .... (announce) that the two prisoners who .... (escape) from Dartmoor prison earlier this morning .... (give themselves up) to local police.

e) .... (you make up) your minds? What .... (you decide) to do?

f) Harry .... (leave) home rather suddenly and we .... (not hear) from him since.

g) Recent research .... (show) that Columbus .... (not discover) America, but that Vikings .... (land) there five hundred years before him.

h) I think that people .... (become) tired of the poor quality of television programmes, though they .... (improve) lately.

i) .... (something happen) to the lines? I .... (try) to get through to Glasgow for the past hour.

j) Bill .... (get) that new job, but he .... (complain) about it ever since.

3
Complete each sentence a) to j) with an appropriate ending from 1) to 10). Do not use an ending more than once.

a) I haven't been feeling very well ....5......
b) I went to the dentist's ....
c) I've lived here ....
d) Don't worry. I haven't been waiting ....
e) I've written two pages ....
f) I waited outside your house ....
g) I've warned you about this ....
h) I haven't made a decision ....
i) The repair worked ....
j) I've decided to believe you ....

1) .... time and time again.
2) .... all my life.
3) .... so far.
4) .... for the time being.
5) .... for the past hour or two.
6) .... yet.
7) .... till half past eight.
8) .... for a while.
9) .... the other day.
10) .... long.

4

Rewrite each sentence, beginning as shown, so that the meaning stays the same.

a) It's a long time since I last went to a football match.
   I haven't *been to a football match for a long time.*

b) This is my second visit to Hungary.
   This is the second time ....

c) I paid this bill earlier, actually.
   Actually I've ....

d) We haven't been swimming for ages.
   It's ages ....

e) Mary started learning French five years ago.
   Mary has ....

f) I am on the tenth page of the letter I am writing.
   So far I ....

g) After I arrived here, I started to feel better.
   Since arriving here, ...

h) It's over twenty years since we got married.
   We have ....

i) The last time I saw Dick was in 1985.
   I haven't ....

j) There is a definite improvement in your work.
   Lately your work ....

5

Rewrite each sentence so that it contains the word in capitals, and so that the meaning stays the same.

a) You have missed the beginning of the film.   HAS
   The film has already started.

b) I can't seem to stop sneezing lately.   BEEN
   ....

c) Paul is different from what he used to be.   HAS
   ....

d) This has been my home for thirty years.   HAVE
   ....

e) Eating Chinese food is new to me.   BEFORE
   ....

f) Is there any news?   HAPPENED
   ....

g) I bought my car in 1985 and I'm still driving it.   BEEN
   ....

h) I don't know where my keys are.   HAVE
   ....

i) Sue doesn't have her dictionary with her; it's at home.   HAS
   ....

j) Tony hasn't been to Paris before.   FIRST
   ....

6

Choose the most appropriate phrase for each situation.

a) The price of petrol has risen/has been rising by 15% over the past year.

b) No wonder you are overweight! You have eaten/You have been eating chocolates all day long!

c) I've read/I've been reading *War and Peace* this morning.

d) Doesn't this room look better? I've put/I've been putting some posters up on the walls.

e) Don't disappoint me! I've counted on you/I've been counting on you.

f) Don't forget your pills today. Have you taken them/Have you been taking them?

g) Who has worn/has been wearing my scarf?

h) I think there's something wrong with your motorbike. It's made/It's been making some very funny noises.

i) Jack has asked/has been asking for a pay-rise three times this year.

j) I've been phoning/I've phoned Ann all evening, but there's no reply.

7

Choose the most appropriate word or phrase underlined.

a) It's a long time since/when I last saw you.

b) I've seen Bill quite often lately/from time to time.

c) Have you spoken to the director beforehand/already?

d) I've lived in the same house for years/for ever.

e) I've read the paper now/still.

f) Diana has bought a computer two years ago/since then.

g) Nothing much has been happening by now/so far.

h) I've finished reading her new book at last/this evening.

i) Sue bought a CD player last week and she's been listening to music ever since/for a while.

j) Sorry, but I haven't got that work finished already/yet.

8

Put each verb in brackets into either the past simple, present perfect simple or present perfect continuous.

Ever since the day I (1) *decided* (decide) to move to London, I (2) .... (worry) whether the decision I (3) .... (take) was the right one. As I (4) .... (already sell) my house and (5) .... (arrange) a new job, it is too late to change my mind. However, since then I (6) .... (hear) a lot of negative things about living in the capital, and lately some of them (7) .... (begin) to bother me. I (8) .... (grow up) in a fairly small town and I (9) .... (spend) all of my life there. I (10) .... (always want) to live in a big city and so when my company (11) .... (offer) me a job in their London office, I (12) .... (grab) at the chance. But according to a programme I (13) .... (just hear) on the radio, more and more people (14) .... (stop) working in London recently, and a lot of large companies (15) .... (choose) to move away from the centre. Of course I (16) .... (tell) my parents that I'm moving and they (17) .... (accept) my decision, but when I (18) .... (tell) my friends they (19) .... (seem) rather shocked. Since then I (20) .... (hope) secretly that the company would tell me that the move was off!

Unit 5 Progress Test (Units 1, 2, 3, 4)

1

Put each verb in brackets into an appropriate tense.

Farmers, as we all (1) ..know....... (know), (2).are having..(have) a hard time of it in Britain lately, and (3).are turning..(turn) to new ways of earning income from their land. This (4) ..involves.. (involve) not only planting new kinds of crops, but some strange ways of making money, the most unusual of which has got to be sheep racing. Yes, you (5) ..heard........ (hear) me correctly! A farmer in the West of England now (6) ..holds..... (hold) sheep races on a regular basis, and during the past year over 100 000 people (7) ..turned up (turn up) to watch the proceedings. 'I (8) ..passed.... (pass) the farm on my way to the sea for a holiday,' one punter told me, 'and I (9) ..thought... (think) I'd have a look. I (10)didn't believe(not believe) it was serious, to tell you the truth.' According to a regular visitor, betting on sheep is more interesting than betting on horses. 'At proper horse races everyone (11)has already studied... (already study) the form of the horses in advance, and there are clear favourites. But nobody (12) ..hear....... has heard (hear) anything about these sheep! Most people (13) ..find.... (find) it difficult to tell one from another in any case.' I (14) ..stayed.... (stay) to watch the races, and I must admit that I (15) ..found.. (find) it quite exciting. In a typical race, half a dozen sheep (16) ..race.......... (race) downhill over a course of about half a mile. Food (17) ..waits...... (wait) for them at the other end of the track, I ought to add! The sheep (18) ..run......... (run) surprisingly fast, although presumably they (19) have not eaten..(not eat) for a while just to give them some motivation. At any rate, the crowd around me (20) obviously enjoyed.. (obviously enjoy) their day out at the races, judging by their happy faces and the sense of excitement.

2

Rewrite each sentence, beginning as shown, so that the meaning stays the same.

a) This matter is none of your business.
   This matter does ....

b) This bridge will take us three years to complete.
   In three years time we ....

c) Patsy wasn't always so unfriendly.
   Patsy didn't ....

d) We'll be at your house soon.
   It won't ....

e) I haven't seen Anne for years.
   It's years ....

f) The dog keeps stealing my socks!
   The dog is ....

g) After taking the pills, I began to feel much better.
   Since taking ....

h) We'll have to leave immediately at the end of the film.
   The moment ....

25

i) Harry left before we reached the hotel.
By the time ....

j) Is there such a place as Eldorado?
Does ....

3

Rewrite each sentence so that it contains the word in capitals, and so that the meaning stays the same.

a) When is the train due to arrive?   GET
....

b) I shouldn't think Paul knows the answer.   DOUBT
....

c) I've had to wait all afternoon.   BEEN
....

d) To get to work on time I have to get up at 6.00.   MEANS
....

e) Today is Liz and John's thirtieth wedding anniversary.   FOR
....

f) By the end of the week, Harry was well again.   GOT
....

g) Whose watch is this?   BELONG
....

h) Cathy hasn't been on holiday with her sister before.   FIRST
....

i) My dentist's appointment is for next Wednesday.   TO
....

j) Brenda had no idea of her next move.   WHAT
....

4

Complete each sentence with an appropriate word or phrase.

a) Can you remember what you .... ten years ago today?

b) This is the first jazz concert I .... to.

c) Don't eat any more ice cream, you .... sick.

d) I have hated this place ever .... here.

e) I hope that by the end of the month I .... all the decorating.

f) Sheila and Ken .... to each other since their quarrel last week!

g) Do .... going to the cricket match tomorrow?

h) We can't go skiing because it .... enough yet.

i) Penny .... to going on holiday, but she ended up very disappointed.

j) I began to recover my strength later, once I .... a good meal.

5

Choose the most appropriate word or phrase.

a) .... we get to the theatre, the play will have started.
A) As soon as   B) Until   C) By the time   D) Whenever

b) What's the matter? Haven't you started ....?
A) already   B) yet   C) by now   D) soon

c) The trouble with you is that you're .... complaining.
A) forever   B) often   C) still   D) each time

d) Can you remember what you were doing ....?
A) the time   B) usually   C) every day   D) at the time

e) The new school opens ....
   A) now   B) at once   C) next week   D) day by day

f) I haven't been feeling very well ....
   A) of late   B) not long ago   C) currently   D) by now

g) .... we get to the top of this hill, we'll be all right.
   A) Eventually   B) Once   C) Now   D) At the time

h) It's ages .... I last saw a decent comedy film on television.
   A) that   B) ago   C) since   D) when

i) I don't go swimming very much ....
   A) nowadays   B) in those days   C) recently   D) now and again

j) .... we haven't managed to find what we are looking for.
   A) To now   B) On and off   C) Formerly   D) So far

6

Put each verb in brackets into a suitable tense, in either continuous or simple form, according to the context.

a) This is my new car. What .... (you think) of it?

b) – Who are you?
   – What do you mean? I .... (live) here.

c) I can't find the car keys. What .... (you do) with them?

d) Sorry I haven't fixed the plug. I .... (mean) to get round to it, but I just haven't found the time.

e) What .... (you do) on Saturdays?

f) I don't know what time we'll eat. It .... (depends) when Helen gets here.

g) I supported you at the time because I .... (feel) that you were right.

h) Peter couldn't understand what had been decided because too many people .... (talk) at once.

i) Jean, I'm so glad you've got here at last. I .... (expect) you all day.

j) Please don't let me down this time! I .... (depend) on you.

7

Put each verb in brackets into an appropriate tense.

a) Sam .... (not receive) the parcel the last time I .... (speak) to him.

b) I .... (consider) buying a house but now I .... (change) my mind.

c) When you .... (feel) hungry later, room service .... (bring) you whatever you .... (want).

d) I .... (find) it difficult to convince the ticket inspector that I .... (lose) my ticket.

e) Since I .... (pay) for our lunch, I .... (try) to attract the waiter's attention.

f) As soon as I .... (have) a good look at the designs, I .... (send) them back to you.

g) I .... (hope) to meet you ever since I .... (read) your first novel.

h) Whatever .... (happen), I .... (meet) you here in a week's time.

i) By the time you .... (finish) getting ready, we .... (miss) the train!

j) Sally! I .... (not expect) to see you here! What .... (you do) in New York?

8
Put each verb in brackets into an appropriate tense.

Ask hundreds of people what they (1) .... (do) on a certain day in August next year, or the year after, and there (2) .... (be) only one reply. Provided of course that the people you (3) .... (ask) (4) .... (belong) to the Elvis Presley Fan Club. Although the King of Rock and Roll (5) .... (die) nearly two decades ago, his fans (6) .... (meet) every year since then outside his home in Memphis, Tennessee, to show respect for the singer they (7) .... (love) so much. Fans like Jean Thomas, from Catford in South London. Jean (8) .... (visit) Gracelands, the house where Elvis (9) .... (suffer) his fatal heart attack, twice in the past five years. 'The first time I (10) .... (borrow) the money from my Mum, as I (11) .... (not work) then. But two years ago I (12) .... (get) married and since then I (13) .... (work) in my husband Chris's garage. Chris and I (14) .... (go) together last year, and we (15) .... (think) of spending two or three months in the USA next year. I (16) .... (always want) to visit some of the places where Elvis (17) .... (perform). Like Las Vegas for example.' Jean says that Elvis (18) .... (be) her obsession ever since she (19) .... (be) ten years old, and she (20) .... (own) every single one of his records, good and bad.

9
Rewrite each sentence, beginning as shown, so that the meaning stays the same.

a) The last time I was in Prague was in 1986.
I haven't ....

b) This will be the team's first match outside England.
This will be the first time ....

c) Terry will get over his illness. Then his work will improve.
Once ....

d) There will be someone to meet you on arrival.
When ....

e) The number of people who attended the fair exceeded our expectations.
More people ....

f) I didn't receive the results of my test for a month.
It was ....

g) My work won't be finished by the end of the month.
I ....

h) Go to the international ticket desk immediately on arrival.
As ....

i) I didn't know about John's departure.
I didn't know that ....

j) Quite a few books are missing from the class library.
Several members of the class have not ....

10

Put each verb in brackets into an appropriate tense.

a) I .... (not understand) what you .... (wait) for.
b) .... (anyone see) my pencil? I .... (leave) it here somewhere.
c) When he .... (not arrive) by 6.00, I .... (know) he .... (miss) the bus.
d) .... (you go away) this weekend? Or .... (you run out) of money?
e) What .... (you think) you .... (do) in ten years' time?
f) I .... (really enjoy) myself at the moment.
g) .... (you let) me know the minute you .... (hear) any news?
h) Something .... (tell) me that you .... (not listen) to a single word I .... (say) in the past ten minutes!
i) What's the matter? .... (you hurt) your ankle? How .... (you do) it?
j) That's definitely the last time that I .... (lend) you any money!

11

Complete each sentence with *one* appropriate word.

a) It's .... since I last had a good Chinese meal.
b) Funnily enough I saw Bob quite .... at the sports club.
c) I've loved you ever .... the first day I set eyes on you!
d) How long .... was it that you lived in Inverness?
e) I've .... to see anyone who can dance as well as Diana.
f) Could you phone me the .... you arrive at the hotel so I don't worry?
g) I promise to get everything ready .... eight o'clock at the latest.
h) Have you finished ....? Wow, you are a fast worker, aren't you!
i) I'm sorry you've been waiting so long, but it will be some time .... Brian gets back.
j) Just sit here, would you? The doctor will be with you ....

12

Decide whether each underlined phrase is appropriate, and rewrite the phrase more appropriately where necessary.

a) <u>Will you be seeing</u> Rob Jones tomorrow? I wonder if you could give him a message from Sally Gordon?
b) I had a great time in the Greek Islands. <u>We would own</u> a small boat and <u>go</u> fishing every day.
c) Julie, hi! <u>I've been hoping</u> I'd see you. I've got some good news!
d) We had a terrible time looking after your dog. <u>It was constantly chasing</u> the cats next door.
e) We had a lovely time in Madrid. Every day <u>we were exploring</u> the city, and in the evening <u>we were going</u> to exciting bars.
f) The steam engine is usually thought of as a relatively modern invention, but the Greeks <u>had built</u> a kind of steam engine in ancient times.
g) I felt rather worried. <u>It was growing</u> darker and colder, and there was still no sign of the rescue helicopter.
h) Don't worry! All we have to do is wait here until someone <u>will find</u> us.
i) This meat <u>is really tasting</u> awful! Are you quite sure it was fresh?
j) The radiator in my room has burst, and there is water all over the floor! You're the manager, what <u>will you do</u> about it?

Unit 6 Passive 1

Explanations

Basic uses of the passive

1 Agent and instrument
The person who performs an action in a passive sentence is called the agent, introduced by *by*. The agent may or may not be mentioned.
*My purse was found by **one of the cleaners**.*
An object which causes something to happen is called an instrument, introduced by *with*.
*He was hit on the head with **a hammer**.*

2 Most verbs with an object (transitive verbs) can be made passive. Common verbs not used in the passive include:
become, fit (be the right size) get, have, lack, let, like, resemble, suit
Some verbs have both transitive and intransitive meanings.
We arrived at the hotel at eight. (cannot be made passive)
How was the answer arrived at? (passive with a different meaning)

3 Verbs with two objects
Verbs which have two objects can be made passive in two ways.
*I was handed **a note**. **A note** was handed **to me**.*
Other common verbs of this type are: *bring, give, lend, pass, pay, promise, sell, send, show, tell*

4 Verbs with object and complement
Some verbs have a noun or adjective which describes their object.
*We elected Jim **class representative**.*
*Everyone considered him **a failure**.*
When these are made passive, the complement goes directly after the verb.
*Jim was elected **class representative**.*
*He was considered **a failure**.*

5 Translation
The uses of the passive in English and in other languages are not necessarily the same. Some languages may use passive forms where English uses active ones, and vice versa.

6 Tenses
Although it is possible to form a wide range of passive tenses, the most used are present simple and continuous, past simple and continuous, present perfect simple, past perfect simple, *will* future, and future perfect. There are also present and past passive infinitives.

Using and not mentioning the agent

1 Change of focus
The passive can change the emphasis of a sentence.
Jack won the prize. (focus on Jack)
The prize was won by Jack. (focus on the prize)

2 Unknown agent
The agent is not mentioned if unknown.
*My wallet **has been taken**.*
In this case, there is no point in adding an agent: 'by somebody'

3 Generalised agent
If the subject is 'people in general' or 'you' the agent is not mentioned.
*Bicycles **are** widely **used** in the city instead of public transport.*

4 Obvious agent
If the agent is obvious or has already been mentioned, it is not mentioned.
*Linda **has been arrested**! (we assume by the police)*
*The company agreed to our request and a new car-park **was opened**.*

5 Unimportant agent
If the agent is not important to the meaning of the sentence it is not mentioned.
*I **was advised** to obtain a visa in advance.*

6 Impersonality
Using the passive is a way of avoiding the naming of a specific person who is responsible for an action.
*It **has been decided** to reduce all salaries by 10%.*
In descriptions of processes, there is emphasis on the actions performed rather than on the people who perform them.
*Then the packets **are packed** into boxes of twenty four.*

Activities

1
Correct any verb forms which are impossible or inappropriate.

a) A lot of homes in the area have been being broken into by burglars. *(have been broken into)*
b) As I drove south, I could see that the old road was rebuilding.
c) I suppose the letter will have been delivered by now.
d) There is nothing more annoying than been interrupted when you are speaking.
e) Jim was been given the sack from his new job.
f) Somehow without my noticing my wallet had been disappeared.
g) The new shopping centre was opened by the local MP.
h) Harry is been questioned by the police about the accident.

i) A lot of meetings have been held, but nothing has being decided yet.

j) Last week it is decided not to have an office party after all.

2

Both sentences in each pair have the same meaning. Complete the second sentence.

a) The crowd was slowly filling the huge stadium.
The huge stadium *was slowly being filled* by the crowd.

b) The invention of the computer simplified the work of accountants.
Since the computer .... the work of accountants ....
simplified.

c) Someone has suggested that the shop should close.
It .... that the shop should close.

d) 'I'd take out some travel insurance if I were you, Mr Smith.'
Mr Smith .... take out some travel insurance.

e) The waitress will bring your drinks in a moment.
Your drinks .... in a moment.

f) Someone used a knife to open this window.
This window .... a knife.

g) You will hear from us when we have finshed dealing with your complaint.
After your complaint ...., you will hear from us.

h) An announcement of their engagement appeared in the local paper.
Their engagement .... in the local paper.

i) Nobody ever heard anything of David again.
Nothing .... David again.

j) They paid Sheila £1000 as a special bonus.
£1000 .... Sheila as a special bonus.

3

Rewrite each sentence so that it does not contain the words underlined and so that it contains a passive form.

a) <u>Someone</u> left the phone off the hook all night.
The phone was left off the hook all night.

b) <u>The government</u> has announced that petrol prices will rise tomorrow.

....

c) <u>A burglar</u> broke into our house last week.

....

d) <u>People</u> asked me the way three times.

....

e) <u>The fruit-pickers</u> pick the apples early in the morning.

....

f) It's time <u>the authorities</u> did something about this problem.

....

g) Lots of <u>people</u> had parked their cars on the pavement.

....

h) The government agreed with the report and so <u>they</u> changed the law.

....

i) <u>You</u> have to fill in an application form.

....

j) <u>They</u> don't know what happened to the ship.

....

4

Put each verb in brackets into the passive in an appropriate tense.

a) The boxes *have not been packed* (not pack) yet.
b) Your food .... (still prepare).
c) The new ship .... (launch) next week.
d) Luckily by the time we got there the painting .... (not sell).
e) We had to go on holiday because our house .... (decorate).
f) I'm afraid that next week's meeting .... (cancel).
g) If we don't hurry, all the tickets .... (sell) by the time we get there.
h) All main courses .... (serve) with vegetables or salad.
i) The second goal .... (score) by Hughes in the 41st minute.
j) The cathedral .... (build) in the fourteenth century.

5

Underline any uses of the agent which are unnecessary.

a) My jewellery has been stolen <u>by a thief</u>!
b) It has been decided by the school that Wednesday will be a school holiday.
c) Harry was pushed over by someone standing next to him in the queue.
d) The goods are transported by rail to our warehouse in the Midlands.
e) I was told by someone that you have a vacancy for a computer operator.
f) Sue has been picked by the selectors for the national team.
g) The letter was sent by post on the 21st of last month.
h) The larger portrait was painted by a little-known Flemish artist.
i) It has been agreed by everyone that no smoking should be allowed.
j) As I arrived at the conference a note was handed to me by one of the delegates.

6

Rewrite each sentence, beginning as shown, so that the meaning stays the same.

a) A friend lent George the motorbike he rode in the race.
The motorbike George rode in the race *was lent to him by a friend*.
b) At the time my aunt was looking after the children for us.
At the time our children ....
c) The police have issued a description of the wanted man.
A description ....
d) It was a mistake to enter Brian for the exam.
Brian should not ....
e) They said they would rather Diana didn't listen to music at work.
Diana ....
f) Johnson first became a member of parliament in 1983.
Johnson was first ....
g) My legal advisers have told me not to say any more at this time.
I have ....
h) Nobody had invited Jean to the party, which annoyed her.
As she ....
i) Tony has another six months to finish his thesis.
Tony has been ....
j) There is no definite decision yet about the venue of the next Olympic Games.
Nothing ....

7

Rewrite each sentence in a more formal style so that it contains a passive form of the word given in capitals.

a) Sorry, but we've lost your letter.
Unfortunately your letter has been mislaid.   MISLAY

b) The police are grilling Harry down at the station.   QUESTION
....

c) They've found the remains of an old Roman villa nearby.   DISCOVER
....

d) You'll get a rise in salary after six months.   RAISE
....

e) You go in the cathedral from the south door.   ENTER
....

f) They stopped playing the match after half an hour.   ABANDON
....

g) They've stopped traffic from using the centre.   BAN
....

h) They took Chris to court for dangerous driving.   PROSECUTE
....

i) You usually eat this kind of fish with a white sauce.   SERVE
....

j) I don't know your name.   INTRODUCE
....

8

Put each verb in brackets into the passive in an appropriate tense.

a) Nothing *has been seen* (see) of Pauline since her car .... (find) abandoned near Newbury last week.

b) As our new furniture .... (deliver) on Monday morning I'll have to stay at home to check that it .... (not damage) during transit.

c) The new Alhambra hatchback, which in this country .... (sell) under the name 'Challenger', ... (fit) with electric windows as standard.

d) For the past few days I .... (work) in Jack's office, as my own office .... (redecorate).

e) The last time I went sailing with friends the boat .... (sink) in a gale. Luckily I .... (not invite) again since then!

f) It .... (announce) that the proposed new office block .... (now not build) because of the current economic situation.

g) A major new deposit of oil .... (discover) in the North Sea. It .... (think) to be nearly twice the size of the largest existing field.

h) Pictures of the surface of the planet Venus .... (receive) yesterday from the space probe 'Explorer' which .... (launch) last year.

i) A large sum .... (raise) for the Fund by a recent charity concert but the target of £250 000 .... (still not reach).

j) No decision .... (make) about any future appointment until all suitable candidates .... (interview).

Unit 7 Passive 2

Explanations

Have and *get*
something done,
need doing

1 *Have* something *done*
This usually describes a service performed for us by someone else.
>   *I've just **had** my car **serviced**.*
It can also describe something unfortunate that happens to someone.
>   *We **have had our car stolen** so we need a lift.*
This applies to a range of tenses:
>   *I'm **having** my flat **painted** next week.*
>   *I **have** it **done** every year.*
>   *Sheila **had** her hair **done** yesterday.*
>   *I **was having** the roof **repaired** when it happened.*
Note the quite different colloquial expressions *have someone round/over*.
In this case, there is no sense of a service.
>   *We **had some friends round** for dinner last night.*

2 *Get* something *done*
Get cannot be used in all the same contexts as *have* in this case. *Get* is
common where there is a feeling that something must be done:
>   *I must **get** my car **serviced**.*
It is also common in orders and imperatives:
>   *Get your hair cut!*
There is also a feeling of eventually managing something in some uses:
>   *I eventually **got the car fixed**.*
>   *Sue always **gets things done** in this office.*

3 The need to have a service done can be described with *need doing*.
>   *Your hair **needs cutting**.*

Passive *get*

Get can be used instead of *be* to form the passive in spoken language.
>   *Martin **got arrested** at a football match.*

Reporting verbs

1 Present reference
With verbs such as *believe, know, say, think* which report people's opinions,
a passive construction is often used to avoid a weak subject, and to give a
generalised opinion.
With present reference, the passive is followed by the present infinitive.
>   *People think that Smith is in England.*
>   *Smith **is thought to be** in England.*

35

2 Past reference
With past reference, the passive is followed by the past infinitive.
> *People believe that Smith left England last week.*
> *Smith **is believed to have left** England last week.*

3 Past reporting verb
If the reporting verb is in the past, the past infinitive tends to follow, though not always if the verb *be* is used.
> *People thought Sue had paid too much.*
> *Sue **was thought to have paid** too much.*
> *The police thought that the thief was still in the house.*
> *The thief **was thought to still be** in the house.*

4 With passive infinitive
> *Everyone knows the portrait was painted by an Italian.*
> *The portrait **is known to have been painted** by an Italian.*

5 If there are two objects, two versions are possible.
> *The portrait **is known to have been painted** by an Italian.*
> *An Italian **is known to have painted** the portrait.*

6 Continuous infinitive
Past and present continuous infinitives are also used.
> *Mary is thought **to be living** in Scotland.*
> *The driver is thought **to have been doing** a U-turn.*

Verbs with prepositions

1 Ending a sentence with a preposition
It is possible to end a sentence with a preposition in a sentence where a prepositional verb is made passive.
> *Someone broke into our house.*
> *Our house was broken **into**.*

2 *By* and *with*
With is used after participles such as *filled, packed, crowded, crammed.*
> *The train **was packed with** commuters.*
The difference between *by* and *with* may involve the presence of a person:
> *Dave was hit **by** a branch. (an accident)*
> *Dave was hit **with** a branch. (a person hit him with one)*

3 *Make* is followed by *to* when used in the passive.
> *My boss made me work hard.*
> *I **was made to** work hard by my boss.*

4 *Cover* and verbs which involve similar ideas, such as *surround, decorate* can use *with* or *by. Cover* can also be followed by *in.*

Common contexts for the passive

1 Formality
The passive is probably more common in written English, where there tends to be less use of personal reference in some contexts, since the audience may be unknown.

2 Points mentioned in Unit 6
The passive is used to change the focus of the sentence, to avoid generalised subjects, and to make an action impersonal. It is common in descriptions of processes, and in scientific and technical language in general.

Activities

1
Decide whether the sentences in each pair have the same meaning.

a) Someone is painting our house at the moment.
We are painting our house at the moment.   *(different)*

b) The dentist is going to take out two of my teeth tomorrow.
I'm having two teeth taken out tomorrow.   *(same)*

c) Someone stole Mary's motorbike last week.
Mary had stolen her motorbike last week.

d) I've just been to the hairdresser's. What do you think?
I've just cut my hair at the hairdresser's. What do you think?

e) Someone has broken into my car.
My car has been broken.

f) Just a minute. I'll ask someone to wrap this for you.
Just a minute. I'll have to wrap this up for you.

g) The car hasn't been serviced for a long time.
We haven't had the car serviced for a long time.

h) They're coming to put in a new water-heater next week.
We're putting in a new water-heater next week.

i) Would you consider having plastic surgery to alter your nose?
Would you consider having your nose altered by plastic surgery?

j) A qualified electrician checked the wiring.
We had checked the wiring with a qualified electrician.

2
Decide in each sentence whether only one or both verbs underlined are suitable.

a) Jean had/got her handbag snatched.

b) Unfortunately my uncle was/got killed in the war.

c) I work slowly, but I have/get my jobs done in the end.

d) I must have/get these trousers altered.

e) It took all day, but I eventually had/got the washing-machine repaired.

f) Several people were/got left behind when the bus drove off.

g) We have had/got all our money stolen, so we need help.

h) Why don't you <u>have/get</u> the cooker seen to?

i) Paul <u>was/got</u> injured after he had been playing for only five minutes.

j) Helen <u>had/got</u> her house painted last year as usual.

3

Rewrite each sentence, beginning as shown, so that the meaning stays the same.

a) People think that neither side wanted war.
   Neither side is *thought to have wanted war.*

b) Everyone knows that eating fruit is good for you.
   Eating fruit ....

c) Everyone thought the painting had been destroyed.
   The painting ....

d) People say that the company bid fifty million pounds for the shares.
   The company ....

e) People say the late Mr Johnson was difficult to work with.
   The late ....

f) People think the jewels were stolen by one of the guests.
   One of the guests ....

g) It is believed that the Chinese invented gunpowder.
   The Chinese ....

h) Apparently the ship did not sustain any damage.
   The ship ....

i) It is thought that the two injured men were repairing high-tension cables.
   The two injured men ....

j) There is a rumour that the escaped prisoner is living in Spain.
   The escaped prisoner ....

4

Rewrite each sentence so that it contains the word in capitals.

a) We believe that the government has prepared a plan.   HAVE
   The government is believed to have prepared a plan.

b) We are thinking of getting someone to paint the outside of the house.   PAINTED

   ....

c) In the end I was unable to find a garage to service my car.   GET

   ....

d) People say that Mrs Turner was having business difficulties.   BEEN

   ....

e) The treasure is thought to date from the thirteenth century.   IT

   ....

f) The police towed away Alan's car.   GOT

   ....

g) Your hair needs cutting.   GET

   ....

h) The police believe that a professional thief stole the statue.   BEEN

   ....

i) Jill's parents are making her study hard.   MADE

   ....

j) Everyone thought that Helen had missed the train.   TO

....

5
Rewrite each
sentence so that it
ends with the
word underlined.

a) Another company has taken <u>over</u> our company.
Our company has been taken over.

b) We are dealing <u>with</u> your complaint.

....

c) We have not accounted <u>for</u> all the missing passengers.

....

d) Someone had tampered <u>with</u> the lock of the front door.

....

e) We don't know how they disposed <u>of</u> the body.

....

f) I must insist that you keep <u>to</u> the rules.

....

g) We are looking <u>into</u> this allegation.

....

h) We will frown <u>upon</u> any attempts to cheat in the exam.

....

i) The youngest complained that people were picking <u>on</u> him.

....

j) Ann was well provided <u>for</u> in her husband's will.

....

6
Choose the most
appropriate word
underlined.

a) The busy shopping street was thronged <u>by/with</u> people.
b) The emergency exit was concealed <u>by/from</u> a red curtain.
c) The price of excursions is included <u>in/with</u> the cost of the holiday.
d) All through January, the fields were covered <u>by/from</u> snow.
e) The room was crammed <u>by/with</u> furniture of all descriptions.
f) Two of the climbers were injured <u>by/with</u> falling rocks.
g) The island is inhabited <u>by/from</u> people of mainly Chinese origin.
h) The bank was quickly surrounded <u>from/with</u> armed police.
i) The window had been smashed <u>from/with</u> a hammer taken from the tool-shed.
j) The stadium was packed <u>from/with</u> cheering fans.

7
Put a suitable
preposition in
each space.

a) The tree had been decorated *with* coloured balls.
b) The answers have been included .... the book.
c) After the rugby match, Jim's shorts were covered .... mud.
d) The victim was struck from behind .... a heavy object.
e) The house was built .... money that David borrowed from the bank.
f) The cat narrowly escaped being run over .... a car.
g) When the accident happened, Sue was struck .... flying glass.
h) The turkey was stuffed .... chestnuts, and was very tasty.
i) No one knew that Peter had been involved .... the investigation.
j) When I left the casino, my pockets were crammed .... money.

8
Rewrite each sentence so that it begins *It* ....

a) They have decided to cancel the match.
   It *has been decided to cancel the match.*
b) We thought it was necessary to send a telegram.
   It ....
c) We have agreed to meet again in a fortnight.
   It ....

d) There is a rumour that the couple are to seek a divorce.
   It ....
e) There is confirmation of Mr Jackson's resignation.
   It ....
f) We believe that the ship has sunk.
   It ....
g) There was a proposal that a new offer should be made.
   It ....
h) We didn't think it was a good idea.
   It ....
i) We decided to try again later.
   It ....
j) There has been a suggestion that I should take a holiday.
   It ....

9
Rewrite the text using the passive where possible and so that the words underlined do not appear.

<u>Nobody</u> knows exactly when <u>someone</u> invented gunpowder. <u>People</u> know for a fact that the Chinese made rockets and fireworks long before <u>people</u> used gunpowder in Europe, which occurred at about the beginning of the thirteenth century. <u>We</u> generally believe that gunpowder brought to an end the 'Age of Chivalry', since anyone with a firearm could bring down a mounted knight. In fact, <u>people</u> did not develop efficient firearms until the sixteenth century. <u>They</u> used gunpowder mainly in siege cannon when <u>people</u> first introduced it. Later <u>they</u> used it in engineering work and in mining, but <u>they</u> found that it was extremely dangerous. Modern explosives have now replaced gunpowder, but <u>we</u> still use it for making fireworks, just as the Chinese did.

It is not known exactly ....

Unit 8 Conditionals and *If* Sentences

Explanations

Basic contrasts

1 What is always true: present + present
Both present simple and continuous are possible after *if* meaning *when*.
*If I **work** late, I get tired.*
*If the water **is boiling**, it means the food is nearly ready.*

2 What was always true: past + past
Both past simple and continuous are possible after *if* meaning *when*.
*We went home early if it **was** foggy.*
*If it **was snowing**, we stayed at home.*

3 Real situations: present + *will*
Here we think that the outcome is really possible.
*If you **keep** driving like that, you'**ll have** an accident.*

4 Hypothetical situations: past + *would*
These are imaginary situations.
*If I **knew** the answer, I'**d** tell you.*
The verb *be* usually takes the form *were* for all persons in these sentences, though *was* is used in everyday speech. Note that in the first person it is possible to use *should* instead of *would*.
*If I **left** home, I think **I should** be lonely.*

5 Hypothetical past situations: past perfect + *would have*
These refer to past events.
*If I **had known** you were coming, I **would have met** you at the station.*

6 With modals
Possible situations in the present
*If you **get** wet, you **should** change your clothes immediately.*
*If you **come** early, we **can** discuss the problem together.*
Hypothetical situations
*If I **had** the money, I **could** help you.*
Hypothetical past situations
*If you **hadn't** reminded me, I **might have** forgotten.*

7   *If only*
This adds emphasis to hypothetical situations. With past events it adds a sense of regret. The second part of the sentence is often left out.
*   **If only** I had enough time!*
*   **If only** I hadn't drunk too much, this wouldn't have happened!*

8   *Unless* and other alternatives to *if*
Unless means *only if not*. Not all negative *if* sentences can be transformed into *unless* sentences.
*   If he wasn't told by Jane, he couldn't have known.*
*   **Unless** he was told by Jane, he couldn't have known. (can be changed)*
*   If Mr Smith doesn't come back, he'll phone you. (cannot be changed)*
If one situation depends on another, *if* can be replaced by *as/so long as*, *provided* or *only if*. See Unit 13 for *only if*.
*   I'll do what you say **provided** the police are not informed.*
Even if describes how something will happen whatever the condition.
*   **Even if** it rains, we'll still go for a picnic.*

9   Past events with results in the present: past perfect + *would*
*   If Jim **hadn't missed** the plane, he **would** be here by now.*

10 Colloquial past situations
This is technically 'incorrect' but many native speakers say this, perhaps to balance the 'have' in each part of the sentence.
*   If I'**d have been there**, I would have seen her.*

Other tenses in conditional sentences

1   *Going to*
Going to can replace *will*.
*   If you fall, you'**re going to** hurt yourself.*
It can also be used to mean 'intend to' after *if*.
*   If you'**re going to** make trouble, we'll call the police.*

2   Present perfect
This can be used to emphasis completion after *if*.
*   If you'**ve finished**, then we'll go.*
It is also possible in both parts of the sentence.
*   If I'**ve told** you once, I'**ve told** you a hundred times!*

3   Doubt and uncertainty
An additional *not* can be added in formal expressions involving doubt. This emphasises the uncertainty and does not add a negative meaning.
*   I wouldn't be surprised if it **didn't** rain. (I think it will rain.)*
The intonation falls on *rain*; there is no stress on *didn't*.

4 *Should*
   After *if,* this makes the possibility of an event seem unlikely.
   > *If you **should see** Ann, could you ask her to call me?*
   This implies that I do not expect you to see Ann.

5 *Were to*
   This also makes an event seem more hypothetical.
   > *If I **were to ask** you to marry me, what would you say?*

6 *Happen to*
   This emphasises chance possibilities. It is often used with *should.*
   > *If you **happen to see** Helen, could you ask her to call me?*
   > *If you **should happen to be passing**, drop in for a cup of tea.*

7 *If it were not for/If it hadn't been for*
   This describes how one event depends on another.
   > *If it **weren't for** Jim, this company would be in a mess.*
   > *If it **hadn't been for** their goalkeeper, United would have lost.*

8 *Will* and *would*: politeness and emphasis
   These can be used as polite forms.
   > *If you **will/would wait** here, I'll see if Mrs Green is free.*
   Will can also be used for emphasis, meaning 'insist on doing'.
   > *If you **will** stay out late, no wonder you are tired! (insist on staying)*

Other ways of
making a
conditional
sentence

1 *Supposing, otherwise*
   Supposing or *suppose* can replace *if,* mainly in everyday speech.
   > ***Supposing you won** the football pools, what would you do?*
   Otherwise means 'or if not'. It can go at the beginning or end of the sentence.
   > *If you hadn't given us directions, we wouldn't have found the house.*
   > *Thanks for your directions to the house. We wouldn't have found it*
   > ***otherwise.***

2 *But for*
   This can replace *if not.* It is used in formal language, and must be followed by
   a noun form.
   > *If you hadn't helped us, we would have been in trouble.*
   > ***But for your help**, we would have been in trouble.*

3 *If so/If not*
   These can refer to a sentence understood but not stated.
   > *There is a possibility that Jack will be late. **If so,** I will take his place.*

4 Colloquial omission of *if*
An imperative can be used instead of an *if* clause in everyday speech.
Sit down, *and I'll make us a cup of tea.* (If you sit down ...)

5 *If* and adjectives
In expressions such as *if it is necessary/possible* it is possible to omit the verb *be*.
If interested, *apply within.* **If necessary**, *take a taxi.*

6 Formally *if* can mean *although*, usually as *if* + adjective.
The room was well-furnished, **if** *a little* **badly decorated.**

Activities

1
Put each verb in brackets into an appropriate tense.

a) Now we're lost! If you *had written down* (write down) Mary's directions, this .... (not happen).
b) Why don't we emigrate? If we .... (live) in Australia, at least the weather .... (be) better!
c) I'm afraid that Smith is a hardened criminal. If we .... (not punish) him this time, he .... (only commit) more crimes.
d) Thanks to Dr Jones, I'm still alive! If it .... (not be) for her, I .... (be) dead for certain!
e) I'm sorry I can't lend you any money. You know that if I .... (have) it, I .... (lend) it to you.
f) Don't be afraid. If you .... (touch) the dog, it .... (not bite).
g) In those days, if you .... (have) a job, you .... (be) lucky.
h) It's always the same! If I .... (decide) to leave the office early, my boss .... (call) me after I've left!
i) What a terrible thing to happen! Just think, if we .... (not miss) the plane, we .... (kill) in the crash.
j) Did you enjoy your meal? If you .... (finish) eating, I .... (clear away) the plates.

2
Rewrite each sentence so that it contains the word in capitals.

a) If you do have any time free, could you give me a ring? SHOULD
If you should have any time free, could you give me a ring?

b) We won't go away if the weather is bad. UNLESS
....

c) I didn't have the money so I didn't buy a new suit. WOULD
....

d) I regret not studying hard last term. ONLY
....

e) If you hurry up, you won't be late. GOING
....

f) If they offered you the job, would you accept? WERE
....

g) If you are in London by any chance, come and see me.　　HAPPEN

....

h) Without you, I would have given up years ago.　　BEEN

....

i) If you insist on doing everything yourself, of course you feel tired!　WILL

....

j) Please take a seat, and I'll inquire for you.　　WILL

....

3

Complete each sentence with a suitable word or phrase.

a) That was a narrow escape! If I had *fallen, I would have* broken my leg.
b) If it hadn't ...., ... gone out for a walk.
c) If you ...., then I'd like it back please.
d) I .... if Harry didn't win the competition!
e) Unless Brenda .... lose the race.
f) If you .... see Mary, give her my love.
g) I wouldn't accept the job, even .... to me.
h) If I were .... loved you, what would you say?
i) Thanks for your help with the garden. I .... otherwise.
j) But for Sally, Jim .... drowned.

4

Rewrite each sentence, beginning as shown, so that the meaning stays the same.

a) Working so much will make you tired.
   If *you work so much, you will get tired.*
b) I regret drinking so much last night!
   If only ....

HELP

c) What would you do if there was an earthquake?
   Supposing ....
d) If you do the shopping, I'll cook lunch.
   You ....
e) What would you do if you found some buried treasure?
   If you were ....
f) If Pauline hadn't been interested, the project would have been abandoned.
   But for ....
g) If by any chance you find my wallet, could you let me know?
   If you happen ....
h) I might be late. If so, start without me.
   If I ....
i) The fire was brought under control thanks to the night-watchman.
   If it hadn't ....
j) Dick is in prison because a detective recognised him.
   If a detective ....

5
Rewrite each sentence so that it contains the word in capitals.

a) Don't take this job if you don't really want it.   UNLESS
   Don't take this job unless you really want it.

b) I wasn't tall enough to reach the shelf.   TALLER
   ....

c) I won't sell the painting, not even for £1000.   IF
   ....

d) If the ship sank, what would you do?   WERE
   ....

e) If you should notice what's on at the cinema, let me know.   HAPPEN
   ....

f) If you hadn't encouraged me, I would have given up.   BUT
   ....

g) Although it is a good car, it is expensive.   IF
   ....

h) If you insist on smoking so much, of course you feel ill.   WILL
   ....

i) I don't have any scissors so I can't lend you any.   IF
   ....

j) But for Helen, the play would be a flop.   WERE
   ....

6
Rewrite each sentence, beginning as shown, so that the meaning stays the same.

a) It's a pity your parents can't be here too.
   If only *your parents could be here too.*

b) If Jane hadn't refused to work overtime, she would have got promotion.
   If it hadn't ....

c) If you left out that chapter, you can't really say you read the whole book.
   Unless ....

d) If you want my advice, I'd think twice about buying a car like that.
   If I ....

e) It won't make any difference if City score first, United will still win.
   United will still win ....

f) If the painting is finished by Saturday, we'll pay you extra.
   Finish ....

g) Provided your voice is audible, the audience will get the point of this scene.
   As long as the audience ....

h) If you refuse to stop eating sweets, you can't expect to lose weight easily.
   If you won't ....

i) Without your help, I wouldn't have found the house.
   If you ....

j) Getting up early makes me feel hungry.
   If ....

7
Complete each sentence with a suitable word or phrase.

a) If you had really wanted to come, you *could have left* a few hours early.
b) I'll lend you my radio as .... you bring it back before Saturday.
c) .... the phone bill today, the phone will be cut off.
d) I shall call off the sale .... to pay me the whole amount in cash.
e) If I .... your tools, I wouldn't have been able to fix the car.
f) If you'd told me you were coming, I .... something to eat.
g) If you took more time over your work .... so many mistakes in it.
h) Those wires look a bit dangerous; .... I were you.
i) If you've finished .... home.
j) If Sue had known her sister wasn't coming, she .... to such trouble.

8
Decide whether each sentence is grammatically possible or not.

a) If you haven't received a letter yet, you haven't got the job. (*possible*)
b) If it isn't for David, we are missing the bus.
c) If it's raining, we go to the pub on the corner instead.
d) If you didn't lend us the money, we would have gone to the bank.
e) If you should happen to change your mind, drop me a line.
f) If it wasn't for the rain, we would have been home by now.
g) If you will drive so fast, no wonder the police keep stopping you.
h) If I knew you were coming, I would have met you at the airport.
i) But for you helped us, we would have taken much longer.
j) If Jack joins the team, I'm leaving.

Unit 9 Unreal tenses and subjunctives

Explanations

It's time

1 *It's time, It's high time*
These are followed by past simple or continuous, though the time referred to is unreal. See Unit 8.
*It's time we **left**. It's high time **I was/were going**.*

2 *Was* or *were*
As in conditional sentences, *were* can be used for all persons of *be*, though *was* is more common in everyday speech.

Wishes

1 Present
These are wishes where you want to change a present state.
I wish I had a motorbike. (I don't have one now.)
I wish you weren't leaving. (You are leaving.)
I wish I was going on holiday with you. (I am not going.)

2 *Would* and *could*
If the verb is an event verb, the reference is to the future. We use *would* or *could* after wish. *Would* here means 'decided to'.
*I wish you **would** leave.*
*I wish I **could** come on holiday with you next year.*
The use with *would* is often used to describe an annoying habit.
*I wish you **wouldn't make such a mess**.*

3 Past
These are wishes referring to a past event, which cannot be changed.
*I wish **I hadn't eaten so much**.*
This use is common after *if only* to express regrets. See Unit 8

4 Hope
Wishes about simple future events are expressed with *hope*.
*I hope it doesn't rain **tomorrow**.*
*I hope he'll stop talking **soon**!*

I'd rather/I prefer (followed by a clause)

1 *I'd rather* is followed by past tenses in the same way as wishes about the present. It expresses a personal preference about actions.

  I'd rather you didn't smoke in here.

  I'd sooner works in the same way.

  Both *I'd rather* and *I'd sooner* are used with normal tenses when comparing nouns or phrases.

  I'd rather be a sailor than a soldier. (present)

  I'd rather have lived in Ancient Greece than Ancient Rome. (past)

2 *I'd prefer* can be used as part of a conditional 2 sentence. Note that 'prefer' in this type of sentence has an object 'it'.

  I'd prefer it if you didn't go.

  I'd prefer is not followed by an unreal tense.

  I'd prefer tea to coffee.

  I'd prefer you not to go.

As if, As though

1 Real and unreal

  The tense here depends on whether the comparison is true or unreal.

  *He acts as if he **were** in charge. (He isn't in charge.)*

  *He acts as if he **is** in charge. (He is in charge.)*

  The difference is clearer with obviously unreal comparisons.

  *You look as if you **had just seen** a ghost!*

  In everyday speech, there is often no obvious difference made.

2 Present and past reference are both possible.

  *I feel **as if I were flying**. (I'm not.)*

  *I feel **as if** an express train **had hit me**. (It didn't.)*

Suppose and *imagine*

1 Understood conditions

  The conditional part of these sentences is often understood but not stated.

  Imagine we won the pools!   *(Imagine what we would do if ...)*

  Suppose someone told you that I was a spy! (What would you say?)

  As with conditional sentences, if the event referred to is a real possibility, rather than imaginary, a present tense is possible:

  *Suppose it **starts** raining, what'll we do?*

2 Present or past

  Present and past reference are both possible.

  Imagine we'd never met!

  Suppose we went to Wales for a change.

Formal Subjunctives	**1**	Insisting, demanding etc.

After verbs such as *demand, insist, suggest, require* which involve an implied obligation, the subjunctive may be used in formal style. This has only one form, that of the infinitive, and there is no third person -s, or past form. The verb *be* has *be* for all forms.

> They demanded that he **leave** at once.

The same applies after expressions such as *it is necessary/essential/important that ...*

> It is essential that you **arrive** before six.

2 Less formal usage

Less formally, *should* can be used, and colloquially no tense change is made, or an infinitive construction is used.

> They demanded that he **should leave**.
> They demanded that he left. (informal)
> It is essential for you **to arrive** before six.

Formulaic Subjunctive

These are fixed expressions all using subjunctive. Typical examples are:

> God save the Queen!
> Be that as it may ...
> Come what may ...

Activities

1

Choose between *hope* and *wish* in each sentence.

a) I hope/wish I'll see you again soon.
b) I hope/wish the weather improves soon.
c) I hope/wish I knew the answer.
d) I hope/wish you didn't have to go.
e) I hope/wish you'd stop shouting so much.
f) I hope/wish nothing goes wrong.
g) I hope/wish it would stop raining.
h) I hope/wish you can come to my party.
i) I hope/wish you don't mind.
j) I hope/wish we could meet next week.

2

Put each verb in brackets into a suitable tense.

a) I would say it was time you *started* (start) working seriously.
b) I'd rather you .... (not watch) television while I'm reading.
c) I wish I .... (spend) more time swimming last summer.
d) Helen is so bossy. She acts as if she .... (own) the place.
e) I wish you .... (not keep) coming late to class.
f) Suppose a complete stranger .... (leave) you a lot of money in their will!
g) I wish I .... (go) to your party after all.

h) I'd rather you .... (sit) next to Susan, please.

i) The government demanded that the ambassador .... (be) recalled.

j) You are lucky going to Italy. I wish I .... (go) with you.

3

Correct the error or errors in each sentence.

a) I wish I bought that old house.

b) I'd rather you don't eat all the bread.

c) It's time I go.

d) I wish I own a motorbike.

e) I wish we are not leaving in the morning.

f) Sue would rather reading than watching television.

g) Come what comes, I'll be on your side.

h) I hope it would stop raining.

i) I'd prefer you didn't wait.

j) I wish I didn't listen to you before.

4

Complete each sentence with a suitable word or phrase.

a) I wish you *would stop* making so much noise late at night!

b) I'd rather the children .... on the television without permission.

c) Suppose .... half the money I owe you. Would that satisfy you?

d) I hope .... get into trouble on my account.

e) This is an awful hotel. I wish we .... to the Grand instead.

f) It is absolutely .... you contact head office in advance.

g) I think it's high time we .... locking all the windows at night.

h) Would you rather I .... the lunch, if you feel tired?

i) I wish my car .... as fast as yours.

j) I'd prefer you .... smoke in here, if you don't mind.

5

Complete each sentence with *one* word.

a) It's *high* time you learned to look after yourself!

b) I wish you .... try listening to me just for once!

c) I .... rather not go by bus, if possible.

d) .... that as it may, it doesn't alter the seriousness of the problem.

e) I wish Carol .... be here to see you all.

f) We both wish you .... staying longer.

g) You .... as if you had played in the match instead of watching it!

h) .... they offered you the job of managing director!

i) I really wish we .... married.

j) I .... you didn't mind my phoning so late.

6
Rewrite each sentence so that it contains the word in capitals, and so that the meaning stays the same.

a) Do you ever regret not going to university?   WISH
   Do you ever wish you had gone to university?

b) I should really be leaving.   TIME

c) I'd rather have beer than wine.   PREFER

d) Jack doesn't know all the answers, though he pretends to.   ACTS

e) I'd love to be able to go with you to the opera.   WISH

f) I wish I hadn't sold that old painting.   PITY

g) It would be better if you didn't stay long.   RATHER

h) The management insisted on our wearing dark suits.   WEAR

i) Why do you have to complain all the time?   WISH

j) I don't want to go to the meeting.   RATHER

7
Rewrite each sentence, beginning as shown, so that the meaning stays the same.

a) It would be nice to be able to fly.
   I wish *I could fly!*

b) I wish I hadn't heard that!
   I'd rather you ....

c) Everyone wished they had listened more carefully to the lecture.
   Everyone regretted ....

d) Unfortunately I've got to work late tonight.
   I wish ....

e) Is it better for me to leave?
   Would you.....................................

f) It's a pity I can't borrow your car.
   I wish you would ....

g) We really must discuss this again.
   It's important that ....

h) It's a pity you were driving so fast.
I wish you..

i) May the President live a long time!
Long ....

j) Jack prefers me not to say anything about the missing money.
Jack would rather..

8

Complete each
sentence with a
suitable word or
phrase.

a) It's time all of us *were* in bed.
b) I'd rather you .... slowly and more carefully.
c) .... may, I will always be on your side!
d) I wish you .... the lecture instead of Professor Brown!
e) Don't rush your decision. I'd rather you .... over.
f) The authorities .... the money be paid at once.
g) I wish I could .... at your party, but I was busy I'm afraid.
h) Mary sometimes acts as if she .... either way what happened.
i) What .... did about that problem we discussed?
j) It's time I .... my way.

Unit 10 Progress Test (Units 6, 7, 8, 9)

1

Put each verb in brackets into an appropriate form.

Employees protesting at the planned closure of the Magnet electronics factory have begun a protest outside the factory in Brook Road. It (1) .... (reveal) last week that production at the factory, where over 3000 local people (2) .... (employ), (3) .... (transfer) to the Magnet plant in Luton next month. 'Why (4) .... (we not inform) about this earlier? We (5) .... (only tell) about this two days ago,' said Marjory Calder, representing the workforce. 'It's about time companies such as this (6) .... (start) thinking about how local communities (7) .... (affect) by their policies. Most people here are buying houses. How (8) .... (their mortgage payments keep up)? And how are we going to find jobs? I wish I (9) .... (know).' Reg Reynolds of Magnet (10) .... (ask) what (11) .... (do) to help those who (12) .... (make) redundant. 'The majority of our employees (13) .... (offer) work at our plant in Luton,' he told our reporter, 'and every effort (14) .... (make) over the past month to offer early retirement to those who qualify.' When he (15) .... (question) about why the workers (16) .... (not tell) about the closure earlier, he revealed that the company (17) .... (promise) a government loan to keep the factory open, but that at the last minute it (18) .... (decide) not to provide the loan after all. 'So don't blame the company, we've done our best.' Local MP Brenda Stone (19) .... (ask) to raise the matter in the House of Commons, and told us that a letter (20) .... (send) to the Minister responsible within the next few days.

2

Rewrite each sentence, beginning as shown, so that the meaning stays the same.

a) It is thought that the prisoner was recaptured while drinking in a pub.
   The prisoner ....

b) Someone broke into John's flat last week.
   John ....

c) Please don't turn on the radio.
   I'd rather you ....

d) The wind was bending the young tree to the ground.
   The young tree ....

e) If you missed the first half, you can't really say you understood the film.
   Unless ....

f) Everyone believed that the house had been sold.
   The house ....

g) What would you do if you lost your job?
   Supposing ....

h) When we have finished building the house, we'll plan the garden.
   After the house ....

    i) It's a pity I am going to work tomorrow.
        I wish ....

    j) The living-room hasn't been painted for two years.
        We ....

3
Complete each sentence with a suitable word or phrase.

a) I don't like this restaurant, I wish we had .... to the 'Taj Mahal'.
b) It's time .... done about this problem.
c) The late Prime Minister is said .... difficult to work with.
d) That was lucky! If I .... this bus, I .... met you.
e) Your order .... with at the moment.
f) But for Pauline, I .... passed the exam.
g) All dishes .... with french fries and a green salad.
h) It is absolutely .... you cash this cheque tomorrow.
i) Jim is being .... the police station.
j) If I were .... where the treasure is, what would you do?

4
Rewrite each sentence so that it contains the word in capitals, and so that the meaning stays the same.

a) Everyone thought the book was written by the princess herself. HAVE
    ....

b) I can't lift this table on my own. UNLESS
    ....

c) I won't stay in this job, not even for double the salary. IF
    ....

d) The coins are believed to have been buried for safe-keeping. IT
    ....

e) If you insist on eating so fast, of course you get indigestion. WILL
    ....

f) It's a pity you aren't going to Ann's party. WISH
    ....

g) Someone punched Sam in the face at a football match. GOT
    ....

h) If you found the missing money, what would you do? WERE
    ....

i) They suspended Jackson for the next two matches. BANNED
    ....

j) Please come this way, and I'll see if Mr Francis is in. WILL
    ....

5
Put each verb in brackets into an appropriate tense.

a) The second film we saw .... (direct) by Howard Hughes.
b) If I .... (know) that you .... (arrive) on that train, I .... (come) to meet you.
c) I wish you .... (not eat) all the food! I'm hungry!
d) Be careful! If you .... (tease) the cat it .... (scratch) you!
e) Thanks very much! If you .... (not help) me, we .... (not finish) the work so quickly.

f) Hurry up, or all the best seats .... (take).

g) What a shame that it .... (decide) to cancel the school play!

h) Carol now wishes she .... (marry) in a church.

i) If it .... (not be) for you, I .... (still be) in prison today!

j) Unfortunately tomorrow's match .... (call off).

6

Rewrite each sentence so that it does not contain the words underlined, and so that it contains a passive form.

a) Mushroom-gatherers usually <u>work</u> in the early morning.
....

b) It's time <u>the government</u> brought the economy under control.
....

c) <u>A thief</u> stole several coats from the cloakroom.
....

d) <u>The management</u> has decided to reduce the workforce by 10%.
....

e) The decorators only <u>took</u> a day to do our house.
....

f) <u>They</u> have no idea what caused the accident.
....

g) <u>You</u> have to make an application for a visa in advance.
....

h) Ticket collectors <u>work</u> on the train on this line.
....

i) Lots of <u>people</u> had left their luggage on the platform.
....

j) <u>A person</u> directed Sally to the wrong address.
....

7

Complete each sentence with *one* appropriate word.

a) .... that as it may, it is still no excuse.

b) Graham .... his car towed away by the police.

c) I am going to call the police .... you leave at once.

d) I think it's high time you .... taking yourself seriously.

e) If you .... to think of moving, we could offer you a job.

f) I .... you can come to my birthday party.

g) Just imagine! .... they told you that you had won first prize!

h) I wish Harry .... see the children now!

i) If only you .... just stop talking for a moment and try listening!

j) It was not .... necessary to call the fire-brigade.

8

Rewrite each sentence, beginning as shown, so that the meaning stays the same.

a) If you pay me back the money you took, I won't tell the police.
Pay me back ....

b) The discovery of new drugs is helping the fight against this disease.
The fight ....

c) It wouldn't make any difference if you offered me a million pounds, I still wouldn't sell!
Even if ....

d) I'll get someone to press your trousers.
I'll have ....

e) Everyone knows that taking exercise is good for your health.
Taking exercise ....

f) Brenda is a star because a famous director saw her act in a school play.
If a famous ....

g) Someone has suggested the resignation of the minister.
It ....

h) I have an appointment for a haircut this afternoon.
I'm having ....

i) I regret not buying some tickets for the concert.
I wish ....

j) Someone will deliver the tickets to your house next week.
The tickets ....

9

Complete each sentence with a suitable word or phrase.

a) I .... to chair the meeting, and I have accepted.

b) It's time the children .... in class.

c) All the missing papers have .... for.

d) I'd rather your cat .... on my armchair.

e) Nothing has .... of Sue since she left for Glasgow.

f) If the weather ...., we would have gone to the seaside.

g) The ship is .... been sunk by pirates.

h) If you'd told me .... rain, I would have stayed at home.

i) I'd prefer you .... sit at the back of the room.

j) I was .... way by a helpful traffic warden.

10

Put *one* suitable word in each space.

By the time we reached the town centre it was packed (1) .... people (2) .... their shopping done. Trees decorated (3) .... coloured lights blinked at every corner and (4) .... I hadn't known about the centenary celebrations, I would (5) .... thought it was Christmas. Banners had (6) .... stretched across the street proclaiming 'MARSHLAND NEW TOWN – THE FIRST HUNDRED YEARS', as (7) .... the shoppers needed to (8) .... reminded. Nothing else had been (9) .... of in the town for weeks. Committees had (10) .... formed, and every day more and more money was (11) .... collected by local schoolchildren selling flags and buttons. Posters printed (12) .... the words LONG LIVE MARSHLAND dangled from every lamp post. If I hadn't (13) .... it with my own eyes, I (14) .... never have believed it. And (15) .... for the Mayor, Mrs Biggs, the centenary would have passed by unnoticed.

11
Rewrite each sentence so that it contains the word given in capitals, and so that the meaning stays the same.

a) John's school is making him sit his exams again. — MADE

....

b) If you don't pay the bill, they'll cut off the electricity. — BE

....

c) If you see Tina by any chance, could you ask her to get in touch? — HAPPEN

....

d) I should really be starting my homework. — TIME

....

e) Without Jane, I would never have made it to the top. — BEEN

....

f) Everyone thinks that Mary has not accepted the job. — THOUGHT

....

g) I haven't got an aspirin, so I can't give you one. — IF

....

h) If you do change your mind after all, let me know. — SHOULD

....

i) It would be better if you didn't bring Jim to the party. — RATHER

....

j) I'm going to the dentist's for a filling tomorrow. — FILLED

....

12
Put *one* suitable word in each sentence.

a) You are the person who .... things done around here!

b) The victim is thought to have been .... a bath at the time.

c) As I cycled along the lane I was hit .... an overhanging branch.

d) If the baby looked unhappy we .... it a toy to play with.

e) If .... you had asked me earlier, I could have helped you.

f) .... if I had got there in time, it wouldn't have made any difference.

g) I wouldn't be surprised if Patrick .... win.

h) .... for the bad weather, our holiday would have been perfect.

i) I .... rather you didn't stay any longer.

j) I wouldn't be surprised if Jack .... to call round this evening.

Unit 11 Modal auxiliaries 1: present and future

Explanations

Don't have to
and *must not*

1 *Don't have to* refers to an absence of obligation.
*You **don't have to** work tomorrow.*

2 *Must not* refers to an obligation not to do something.
*You **must not** leave the room before the end of the test.*

Should

Where **should* appears, *ought to* can also be used.

1 Expectation
*This film ***should** be really good.*

2 Recommendation
*I think you ***should** talk it over with your parents.*
In writing, *should* can be used to express a strong obligation politely.
*Guests **should** vacate their rooms by midday.*

3 Criticism of an action
*You ***shouldn't** eat so much late at night.*

4 Uncertainty
***Should** I leave these papers on your desk?*

5 *Should* and verbs of thinking
Should is often used with verbs of thinking, to make an opinion less direct.
*I **should think** that model would sell quite well.*

6 With *be* and adjectives describing chance
This group of adjectives includes *odd, strange, funny (=odd)* and the
expression *What a coincidence.*
*It's strange that you **should** be staying in the same hotel!*

7 After *in case* to emphasise unlikelihood:
*I'm taking an umbrella **in case it should rain**.*
See Unit 8 for similar uses in conditional sentences.

Could

1 *Could* is used to express possibility or uncertainty.
*This **could** be the house.*

2 *Could* is used with comparative adjectives to express possibility or impossibility.
*The situation **couldn't** be worse.*
*It **could** be better.*

59

3 *Could* is used to make suggestions.
We **could** *go to that new restaurant opposite the cinema.*

4 *Could* is used to express unwillingness.
I **couldn't** *possibly leave Tim here on his own.*

Can

1 *Can* with *be* is used to make criticisms.
You **can be** *really annoying, you know!*

2 *Can* is also used with *be* to refer to capability.
Winter here **can be** *really cold.*

Must and *can't*

These refer to present time only. (See *bound to.*) In expressing certainty, they are opposites.
This **must** *be our stop. (I'm sure it is.)*
This **can't** *be our stop. (I'm sure it isn't.)*

May and *might*

1 *May* can be used to express *although* clauses:
She **may** *be the boss,* **but** *that is no excuse for shouting like that.*
See also Unit 14 Emphasis.

2 *May/might as well*
This describes the only thing left to do, something which the speaker is not enthusiastic about.
Nobody else is going to turn up now for the lesson, so you **may as well** *go home.*

3 *May* and *might* both express possibility or uncertainty. *May* is more common in formal language.
The peace conference **may** *find a solution to the problem.*

4 There is an idiomatic expression with *try*, using *may* for present reference, and *might* for past reference.
Try as I might, *I could not pass my driving test.*
Although I tried hard, I could not pass my driving test.

Shall

1 *Shall* can be used with all persons to emphasise something which the speaker feels is certain to happen or wants to happen.
I **shall** *definitely give up smoking this year.*
We **shall** *win! (shall is stressed in this sentence)*

2 Similarly, *shall* is used in formal rules and regulations.
No player **shall** *knowingly pick up or move the ball of another player.*

Will	**1**	*Will* can be used to express an assumption.
		–The phone's ringing. – That'll be for me.

2 *Will /won't* can be used emphatically to tell someone of the speaker's intention, or to forbid an action, in response to a *will* expression.
– *I'll take the money anyway, so there!*
– *You **won't**!*
– *I **will**!*
Similarly *I won't* can mean *I refuse*, and *I will* can mean *I insist*.
– *I won't do it!   – Yes, you **will**!*

Would	**1**	*Would* can refer to an annoying habit, typical of a person.
		*Jack **would** get lost, **wouldn't he**! It's typical!*

2 *Would* is used in sentences expressing certainty, where the sentence is a suppressed conditional sentence.
*Nobody **would** agree with that idea. (if we asked them)*
*Life **wouldn't** be worth living without you. (if you weren't there)*

3 *Would* can be used after *be* followed by adjectives *doubtful, unlikely* to emphasise a tentative action.
*It's **unlikely** that Jim **would** do something like that.*
Would can be used after after *doubt* in the same way.
*I **doubt** whether Helen **would know** the answer.*

Need	**1**	*Need to* is not a modal auxiliary, and behaves like a normal verb.
		*Do you **need to** use the photocopier?*

2 *Need* is a modal auxiliary, but mainly in question and negative forms.
***Need you** make so much noise?*

3 See Unit 7 for *need doing*

Related non-modal expressions	**1**	*Had better*
		This is a recommendation and refers only to the present or future.
		*You'd **better** not phone her again.*

2 *Be bound to*
This makes a future prediction of certainty.
*It's **bound to rain** tomorrow.*

Activities

1

Choose the most suitable words underlined.

a) I don't think you could/should tell anyone yet.
b) I couldn't/shouldn't possibly leave without paying.
c) That mustn't/can't be the hotel Jane told us about.
d) There are times when the traffic here can/could be really heavy.
e) We are enjoying our holiday, though the weather could/must be better.
f) You couldn't/shouldn't really be sitting here.
g) You could/may be older than me, but that doesn't mean you're cleverer.
h) I might/should suppose your job is rather difficult.
i) I'm afraid that nobody should/would help me in that kind of situation.
j) No member of the association must/shall remove official documents from these premises without written permission.

2

Put *one* suitable word in each space.

a) Quite honestly, you might as *well* not bother.
b) It's .... that you should know Wendy too!
c) You .... better not take any more medicine now.
d) All students .... report to the registrar's office on arrival.
e) How about going to the lake? We .... take a cold lunch with us.
f) If I say you have to do it, you .... do it!
g) I'm not sure about my application. .... I send two copies or three?
h) .... that really be Paula's husband? He looks so young.
i) This .... be the place I suppose, but it doesn't look like it.
j) Both the clocks say 4.30, so that .... be the time.

3

Rewrite each sentence, beginning as shown, so that the meaning stays the same.

a) Although you are in charge, it doesn't give you the right to be rude.
You may *be in charge, but it doesn't give you the right to be rude.*
b) I recommend going to Brighton for a week.
I think ....
c) It's typical of Steve to lose his keys!
Steve would ....
d) I suppose Kate is quite well off.
I should ....
e) I am as happy as possible at the moment.
I couldn't ....
f) Although I tried hard, I couldn't lift the suitcase.
Try ....
g) I'm sure that Peter will be on time.
Peter is ....
h) Fancy you and I having the same surname!
It's odd ....
i) If I were you I'd take up jogging.
I think ....
j) Do we have to leave so early?
Need ....

4

Rewrite each sentence so that it contains the word in capitals, and so that the meaning stays the same.

a) I expect this beach will be deserted.
This beach should be deserted. .... SHOULD

b) This climb is possibly dangerous.
.... COULD

c) Arthur is sometimes really irritating! .... CAN

d) You can't borrow my car! .... WON'T

e) How about going to the theatre instead? .... COULD

f) Do you want me to turn off the oven, or not? .... SHOULD

g) I don't think Harry is likely to resign. .... WOULD

h) I'm sure this isn't the way to Norwich. .... CAN'T

i) It would be all the same if we gave up now. .... MIGHT

j) Please turn off the light before leaving. .... SHOULD
....

5

Choose the sentence closest in meaning to the sentence given.

a) It's possible that we'll know the answers tomorrow.
  A) We may know all the answers tomorrow.
  B) We should know all the answers tomorrow.

b) I don't think you should ring him now. It's rather late.
  A) You might not ring him now. It's rather late.
  B) You'd better not ring him now. It's rather late.

c) You needn't come if you don't want to.
  A) You won't come if you don't want to.
  B) You don't have to come if you don't want to.

d) I think it's wrong for you to work so hard.
  A) You don't have to work so hard.
  B) You shouldn't work so hard.

e) Perhaps these are the keys.
  A) These might be the keys.
  B) These must be the keys.

f) I know. Why don't we go out to eat instead.
  A) I know. We must go out to eat instead.
  B) I know. We could go out to eat instead.

g) It would be quite wrong for us to lock the cat in the house for a week.
  A) We'd better not lock the cat in the house for a week.
  B) We can't lock the cat in the house for a week.

h) It's possible that the decision will be announced next week.
  A) The decision might be announced next week.
  B) The decision will be announced next week.

i) Although I try hard, I can never solve *The Times* crossword.
   A) Try as I may, I can never solve *The Times* crossword.
   B) Try as I can, I may never solve *The Times* crossword.

6

Complete each sentence with a suitable word or phrase.

a) How funny *that you should* say that!
b) The heating comes on automatically. You .... turn it on.
c) The people here .... be really unfriendly.
d) Of course I'll help! I .... possibly let you do it on your own.
e) The team .... good without Sue at centre-forward.
f) Of course you can't sleep if you .... drink so much coffee!
g) It's a lovely hotel. And the staff .... more helpful.
h) You .... be very critical sometimes.
i) George .... it there if he has stayed there for so long.
j) You .... right, but I still don't agree with you!

7

Rewrite each sentence so that it contains the word in capitals, and so that the meaning stays the same.

a) I'm sure that's Marion.
   That'll be Marion.   WILL
   ....

b) Jim keeps giving me presents.   WILL
   ....

c) It makes no difference if we call it off.   MAY
   ....

d) Don't bother lying to me.   HAVE
   ....

e) The burglar might come back, so change all the locks.   CASE
   ....

f) Although it's summer, the temperature is more like winter.   MAY
   ....

g) You should leave before Jack gets back.   HAD
   ....

h) That is not typical of Helen's behaviour.   WOULDN'T
   ....

i) It would be impossible to tell Sally the truth.   POSSIBLY
   ....

8

Complete each sentence with a suitable word or phrase.

a) What about this meat? *Should/Shall* I roast it or stew it?
b) Thank you for offering but I .... possibly accept.
c) Harry studies a lot. He .... know all the answers.
d) Oh well, things .... much worse I suppose.
e) It's no use waiting here. We .... well start walking.
f) Jack refuses. He says it's wrong and he .... do it.
g) Any letters from Italy .... be for Tina.
h) Cairo .... be quite cold in winter.
i) I love these trees. Without them the garden .... the same.
j) Rule 6. No member .... enter the bar area wearing sports kit.

Unit 12
Modal auxiliaries 2: past

Explanations

Had to and *must have*

Had to is the past form of *must* and refers to a past obligation.
>   *Sorry I'm late, I **had to post** some letters.*
The negative form is *didn't have to.*
Must have refers to past certainty. (see below)

Should have and *ought to have*

Where *should appears, *ought to* is also possible.

1 Expectation
Should have refers to something which was supposed to happen.
>   *The parcel I sent you *****should have arrived** by now.*

2 Criticism of an action
>   *You *****shouldn't have eaten** so much last night.*

3 *Should have* and verbs of thinking
The past form *knew* in the example is an unreal tense, and the *should have* form is used according to 'sequence of tenses'.
>   *I **should have thought** you knew.*

4 With *be* and adjectives describing chance
>   *It was strange that you **should have been staying** in the same hotel last year.*

5 As a polite expression of thanks on receiving a gift or a favour
>   *– I've done the washing up for you. – Oh, you really **shouldn't have!***
The intonation should be friendly, as this is not a criticism.

Could have

1 *Could have* refers to past possibility or uncertainty.
>   *David **could have won** the race if he had tried. (possibility/ability)*
>   *It **could have been** Sue, I suppose. (uncertainty)*
2 *Couldn't have* is also possible for both meanings.
3 *Couldn't have* can be used with comparative adjectives.
>   *We **couldn't have been happier** in those days.*
4 *Could have* can also express unwillingness.
>   *We **couldn't have left** the dog on its own. (so we didn't)*

65

Could	**1**	*Could* refers to past permission or past ability.
		*When I was sixteen I **could stay** out till 11.00. (I was allowed to)*
		*Mary **could swim** when she was three. (she actually did)*
	2	Compare:
		*Mary **could have swum** when she was three. (but she didn't)*

May have and *might have*	**1**	*Might have* refers to past possibility which did not happen.
		*You **might have drowned**!*
	2	*Might have* and *may have* refer to uncertainty.
		*I suppose I **may have been** rather critical.*
	3	Both can be used in the negative to express uncertainty.
		*They **might not have received** our letter yet.*
	4	*Might have* is used to express annoyance at someone's failure to do something. There is strong stress on the words underlined.
		*You **might** have **told** me my trousers were split!*
	5	*I might have known* + *would* is an idiom by which the speaker expresses ironically that an action was typical of someone else.
		*I **might have known** that he **would** be late.*
		– It was Jack who broke the vase.
		*– I **might have known**!*

Must have and *can't have*	**1**	These refer to the speaker's certainty about a past action.
		*Someone **must have taken** it. (I am sure they did.)*
		*You **can't have lost** it. (I am sure you didn't.)*
	2	Both can also be used with *surely* in exclamations.
		*Surely you **can't have** eaten all of it!*
		*Surely you **must have** noticed it!*

Would not		This expresses an unwillingness in the past.
		*Everyone was angry because Sam **wouldn't turn off** the television.*

Would have	**1**	*Would have* can refer to events in the past which did not actually happen.
		*I **would have accepted** the job, but I didn't want to move house.*
	2	Assumptions about the past are also possible with *would have*.
		– Someone called after you left but didn't leave a message.
		*– That **would have been** Cathy, probably.*

Needn't have and *didn't need to*	**1**	*Needn't have done* refers to an unnecessary action which was actually done.
		*You **needn't have paid** all at once. (You did pay.)*
	2	*Didn't need to* refers to an unnecessary action which was not done.
		*I **didn't need to go** to the the dentist again, luckily.*

Adverbs and modals	Adverbs such as *well, easily, obviously, really, just* are often used to emphasise modal expressions, in both present and past time.

*You could **easily** have been killed.*
*I might **well** decide to come.*
*She **obviously** must have left.*
*You couldn't **really** have managed without me.*
*I might **just** take you up on that.*

Activities

1
Choose the most suitable words underlined.

a) That can't have been/shouldn't have been Nick that you saw.
b) You had to give/might have given me a hand!
c) I caught a later train because I had to see/must have seen a client.
d) I suppose Bill should have lost/might have lost his way.
e) I didn't refuse the cake, as it must have been/would have been rude.
f) I don't know who rang, but it could have been/must have been Jim.
g) It was odd that you should have bought/would have bought the same car.
h) I asked them to leave but they couldn't/wouldn't go.
i) It's a pity you didn't ask because I could help/could have helped you.
j) It's your own fault, you can't have/shouldn't have gone to bed so late.

2
Complete each sentence with a suitable word or phrase.

a) Don't worry that Carol is late, she *might /could have* missed the train.
b) I begged David to accept some money, but he .... hear of it.
c) That was a lucky escape! You .... been killed!
d) It was supposed to be a secret! You .... told her!
e) I spent last week at the beach because I didn't .... go to school.
f) The plane is late. It .... landed by now.
g) You .... met my brother. I haven't got one!
h) There is only one solution. The butler .... done it.
i) It was lovely. We .... a better holiday.
j) So it was you who set off the fire alarm for a joke! I .... known!

3
Rewrite each sentence so that it contains the word in capitals, and so that the meaning stays the same.

a) It wasn't very nice of you not to invite me to your party!   MIGHT
You might have invited me to your party! ....

b) Thank you very much for buying me flowers!   SHOULDN'T
....

c) It wouldn't have been right to let you do all the work on your own.   COULDN'T
....

d) I don't believe that you have lost your keys again!   CAN'T
....

e) Mary was a talented violinist at the age of ten.   PLAY
....

f) Perhaps they didn't notice the tyre was flat. **MIGHT**

....

g) The results are expected tomorrow. **KNOW**

....

h) They escaped possible injury when the car crashed. **HAVE**

....

i) A visa wasn't necessary after all. **NEED**

....

j) Apparently someone has borrowed the cassette player. **HAVE**

....

4
Complete the comment at the end of each sentence.

a) Pay no attention to what Martin said. He *can't have been* serious.

b) Fancy accepting the job just like that! You .... asked me first!

c) The test was no problem at all. It .... easier, in fact!

d) I'm sure Jack didn't mean to ignore you. He .... noticed you.

e) That was a lucky escape! We .... killed!

f) Hello, I'm home early. I .... late at the office after all.

g) The meat is a bit burnt. You .... cooked it for so long. I did tell you!

h) There were plenty of tickets left for the concert. We .... them in advance.

i) Sally got home at four o'clock this morning. The party .... really good!

j) This homework is not as good as usual. I think you .... more time on it.

5
Put *one* suitable word in each space. Words with '*n't*' count as one word.

a) I *could* have become a millionaire, but I decided not to.

b) You .... have been here when Helen told the boss not to be so lazy!

c) Peter wasn't here then, so he .... have broken your vase.

d) I .... have bought that car, but I decided to look at a few others.

e) If you felt lonely, you .... have given me a ring.

f) Don't take a risk like that again! We .... have lost because of you.

g) It's been more than a week! You .... have some news by now!

h) We were glad to help. We .... have just stood by and done nothing.

i) You really .... have gone to so much trouble!

j) I .... have thought that it was rather difficult.

6
Correct any
errors in these
sentences.

a) You mustn't have forgotten already! (error: *can't have forgotten*)
b) Paul shouldn't have been more helpful if he had tried.
c) Frances might not have understood what you said.
d) It was funny that she should have remembered me.
e) Harry may have won the match with a bit more effort.
f) You must have told me you had already eaten.
g) Fortunately I needn't have gone to the bank in person.
h) You mustn't have been so unkind!
i) I couldn't have managed without you.
j) I have no idea who it was, but I suppose it would have been Ann.

7
Put *one* suitable
adverb in each
space.

a) Someone <u>obviously</u> must have picked it up by mistake.
b) He could .... have stolen the painting without anyone knowing.
c) I may .... have made a mistake.
d) You .... shouldn't have spent so much on my present.
e) Bill .... wouldn't listen to anything we said.
f) I couldn't .... have left without saying a word.
g) .... you can't seriously believe that I am guilty!
h) I opened the window, I .... had to get some fresh air.
i) I may .... come to your party after all.
j) How dangerous! You could .... have been injured!

8
Complete each
sentence with a
suitable word or
phrase.

a) You should have seen Jim's face! He .... happier!
b) I'm sorry. I suppose I .... been a bit rude.
c) Surely it .... been Ann who told you.
d) You really .... so much trouble over me.
e) One thing is for sure, someone .... known about it.
f) Was it really necessary? You .... to tell the police, you know.
g) They .... saved her from the fire, but the ladder didn't reach her window.
h) Keep your fingers crossed! The traffic warden .... noticed the car is parked on double yellow lines!
i) It's funny .... bought exactly the same dress as me!
j) I should .... would know better.

9
Rewrite each
sentence so that it
contains a modal
auxiliary and so
that the meaning
stays the same.

a) The police refused to do anything about my noisy neighbours.
....
b) Jean's boss was extremely kind to her.
....
c) Why didn't you back me up!
....
d) Our worrying so much was a waste of time.
....

e) It's just not possible for the cat to have opened the fridge!

....

f) George knew how to ride a bicycle when he was five.

....

g) I wanted to go to the party, but it was snowing hard.

....

h) It would have been possible for Helen to give us a lift.

....

i) It's possible that the last person to leave didn't lock the door.

....

j) School uniform wasn't compulsory at my school.

....

Unit 13 Inversion

Explanations

Inversion

The term 'inversion' covers two different grammatical operations.

1   Using a question form of the main verb
    *Not only **did he fail** to report the accident, but also later denied that he*
    had been driving the car.
    *Never **have I enjoyed** myself more!*

2   Changing the normal positions of verb and subject
    *Along the street **came a strange procession**.*
    See Unit 14 for an explanation of this example.

Inversion after
negative
adverbials

1   This only occurs when the adverbial occurs at the beginning of a clause.
    All the examples below are used in formal language, usually for rhetorical
    effect, such as in political speeches. They are not usual in everyday spoken
    language. Compare:
        *Never **have I heard** a weaker excuse!*
        I have never heard a weaker excuse!

2   Time expressions: *never, rarely, seldom*
    These are most commonly used with present perfect or past perfect,
    or with modals such as *can* and *could*. Sentences of this type often contain
    comparatives.
        ***Rarely can a minister** have been faced with such a problem.*
        ***Seldom has the team** given a **worse** performance.*
        ***Rarely had I had** so much responsibility.*

3   Time expressions: *hardly, barely, scarcely, no sooner*
    These refer to an event which quickly follows another in the past. They are
    usually used with past perfect, although *no sooner* can be followed by past
    simple. Note the words used in the contrasting clause.
        ***Hardly had the train left** the station, **when** there was an explosion.*
        ***Scarcely had I entered** the room **when** the phone rang.*
        ***No sooner had I reached** the door **than** I realised it was locked.*
        ***No sooner was the team** back on the pitch **than** it started raining.*

4   After *only*
    Here *only* combines with other time expressions and is usually
    used with past simple.
        ***Only** after posting the letter **did I remember** that I had forgotten*
        to put on a stamp.

71

Other examples are *only if/when, only then, only later*
Note that when *only* refers to 'the state of being the only one', there is no inversion following it.
> *Only Mary realised that the door was not locked.*

5 Phrases containing *no/not*
These include *under no circumstances, on no account, at no time, in no way, on no condition, not until, not only ... (but also)*. Note that the inverted verb is the verb describing the event limited by the negative adverbial.
> **On no condition are they** *to open fire without a warning.*
> **Not until** *I got home* **did I notice** *that I had the wrong umbrella.*

6 *Little*
Little also has a negative or restrictive meaning in this sense:
> **Little does the government appreciate** *what the results will be.*

Inversion after so/such with that

1 This occurs with *so* and adjectives when the main verb is *be*. It is used for emphasis and is more common than the examples in 2.
> **So devastating were the floods that** *some areas may never recover.*

2 *Such* used with *be* means *so much/so great*
> **Such was the force** *of the storm that trees were uprooted.*

3 As in the examples in 2, inversion only occurs if *so/such* is the first word in the clause.

Inverted conditional sentences without If–

1 Three types of *If–* sentence can be inverted without *If–*. This makes the sentences more formal and makes the event less likely.
> *If they were to escape, there would be an outcry.*
> **Were they to escape,** *there would be an outcry.*
> *If the police had found out, I would have been in trouble.*
> **Were the police to have found out,** *I would have been in trouble.*

> *If you should hear anything, let me know.*
> **Should you hear** *anything, let me know.*
> *If he has cheated, he will have to be punished.*
> **Should he have cheated,** *he will have to be punished.*

> *If I had known, I would have protested strongly.*
> **Had I known,** *I would have protested strongly.*

2 Inversion after *as*
This is more common in formal or written language.
> *We were short of money,* **as were most people** *in our neighbourhood.*
> *I thought,* **as did my colleagues,** *that the recession would soon be over.*

3 Inversion after *so*, *neither* and *nor*

These are used in 'echoing' statements, agreeing or disagreeing.

– *I am going home.* – *So am I.*

– *I don't like meat.* – *Neither/Nor do I.*

See Unit 14 for ways of giving emphasis without inverting after *so*.

Activities

1

Choose the most suitable words underlined.

a) Jim promised that <u>he would never/never would he</u> tell anyone else.

b) Not until it was too late <u>I remembered/did I remember</u> to call Susan.

c) Hardly had we settled down in our seats <u>than/when</u> the lights went out.

d) Only after checking three times <u>I was/was I</u> certain of the answer.

e) At no time <u>I was aware/was I aware</u> of anything out of the usual.

f) Only Catherine and Sally <u>passed/did they pass</u> the final examination.

g) <u>So the waves were high/So high were the waves</u> that swimming was dangerous.

h) Only when <u>Pete has arrived/has Pete arrived</u> can we begin the programme.

i) No sooner had it stopped raining <u>than/when</u> the sun came out.

j) <u>If should you leave early/Should you leave early</u> could you give me a lift?

2

Complete each sentence with a suitable word or phrase.

a) *Hardly* had we arrived at the hotel, when there was a power cut.

b) .... are members of staff to accept gratuities from clients.

c) .... Detective Dawson realise what she was to discover!

d) .... so many employees taken sick leave at the same time.

e) .... to pay the full amount now, there would be a ten per cent discount.

f) I supposed, as .... most people, that I would be retiring at 60.

g) .... the doctors seen a more difficult case.

h) .... Jean win first prize, but she was also offered a promotion.

i) .... will late arrivals be admitted to the theatre before the interval.

j) .... one missing child been found, than another three disappeared.

3

Rewrite each sentence, starting as shown, so that the meaning stays the same.

a) It was only when the office phoned me that I found out about the meeting.

Not until *the office phoned me did I find out about the meeting.*

b) The facts were not all made public until later.

Only ....

c) If I had realised what would happen, I wouldn't have accepted the job.

Had ....

d) The response to our appeal was so great that we had to take on more staff.

Such ....

e) Harry broke his leg, and also injured his shoulder.
Not only ....

f) The police didn't at all suspect that the judge was the murderer.
Little ....

g) If you do happen to see Helen, could you ask her to call me?
Should ....

h) The bus driver cannot be blamed for the accident in any way.
In ....

i) The snowfall was so heavy that all the trains had to be cancelled.
So ....

j) If the government raised interest rates, they would lose the election.
Were ....

4
Decide which sentences are inappropriate in the contexts given.

a) Guest to host: 'So nice was that pudding, that I would like to have some more.' (*inappropriate*)

b) Witness to court: 'No sooner had I turned out the light, than I heard a noise outside.'

c) News reader: 'Such was force of the earthquake, that whole villages have been devastated.'

d) Parent to child: 'Should you fancy a pizza, let's order one now.'

e) Friend to friend: 'Never before have I seen this film.'

f) Politician to audience: 'Seldom has the country faced a greater threat.'

g) Celebrity to interviewer: 'Were I to have the time, I'd go climbing more often.

h) Victim to police officer: 'Scarcely had we been introduced when he punched me for no reason.'

i) Printed notice: 'Under no circumstances is this control panel to be left unattended.'

j) Colleague to colleague: 'Should you change your mind, just let me know.'

5
Complete each sentence with a suitable word or phrase.

a) Scarcely *had the plane taken off, when* the pilot had to make an emergency landing.

b) Little .... what has been going on in her absence.

c) No sooner .... than I realised I'd left my bag on the platform.

d) Only when .... on the light did we notice the hole in the ceiling.

e) Not until I asked a passer-by .... where I was.

f) Seldom does .... below freezing at this time of the year.

g) Hardly .... his speech, when the minister was interrupted.

h) On no account am .... while I am in a meeting.

i) Rarely has .... this school written a better composition.

j) In no way .... bear responsibility for injuries to passengers.

6

Rewrite each sentence so that it contains the word or words in capitals, and so that the meaning stays the same.

a) Were Smith to resign, I might stand a chance of getting his job.   IF

   If Smith were to resign/If Smith resigned, I might stand a
   chance of getting his job.

b) Such was the demand for tickets that people queued day and night.   GREAT

c) The money is not to be paid under any circumstances.   NO

d) Three days passed before we arrived at the first oasis.   NOT UNTIL

e) Hardly had the ship left port, than a violent storm developed.   SOON AFTER

f) They would have discovered land sooner had they carried a compass.   IF

g) Little did Brenda know what she was letting herself in for.   IDEA

h) It was only when I stopped that I realised something was wrong.   DID I

i) The accused never expressed regret for what he had done.   AT NO TIME

j) So exhausted were the runners that none of them finished the race.   TOO

7

Rewrite each sentence, beginning as shown, so that the meaning stays the same.

a) As soon as I got into the bath, someone knocked at the door.
   No sooner *had I got into the bath than someone knocked at the door.*

b) There was so much uncertainty that the financial markets remained closed.
   Such ....

c) It's not common for there to be so much rain in March.
   Seldom ....

d) You won't be allowed in until your identity has been checked.
   Only ....

e) Just after the play started there was a power failure.
   Hardly ....

f) The Prime Minister has hardly ever made a speech as inept as this.
   Rarely ....

g) We had only just arrived home when the police called.
   Scarcely ....

h) Press photographers are banned from taking photographs backstage.
   On no ....

i) The way so much money has been spent to so little purpose must be a record!
   Never before ....

j) The judge was taken ill just after the trial proceedings began.
   Barely ....

8
Complete each sentence with a suitable word or phrase.

a) Should *you need* anything, could you let me know?

b) Were ...., everyone in it would have been killed.

c) Had .... harder, I would probably have passed all my exams.

d) Should .... neighbourhood, why don't you drop in?

e) Had .... immediately, your daughter would not be so ill.

f) Were .... you, I would turn you down flat!

g) Should ...., just call room service, and order a meal.

h) Were .... job, we couldn't be sure that she would accept.

i) Had .... measures, this political crisis could have been avoided.

j) Should .... lost, we would have heard from him by now.

Unit 14 Emphasis

Explanations

Changing word order to change focus

1 Passive
Passive constructions vary the way information is given in a sentence, putting more emphasis on what comes first. See Units 6 and 7.
All roads to the north have been blocked by snow.

2 Fronting and inversion
Inversion here refers to changing the normal word order in the sentence so that a prepositional phrase is emphasised before the verb. This also involves putting the verb before the subject.
*Suddenly **down came** the rain!*
***Up into the air** went the balloon.*
Fronting involves changing the order of clauses in a sentence and putting first for emphasis a clause that would usually not be first.
I don't know where the money is coming from.
***Where the money is coming from**, I don't know.*
Time phrases can vary in position, and are often put first because the time reference is important.
***At six o'clock** Monica decided to phone the police.*
May clauses
There is a type of *may* clause introduced by *although* which can be inverted. It is a highly formal expression.
Although it may seem/be difficult, it is not impossible.
***Difficult as/though it may seem/be**, it is not impossible.*

3 Cleft and pseudo cleft sentences
These are sentences introduced by *it is/it was* or by a clause beginning *what*. Different parts of the sentence can be emphasised in this way.
In speech, stress and intonation also identify the emphasis.
With *it is/was*
Sue borrowed my bike last night.
***It was Sue** who borrowed my bike.*
***It was last night** that Sue borrowed my bike.*
***It was my bike** that Sue borrowed.*
Sentences with *because* are also possible.
***It was because** I felt ill that I left.*
Modal auxiliaries are also possible.
You can't have read the same book.
***It can't have been the same book** that you read.*

77

What clauses

These are common with verbs such as *need, want, like, hate.*

> *I hate rainy weather.*
> **What I hate** *is rainy weather.*
> *You need a holiday.*
> **What you need** *is a holiday.*

It is also possible to emphasise events, using auxiliary *do/did.*

> *Peter left the windows unlocked.*
> **What Peter did was** *(to) leave the windows unlocked.*
> *They are destroying the environment.*
> **What they are doing is** *destroying the environment.*

Clauses beginning *all* emphasise 'the only thing'.

> *I only need another £15.*
> **All I need** *is another £15.*

Adding words for emphasis

1 *Own*

This intensifies possessive adjectives.

> *It was **my own** idea.*

2 *Very* and *indeed*

Very can be used emphatically to mean *exactly/precisely.*

> **At the very same moment**, *the telephone rang.*

Very ..... indeed is another way of intensifying adjectives.

> *It was **very cold indeed**.*

3 Emphasising negatives

Ways of emphasising *not* include: *at all, in the least, really.*

> *It was **not at all cold**. It was **not cold at all**.*

In the least/slightest usually adds *bit* if used before an adjective.

> *I wasn't interested **in the slightest**.*
> *I wasn't **the least bit** interested.*

No and *none* can be emphasised by *at all* and *whatsoever.*

> *There were **none left at all**.*
> *There were **no tickets left whatsoever**.*

4 *The*

The can emphasise uniqueness. It is heavily stressed in speech.

> *Surely you are not **the** Elizabeth Taylor, are you?*

5 Question words ending in *-ever*

These add an air of disbelief to the question.

> **Whatever** *are you doing!* **Whoever** *told you that!*

6   Auxiliary *do*

This can emphasise the verb, and is stressed in speech.

>*I **do** like this film! It's really great!*

It is also used in polite forms.

>*I **do** hope you'll come again!*   ***Do** sit down!*

7   Adverbs and adjectives

There is a large number of adverbs and adjectives used to add emphasis. Common examples are:

>*I **actually** went inside one of the Pyramids.*
>*It is **by no means** certain that the match will take place.*
>*Some people were **even** wearing pullovers, it was so cold.*
>*Her performance was **sheer** magic!*
>*This book is **utter** nonsense!*

These examples are only possible with adjectives which express an absolute opinion (non-gradable adjectives).

>*It was **absolutely** fantastic!*
>*The third exam question was **quite** (**completely**) impossible.*
>*This guide book is **utterly** useless.*
>*You were **simply** wonderful!*
>*Don't cook the meat any more. It's **just** right!*

8   Echoing phrases with *so*

These express agreement.

>*– This is the book you are looking for. – **So it is**!*

Other means

1   Time phrases

Common examples are: *day after day; time and time again; over and over again; day in, day out*

>*David reads the same book **over and over again**!*

2   Repetition of main verb.

>*I **tried and tried**, but it was no use.*

3   In the repetition of a phrase with a possessive it is possible to omit the first mention of the noun and use a possessive pronoun.

>***Their marriage** was a successful **marriage**.*
>***Theirs** was a successful marriage.*

Activities

1
Complete each sentence with one suitable word.

a) You can't complain. It's your *own* fault, isn't it?
b) – That looks like Janet.
   – .... it is! My goodness, hasn't she changed.
c) I'm sorry to keep you waiting. I .... hope you haven't been here long.
d) It is by no .... certain that the Prime Minister will attend the meeting.
e) .... I really enjoy in winter is a bowl of hot soup.
f) I searched and .... for my keys but I couldn't find them.
g) .... you are all going to sleep I can't quite work out!
h) What the government then .... was to raise interest rates.
i) There isn't much to eat. .... we've got is some leftovers.
j) Cathy wasn't in the .... put out when I couldn't make it to her wedding.

2
Rewrite each sentence so that it contains the word in capitals, and so that the meaning stays the same.

a) The bad weather continued for days.   AFTER
   The bad weather continued day after day.

b) I can't stand getting up early.   WHAT
   ....

c) The car doesn't need anything else except new tyres.   ALL
   ....

d) Brenda didn't worry at all about her exams.   LEAST
   ....

e) I felt extremely tired.   INDEED
   ....

f) Keith told me about the hotel.   WHO
   ....

g) That's exactly the same book I'm reading!   VERY
   ....

h) Please stay longer.   DO
   ....

i) It was a really awful film.   JUST
   ....

j) I had spent all my money.   WHATSOEVER
   ....

3
Choose the most appropriate word or words underlined.

a) Don't worry, I'm none at all tired/not at all tired.
b) I thought that speech was utter/utterly rubbish.
c) It was because/why the car broke down that we missed our plane.
d) – You are sitting on my hat!   – So am I/So I am !
e) The sea was so rough that actually/even the experienced sailors were seasick.
f) Whatever/Why ever are you looking at me like that for?
g) I would like to make it quite/simply clear that we are just good friends.

h) This is my <u>very private/very own</u> computer.

i) On this course, we <u>absolutely expect/do expect</u> you to work hard.

j) There were warnings, but <u>nothing whatsoever/nothing simply</u> was done.

4

Rewrite each sentence, beginning as shown, so that the meaning stays the same.

a) I don't know who is going to pay for the damage.
Who *is going to pay for the damage I don't know.*

b) Although the ticket may seem expensive, it is good value for money.
Expensive ....

c) I really can't stand lukewarm food.
What ....

d) In the end Martha went to the police.
What ....

e) Every day, it's the same old routine in my job.
Day in ....

f) I think you must have seen a ghost.
It ....

g) Her car was the last car we expected to be stolen.
Hers ....

h) The parcel finally arrived on Wednesday.
It ....

i) I don't understand why you left that job in London.
Why ever ....

j) I bought it because it was a bargain.
It was because ....

5

Choose the most suitable word or phrase given.

a) I expected to receive three letters, but none ......C...... arrived.
   A) all   B) completely   C) whatsoever   D) utterly

b) I was so tired I .... had to take a nap.
   A) simply   B) utterly   C) quite   D) by no means

c) I'll take this tie. It's the .... thing I'm looking for.
   A) just   B) quite   C) sheer   D) very

d) If you ask me, it's a/an .... waste of time.
   A) sheer   B) absolutely   C) very   D) really

e) I .... like your new shoes. Where did you buy them?
   A) would   B) do   C) utterly   D) just

f) Helen's new boyfriend is not .... what I expected.
   A) at all   B) just   C) absolutely   D) very

g) .... do you think you are doing, might I ask?
   A) Actually B) Just   C) Whatsoever   D) Whatever

h) Paul .... had the nerve to blame me for the whole mess!
   A) quite   B) simply   C) actually   D) really

i) No, I don't have a car. I can't .... drive.
   A) quite   B) utterly   C) simply   D) even

j) I .... had to tell you the news! I'm expecting a baby!
   A) just   B) did   C) utterly   D) quite

6

Choose a sentence from 1) to 10) which makes a suitable continuation for each speaker in a) to j).

a) All of the trains were delayed by fog. (*4*)
b) It wasn't so much my qualifications that impressed them.
c) I found that I was spending more and more time staying late at the office.
d) I don't find that the buses are especially late, actually.
e) Actually my fridge is in quite good condition, considering its age.
f) I don't find watching television particularly relaxing.
g) I've decided to buy a new stereo after all.
h) This book didn't teach me everything I know about cooking.
i) The flight itself didn't really bother me at all.
j) Actually I wasn't in the office yesterday.

1) Where I am going to get the money from is another matter.
2) What I really need is a new washing machine.
3) It must have been someone else you spoke to.
4) It was after 10.00 when I finally got home.
5) What really gets on my nerves is people who push into the queue.
6) It was when I got off the plane that I felt ill.
7) What I did in the end was to ask for a pay-rise.
8) It was Sarah who taught me how to make bread.
9) It was because I spoke well at the interview that I got the job.
10) What I like most is a long walk in the country.

7

Complete each sentence with a suitable word or phrase.

a) I know you're busy, but I *do* think you could have helped me with the decorating.
b) It's by .... certain that the president will be re-elected.
c) You may have lots of restaurants where you live, but there are .... all in this part of town.
d) I told you .... again about the leaking pipes, but you wouldn't listen.
e) You don't seem the .... bit interested in my problems!
f) Strange .... seem, the bus is actually faster than the train.
g) In the end .... was to call a plumber.
h) We .... waited all day, but Chris never turned up.
i) Pauline was .... all bothered by our turning up so late.
j) It .... Jim that you saw, he is in Germany at the moment.

8

Rewrite each sentence so that it contains the word in capitals, and so that the meaning stays the same.

a) You did something that was wrong.   WHAT
What you did was wrong.
....

b) The calculator I've got doesn't need a battery.   OWN
....

c) The accident was caused because someone was very careless.   SHEER
....

d) I like cheese best for breakfast.   WHAT
....

e) I seem to want to do nothing but sleep.

.... ALL

f) It did nothing but rain for days.

.... AFTER

g) I can't make any sense of this!

.... UTTER

h) What on earth are you doing here at this time?

.... WHATEVER

i) Actually, you are not right at all.

.... QUITE

j) It's very important for me to know the answer.

.... SIMPLY

Unit 15 Progress Test (Units 11, 12, 13, 14)

1
Put *one* suitable word in each space.

Some people always have good advice to give you, but only after the event. You (1) .... have come across the type, who somehow always know what you (2) .... have done when it has become too late. By now I (3) .... spot them a mile off. It (4) .... be because I have had so much practice. Last week, for example, I (5) .... to take my car to the garage because the lights weren't working. It was an expensive job, but I decided that I (6) .... as well pay, and get it over quickly. 'You (7) .... have told me,' said a friend when I was telling him how much I (8) .... to pay. 'I (9) .... easily have fixed it for you. Then you (10) .... not have wasted so much money.' You (11) .... imagine how I felt! Actually, he (12) .... probably have made a mess of the job, and I (13) .... well have ended up paying more. But it does seem strange that everyone else (14) .... know exactly what I (15) .... to do.

2
Complete each sentence with *one* suitable word.

a) Do you think I had .... catch the earlier train?
b) .... have we eaten a more enjoyable meal!
c) Strange as it .... seem, I have never drunk coffee!
d) You .... have told me the meeting was cancelled!
e) Not .... I woke up did I realise that Diana had left.
f) .... I really need is a new motorbike.
g) You .... be Jane's mother. Pleased to meet you.
h) At the .... end of the film, she meets the murderer.
i) .... did we know what was in store for us later!
j) You know Steve, he's .... to be late, so don't bother waiting for him.

3
Rewrite each sentence so that it contains the word in capitals, and so that the meaning stays the same.

a) I didn't enjoy my holiday at all.   LEAST
....
b) You are not to leave the hospital under any circumstances.   NO
....
c) I tried hard but I couldn't undo the bottle.   MIGHT
....
d) The weather here is sometimes really awful!   CAN
....
e) I wish you wouldn't complain all the time!   DO
....
f) It's not worth staying here.   MIGHT
....
g) Two weeks passed before the letter arrived.   DID
....

h) I expect this film will be good.	SHOULD
....	
i) This food has no taste.	QUITE
....	
j) She was so popular that everyone voted for her.	SUCH
....	

4

Rewrite each sentence, beginning as shown, so that the meaning stays the same.

a) If they offered me the job, I would accept.
Were ....

b) I'm sure you had a good time at the party.
You must ....

c) I have no idea who Sarah is going out with.
Who ....

d) As soon as the police officer left, the neighbours started shouting again.
No sooner ....

e) Luckily it wasn't necessary for Jim to take the exam again.
Luckily Jim ....

f) In the end I had to get a lift with a colleague.
What ....

g) It was only when I got home that I realised I'd forgotten my bag.
Not until ....

h) The guests didn't finally leave until after midnight.
It ....

i) If you're ever in the neighbourhood, please drop in and see us.
Should ....

j) Why didn't you tell me you were ill?
You ....

5

Rewrite each sentence so that it begins with the word underlined, and so that the meaning stays the same.

a) I've <u>never</u> had such a good holiday.
....

b) Three policemen came <u>into</u> the room.
....

c) You must not leave the door unlocked <u>under</u> any circumstances.
....

d) I had <u>hardly</u> sat down, when there was another knock at the door.
....

e) It may seem <u>strange</u>, but I enjoy hard work.
....

f) The company did <u>not</u> pay me until I had been working with them for a month.
....

g) I have no idea <u>where</u> the boat leaves from.
....

h) If you <u>should</u> need me, I'll be in my office all day.
....

i) Time is <u>all</u> I need.

....

j) If the government <u>had</u> acted, the crisis might have been avoided.

....

6

Rewrite each sentence so that it does not contain the word or words underlined and so that the meaning stays the same. Other changes may be necessary.

a) <u>It would</u> have <u>been a good idea to</u> take your umbrella.

....

b) It's <u>certain</u> to rain tomorrow.

....

c) <u>I know you're</u> tired, but that's no reason to be so irritable.

....

d) The hotel <u>was as</u> comfortable <u>as possible</u>.

....

e) <u>It's possible that</u> Ann is out.

....

f) You <u>are quite wrong to</u> eat so much chocolate.

....

g) <u>I'm sure that isn't</u> the road to Canterbury.

....

h) <u>It's typical of</u> Martin to get promoted!

....

i) Connie's mother <u>refused to</u> let the children watch television.

....

j) I <u>don't think</u> anyone would agree with you.

....

7

Choose the most suitable word or phrase given.

a) Don't be silly! That .... possibly be Madonna!
   A) mustn't   B) shouldn't   C) won't   D) can't

b) No sooner had we started the picnic, ... the rain began pouring down!
   A) than   B) when   C) that   D) and

c) At the .... same moment, we both realised what was happening.
   A) quite   B) simply   C) very   D) absolutely

d) I supposed, as .... we all, that the meeting would be cancelled.
   A) did   B) would   C) equally   D) just

e) I've told you time and time .... not to leave the door open!
   A) to   B) over   C) again   D) before

f) Sorry I'm late, but I .... call in at the supermarket on the way.
   A) needed   B) must   C) had to   D) was to

g) You .... have told me that my skirt was split!
   A) needn't   B) must   C) all   D) might

h) If the phone rings, it .... be for me.
   A) can   B) will   C) would   D) shall

i) At the end of the week, all the sales staff were .... exhausted.
   A) utterly   B) even   C) actually   D) to be

j) The team .... be the same without Margaret Hargreaves.
   A) mustn't   B) wouldn't   C) shouldn't   D) needn't

8
Complete each sentence with a suitable word or phrase.

a) But I only lent you the book this morning! You .... it already!
b) I don't know who phoned, but I suppose it .... Sophia.
c) Strange ...., Harry has never been to London.
d) Never .... a more boring film!
e) I told you we would miss the train! We .... earlier!
f) I was just thinking about you. It's strange that .... phoned me!
g) Try ...., I just can't understand how this computer works!
h) Seldom .... fall here in winter, even when it is very cold.
i) It rained every day on my holiday in France, so I ....
   the suntan lotion after all!
j) Well, I thought the food was awful. It .... the same
   restaurant you went to.

9
Rewrite each sentence, beginning as shown, so that the meaning stays the same.

a) It's not necessary for you to wear a uniform.
   You ....
b) Paul smashed a window and damaged the television too.
   Not only ....
c) I remembered I had forgotten to buy any eggs after I arrived home.
   Only ....
d) Public opinion was so strong that the Prime Minister had to resign.
   Such ....
e) We didn't realise how serious the situation was.
   Little ....
f) I wouldn't wake her up now, if I were you.
   You'd ....
g) By law, all rear-seat passengers are obliged to wear seat-belts.
   By law, seat-belts ....
h) It's possible that Mary and Helen have not heard from the bank yet.
   Mary and Helen ....
i) It's impossible that we stayed at the same hotel, in that case.
   We ....
j) If someone had called the fire-brigade immediately, the tragedy might have
   been avoided.
   If the ....

10
Choose the best meaning, A) or B), for each sentence.

a) He might have let me know!
   A) I wish he had let me know.
   B) I'm not sure whether he let me know.
b) It's quite the best film I've ever seen.
   A) I have seen some that were better.
   B) I haven't seen any that were better.

c) You must be joking!
   A) I'm sure you are joking.
   B) You are supposed to make people laugh.
d) I should like to invite her out.
   A) People think it an obligation for me to do this.
   B) I think it would be a good idea.
e) You mustn't work so hard.
   A) It's not necessary to work so hard.
   B) It isn't a good idea to work so hard.

11
Rewrite each sentence so that it contains the word in capitals, and so that the meaning stays the same.

a) I'm sure that City will win the match.   BOUND
   ....

b) It's typical of you to say that!   WOULD
   ....

c) Harry tells the same joke all the time!   OVER
   ....

d) It may seem strange but I like stale cake!   AS
   ....

e) There is not a single seat left.   AT
   ....

f) You are supposed to have finished by now.   SHOULD
   ....

g) I don't believe you have spent all the money I gave you!   SURELY
   ....

h) It was very kind of you to bring me chocolates!   SHOULDN'T
   ....

i) Do you want me to phone them back?   SHOULD
   ....

j) There's nothing better to do, so go home.   MAY
   ....

12
Complete each sentence with *one* suitable word.

a) Jean must .... had a good time in Denmark.
b) I'm sure .... was last week that I paid the bill.
c) I think Phil .... better stay in bed today.
d) The meals in the hotel were .... awful.
e) Really the whole house .... painting.
f) Strange .... it may seem, Mary likes it there.
g) This restaurant is .... place to be seen in this town.
h) This is my .... own recipe, actually.
i) Hardly had I entered the office, ... the phone started ringing
j) After we had been on the beach for an hour, ... came the rain!

Unit 16 Indirect speech and reporting

Explanations

Problems

This unit assumes that the basic rules for forming indirect speech are already known.

1 Indirect speech with modal auxiliaries
If the reporting verb is in a past tense, modals change where there is a 'past' equivalent.

will – would   can – could   may – might

Could, would, and *might* do not change.

    – *I might be late.* She said (that) she **might be** late.

Should changes to *would* if it is used as a first person form of *would.*

    – *I should love to come.* She said (that) she **would** love to come.

Otherwise *should* remains unchanged.

    – *You should rest.* They said (that) I **should** rest.

Must can be reported as either *had to* or remain as *must.*

2 Indirect speech with conditional sentences
After a past tense reporting verb, real situations include tense changes.

    – *If we leave now, we'll catch the train.*

    I **told** him that if we **left we'd catch** the train.

In reported hypothetical situations, tense changes are not made if the event has reference to a possible future.

    – *If you came back tomorrow, I'd be able help you.*

    She said that **if I came back the next day, she'd be able to help** me.

If the event is clearly hypothetical and impossible, time changes are made.

    – *If I had a spanner, I could fix this.*

    He said that if he **had had a spanner he could have fixed** it.

Hypothetical past conditional sentences do not change.

3 *Don't think*
Statements reported with verbs of thinking such as *think, expect, suppose* can transfer the negative from the statement to the verb.

    I suppose she won't come. = *I **don't suppose** she will come.*

4 Past tenses
It is not strictly necessary to report past tenses with a shift into past perfect in spoken language, if the sequence of events is clear.

Reporting verbs   There are numerous reporting verbs, which report the words of others, or our own words or thoughts. Only a selection is given here. Other examples are included in the activities. Only the most useful categories are given here. It is advisable to use a dictionary to check on how reporting verbs are used.
See Units 19, 21 and 22 for prepositions or *-ing* forms following verbs.

1   Verbs followed by *that* + clause (with * can be followed by a person)

add	*confirm*	*feel*	*predict*	*say*
admit	*consider*	*hope*	*promise**	*state*
agree	*decide*	*imply*	*reassure**	*suggest*
announce	*deny*	*insist*	*reckon*	*suppose*
argue	*doubt*	*mean*	*remark*	*tell**
believe	*estimate*	*mention*	*repeat*	*think*
claim	*expect**	*object*	*reply*	*threaten**
complain	*explain*	*persuade*	*report**	*warn**

2   Verbs followed by person + *to*
advise   forbid   invite   persuade   tell
ask   instruct   order   remind   warn

3   Verbs followed by subjunctive or *should*
Most of these verbs can also be used in the other ways given.
As these verbs contain the sense that someone 'should do' something, *should* can follow them.
   *They **suggested that she should** apply again.*
More formally, the subjunctive can be used instead of *should*. This is formed from the base of the verb (without third person 's').
   *They **suggested that she apply** again.*
Some other verbs of this type are:
advise (also: someone to do/against something)
agree (also: to do something, *that* + clause without *should*)
demand (also: to do something)
insist (also: on someone doing something)
prefer (also: someone to do something)
propose (also: doing something)
recommend (also: doing something)
request (also: someone to do something)
suggest (also: *that* + clause without *should*)
urge (also: someone to do something)

4   Verbs which can be followed by *that* + clause containing *would*
All these verbs report statements containing *will*. These verbs can also be followed by 'to do something'.

– I'll leave at 8.00.
She decided to leave at 8.00.
She decided she would leave at 8.00.
Others are: *expect, hope, promise, threaten*

5 Verbs which can be impersonal with *it*
The speaker may not want to take personal responsibility for a statement, or may be reporting the views of a group of people. These verbs can be used in the passive, introduced by *it*. See also Unit 7 Passive.

It has been agreed to close most of the coal mines.

agree	*decide*	*imply*	*rumour*
announce	*estimate*	*know*	*say*
believe	*expect*	*predict*	*state*
claim	*fear*	*reckon*	*suggest*
confirm	*feel*	*recommend*	*suppose*
consider	*hope*	*report*	*think*

Functions

1 Many verbs describe a function, rather than report words.
– Look, if I were you I'd leave early.
She advised me to leave early.
Examples are:
admit   complain   request   suggest
advise   invite   remind   warn
agree   persuade   threaten

2 Some verbs describe actions.
– Hi, Dave, how are you?
He greeted me.
Examples are:
accept, congratulate, decide, greet, interrupt, introduce

Changes of viewpoint: *this* and *that*

Changes of time, place and person reference are assumed known at this level. In a report, there is no longer a clear reference which can be understood by two people in the same place.
*I left the parcel on **this chair**.*
A report would have to specify which chair:
*He said he had left the parcel on **the chair by the window**.*
Or the reference may be replaced by a more general one:
– I love this town.
*She said that she loved **the town**.*

Activities

1

Choose the most suitable word underlined.

a) The government spokesperson denied/refused that there was a crisis.

b) Jane said me/told me there was nothing the matter.

c) Peter persuaded me/insisted me to stay for dinner.

d) The director of studies advised me/suggested me to spend more time in the librar

e) Sheila explained me/warned me not to leave the heater on all night.

f) The chairperson mentioned us/reminded us that time was extremely short.

g) Bill answered them/replied them with a detailed description of his plans.

h) Michael and Sarah announced/reported that they were going to get married.

i) Paul accepted/expected that he had made a mistake, and apologised.

j) The manager confirmed/reassured that our room had been reserved.

2

Match each report 1) to 10) with the actual words spoken from a) to j).

1) Jim admitted that he might have taken it. *(e)*

2) Sue denied that she had taken it.

3) Harry doubted whether he had taken it.

4) Diana explained that she had taken it.

5) Bill insisted he had taken it.

6) Mary suggested that she had taken it.

7) Ted confirmed that he had taken it.

8) Ruth claimed that she had taken it.

9) Charles repeated that he had taken it.

10) Sally reassured us that she had taken it.

a) No, I've definitely taken it.

b) I don't think I took it.

c) Don't worry, I've taken it. It's all right!

d) What about me? Perhaps I took it?

e) OK, perhaps I did take it after all.

f) Yes, I took it. I took it, I tell you!

g) Yes, that's quite correct. I took it.

h) No, I certainly didn't take it, I can assure you.

i) You may not believe me, but actually I took it.

j) You see, it's like this. I've taken it.

3

Rewrite each sentence in indirect speech beginning as shown.

a) 'I wouldn't cook the fish for too long, Bill, if I were you,' said Jean.
Jean advised Bill *not to cook the fish for too long*. ....

b) 'Helen, would you like to come to lunch on Sunday?' said Mary.
Mary ....

c) 'Well, in the end I think I'll take the brown pair,' said the customer.
The customer finally ....

d) 'Me? No, I didn't take Sue's calculator,' said Bob.
Bob denied ....

e) 'Don't forget to buy some milk, Andy,' said Clare.
Clare reminded ....

f) 'Look, I might not be able to come on Saturday,' said David.
David told us ....

g) 'Why don't you go and see 'The Sound of Music' again, Brian?' I said.
I suggested ....

h) 'No, you really must stay the night, Sophia,' Ann said.
Ann insisted ....

i) 'Make sure you don't take the A20 in the rush hour, Tim,' said Jack.
Jack warned ....

j) 'You are not allowed to smoke in your room, Dick,' said his mother.
Dick's mother ....

4
Rewrite each
sentence so that it
contains the
word in capitals,
and so that the
meaning stays the
same.

a) He was warned by the fireman not to re-enter the house.   HIM
The fireman warned him not to re-enter the house.

b) There has been a rumour that the president is ill.   IT
....

c) Sue thought it would be a good idea for me to see a doctor.   ADVISED
....

d) The minister proposed regular meetings for the committee.   MEET
....

e) The management claimed that all strikers had returned to work.   WAS
....

f) The travel agent recommended our staying near the airport.   SHOULD
....

g) There has been no report that any lives were lost.   IT
....

h) Jack demanded action from the police.   SHOULD
....

i) David supposed that we didn't want to watch television.   WANTED
....

j) My bank manager invited me to visit him at home.   COULD
....

5
Match each
report 1) to 10)
with the actual
words spoken
from a) to j).

1) Ann told me that I should take a holiday.(*d*)
2) Ann expected me to take a holiday.
3) Ann insisted that I should take a holiday.
4) Ann invited me to take a holiday.
5) Ann agreed that I could take a holiday.
6) Ann reminded me to take a holiday.
7) Ann proposed that I should take a holiday.
8) Ann asked whether I would take a holiday.
9) Ann reassured me that I could take a holiday.
10) Ann preferred that I take a holiday.

a) Would you like to come on holiday with me?
b) Don't worry. Of course you can take a holiday.
c) Don't forget to take a holiday, will you!
d) You should take a holiday.
e) Are you going to take a holiday?
f) It's all right by me if you take a holiday.
g) Actually, I'd rather you took a holiday.
h) I thought you were going to take a holiday.
i) Taking a holiday would be a good idea.
j) You really must take a holiday.

6
Complete each
sentence with
one suitable
word. Do not use
say.

a) I thought Jim would say something about his new job. But he didn't _mention_ it.
b) Sorry, I wasn't being insulting. I simply .... that you seem to have put on rather a lot of weight lately.
c) The police .... that the crowd was under 50 000, although the organisers of the march put it at nearer 100 000.
d) The children .... that their parents were always checking up on them.
e) It has been .... that by the year 2050 some capital cities will be almost uninhabitable because of the effects of air pollution.
f) During the months before Smith's transfer from City, it had been .... that he and the manager had come to blows in the dressing-room, though this was denied by the club.
g) Brown .... that the arresting officers had treated him roughly, and that one of them had punched him in the eye.
h) An Army spokesman stressed that all troops patrolling the streets had been .... to issue clear warnings before firing any shots.
i) Although he didn't say so directly, the Prime Minister .... that an agreement between the two sides was within reach.
j) The witness .... her name and address to the court before the cross-examination began.

Unit 17 Articles

Explanations

Definite article

Basic uses of articles are assumed known.

1 Classes
This is one way to refer to classes, and is perhaps more formal than using a plural:
  The tiger is threatened with extinction.

2 National groups
Groups as a whole.
  The French eat in restaurants more than the English.
Single examples are not formed in the same way:
  A Frenchman/woman, an Englishman/woman

3 Other groups
If these are clearly plural:
  The Social Democrats, The Rolling Stones
Note the difference:
  Pink Floyd, Queen (no article)

4 Unique objècts
  The moon, the sun
Note that there are other suns and moons in the universe:
  This planet has a small moon.

5 Titles
These tend to be 'unique'.
  The director of studies
If the title is post-modified (has a description coming after the noun), *the* is more likely, but not essential. Compare:
  She became President in 1998.
  She became (the) President of the United States in 1998.

6 Other titles
The may be part of the title, and so is capitalised.
Newspapers: *The Independent, The Sunday Times*
Titles of books and films etc do not have *the* unless there is post-modification.
  The Phantom of the Opera.
'The' is sometimes dropped in everyday speech.
  Have you seen 'Phantom of the Opera'?

7 Musical instruments
The is included if ability to play is mentioned.
> *Jane plays the flute.*

A description of playing might not use *the*.
> *Jane played a flute and Paul played a recorder.*

8 Emphatic use
This is heavily stressed and emphasises the following noun.
> *This hotel is **the** place to stay.*

See also Unit 14.

9 Geographical names
The following use *the*:
rivers: *the Thames*
mountain ranges: *the Alps*
oceans: *the Mediterranean*
unique features: *the Channel, the Arctic*
compass points/areas: *the East, the Middle East*
countries: collective or plural: *The United Kingdom, The Netherlands*
This does not apply to:
lakes: *Lake Geneva*
mountain peaks: *Everest* (but *The Matterhorn*)
continents: *Asia*
countries: *France*
The definite article is sometimes used before Lebanon and Gambia:
The Lebanon The Gambia

10 Place names
Post-modification, especially with ....*of*.... plays a role in place names.
Compare:
> *Leeds University /The University of Leeds*
> *London Bridge /The Tower of London*

If the first part of a place-name is another name, then normal rules about zero article apply.
> *Brown's Restaurant*
> *The Garden House Hotel*

The same applies in geographical names:
> *Canvey Island*
> *The Isle of Man*

11 *Most* and *the most*
Most without an article means 'the greater part'.
> *I live in London **most of the time.***
> *This is **the most expensive** hotel in town.*

12 Importance of context

The definite article refers to already mentioned items, and so its use depends on context.

> *The Smiths had a son and a daughter. **The** son was in the Army and **the** daughter was training to be a doctor.*
> *On **the** Saturday, there was a terrible storm.*

Here, *the Saturday* refers to a day in a area of time already mentioned.

> *On **the** Saturday **of that week** …*

Indefinite article

1 Jobs

Compare: *Tony is a builder. Tony was **the** builder of that house.*

2 In measuring

> *Three times **a** week. Fifty kilometres **an** hour.*
> *£3.50 **a** kilo. £15 000 **a** year.*

Formally, *per* can replace *a/an*.

3 Unknown people

Use of *a/an* emphasises that a person is unknown.

> *A Mr Jones called while you were out.*

Zero article

1 Names

Compare:

> *Matthew Smith is one of my favourite artists. (a person)*
> *A Matthew Smith hangs in their bedroom. (a painting)*

2 Some unique organisations do not use *the*.

> *Parliament,* but *The (House of) Commons*

3 Streets

Most streets do not use an article.

> *Green Road Godwin Street*

Exceptions are:

> *The High Street The Strand*

and street names without preceding adjectives. Compare:

> *Holly Drive The Drive*

Translation problems

Study these sentences. Would you use an article in your language?

> I know how to use *a* computer.
> *A* pound and *a* half of cheese.
> I was holding it *in my* hand.
> It's a film about _ homeless people.
> Terry has _ flu. I've got *a* headache.

Activities

The activities include revision material.

1

In each space put *a/an* or *the*, or leave the space *blank*.

It has been announced that for (1) *the* third consecutive month there has been (2) .... rise in (3) .... number of (4) .... unemployed, rather than (5) .... fall that had been predicted. (6) .... rise was blamed on (7) .... continuing uncertainty over (8) .... government economic policy, and couldn't come at (9) .... worse time for (10) .... Prime Minister, who is facing (11) .... growing criticism over (12) .... way (13) .... present crisis is being handled. (14) .... MPs are increasingly voicing (15) .... fears that despite (16) .... recent devaluation of (17) .... pound and cuts in (18) .... interest rates, (19) .... government still expects (20) .... recovery of the economy to take three or even four years. To make (21) .... matters worse, (22) .... number of small business going into (23) .... liquidation is still at (24) .... record level, and (25) .... housing market is showing no signs of recovery. Some backbenchers expect (26) .... general election before (27) .... end of (28) .... winter unless there is (29) .... rapid change of (30) .... fortune.

2

Correct the errors in these sentences.

a) It's not a first-class accommodation unless it has a private bathroom.
   It's not first-class accommodation unless it has a private bathroom.
b) On this record twins play piano duet.
c) The halfway through meal we realised what waiter had said.
d) If the Mrs Hillier phones, say I'm away on trip.
e) There is a wonderful scenery in eastern part of Turkey.
f) Cocker spaniel is one of most popular pet dogs.
g) There is going to be fog and a cold weather all the next week.

h) The burglaries are definitely on increase.
i) I spent very interesting holiday at the Lake Coniston in England.
j) We are against war in general, so of course we are against war like this between superpower and developing country.

3

Choose the most suitable word underlined. A dash (–) means that no article is needed.

a) Helen doesn't like the/– cream cakes sold in a/the local bakery.
b) The/– basketball is fast becoming a/the popular sport worldwide.
c) We could see that the/– Alps were covered in the/– snow.
d) It's a/– long time since I met a/– lovely person like you!
e) Diana has a/– degree in the/– engineering from the/– University of London.

f) At <u>the/–</u> present moment, <u>the/–</u> man seems to have <u>the/an</u> uncertain future.

g) <u>The/–</u> problem for <u>the/–</u> today's students is how to survive financially.

h) <u>The/–</u> French enjoy spending holidays in <u>the/–</u> countryside.

i) Please do not turn on <u>a/the</u> water-heater in <u>a/the</u> bathroom.

j) Sue bought <u>a/the</u> Picasso I was telling you about <u>the/–</u> last week.

4

In each space put *a/an* or *the*, or leave the space *blank*.

a) I'm going to stand for — Parliament at .... next election.

b) When I left .... station, I had to stand in .... queue for .... taxi for .... long time.

c) We took .... trip around London and saw .... Tower Bridge.

d) ....happiness of the majority depends on .... hard work from everyone.

e) .... most main roads in this part of .... country follow .... line of .... roads built by .... Romans.

f) Have you got .... latest record by .... Gipsy Kings?

g) If I had .... time, I would like to take up .... archery.

h) We spent .... pleasant evening having .... drink at .... Robin Hood.

i) .... Nile flows right though .... city.

j) .... summer I spent in .... USA was one of .... best in my life.

5

In each space put *a/an* or *the*, or leave the space *blank*.

a) Go down — Kingston Street and turn right into .... Mill Road.

b) Please let me carry .... shopping. It's .... least I can do.

c) I don't like .... milk in .... coffee.

d) She was .... first woman to cross .... Atlantic in .... canoe.

e) Jim became .... furniture salesman after leaving .... school.

f) At .... end of .... busy day, ... sleep is .... best tonic.

g) .... James Joyce I knew wasn't .... novelist and wasn't .... Irish either.

h) We'll go for .... walk if .... sun comes out.

i) This is .... last time I do you .... favour for .... while.

j) I'm staying in .... Hilton so you can leave me .... message.

6

Correct the errors in these sentences.

a) The time you spend on the relaxing pastime is good for you.
   The time you spend on a relaxing pastime is good for you.

b) Don't you work in record shop in High Street?

c) A new campaign against the smoking is directed at the young women.

d) The leader of the team is usually called captain.

e) A half the time I get phone call it's wrong number.
f) I saw brilliant rock band perform at the Isle of Wight rock festival.
g) Do you know what the difference there is between the stoat and the weasel?
h) At the half-time the both teams seemed in a difficulty.
i) The earthquake could easily damage the Channel Tunnel.
j) A painting I like best is the one not for a sale.

7
In each space put *a/an* or *the*, or leave the space *blank*.

a) Please watch *the* cabin attendant as she demonstrates .... use of .... oxygen mask.
b) Paul spent .... half of his life in .... Far East.
c) You have to use at .... least .... pint and .... half of milk.
d) Dick has .... sore throat and is taking .... medicine.
e) We arranged .... accommodation on .... outskirts of .... city.
f) There is .... very difficult crossword in .... *Times*.
g) Could you give me .... information I asked for in .... letter I sent you?
h) I bought .... jewellery for my sister but it wasn't .... kind she likes.
i) I always wanted to be .... astronaut but .... ambition wore off.
j) And .... last of all, don't forget to put .... cat out for .... night.

8
Choose the most suitable word underlined. A dash (–) means that no article is needed.

a) Brenda is the/– ideal for a/the job. She has a/– wealth of the/– experience.
    Brenda is ideal for the job. She has a wealth of experience.
b) The/– safety at the/– work is a/– major concern for us.
    ....
c) The/– poorest people in the/– country live in this city.
    ....
d) Have you seen a/the new 'Hamlet' at the/– National Theatre?
    ....
e) There is a/– beautiful countryside within an/– easy reach of a/the hotel.
    ....
f) I have a/– terrible cold and am staying in the/– bed today.
    ....
g) I earn £3 an/the hour as a/– supermarket cashier on the/– Saturdays.
    ....
h) The/– charge for an/– excess luggage is £10 a/the kilo.
    ....
i) The/– most of the/–life is a/– matter of getting on with the/– others.
    ....
j) This country is officially called The/– United Kingdom of The/– Great Britain and The/– Northern Ireland.
    ....

Unit 18 Relative clauses and non-finite clauses

Explanations

Defining and non-defining

1 Defining
A defining clause specifies which person or thing we mean. It cannot be separated from the person or thing it describes.
*By 4.30, there was only one painting **which hadn't been sold**.*

2 Non-defining
A non-defining clause contains extra information. In writing it is separated by commas, and in speech, if used at all, is usually indicated by intonation.
*By 4.30, **which was almost closing time**, nearly all the paintings had been sold.*

3 Some of the points given below depend on the type of clause.

Which and that

1 These are alternatives in a defining clause, although *which* is felt to be more formal.
*By 4.30, there was only one painting **that hadn't been sold**.*

2 *That* is not normally used to introduce a non-defining clause.
*The train, **which** was already an hour late, broke down again.*

3 *That* cannot follow a preposition.
*It was a service **for which** I will be eternally grateful.*

4 *That* is often used instead of *who* in everyday speech in defining clauses.
*Do you know the girl **that** lives next door?*

Who and whom

1 *Whom* is the object form of *who* and is used formally in object clauses.
*He was a person **whom** everyone regarded as trustworthy.*

2 However, this is now felt to be excessively formal by most speakers and *who* is commonly used instead.

3 *Whom* has to be used if it follows a preposition.
***To whom** it may concern.*
***To whom** am I speaking?*
However, in everyday use, it is usual to avoid this kind of construction.
Who am I speaking to?
See *when* and *where* below.

101

Whose	This means *of whom*. It is used in both defining and non-defining clauses.
	    *Several guests, **whose** cars were parked outside, were waiting at the door.*
	    *Several guests **whose** rooms had been broken into complained to the manager.*

When and *where*	**1** Non-defining
	Here they follow a named time or place.
	    *Come back at 3.30, **when** I won't be so busy.*
	    *I stopped in Maidstone, **where** my sister owns a shop.*
	
	2 Defining
	When follows words such as *time, day, moment*.
	    *There is hardly a moment **when** I don't think of you, Sophia.*
	Where follows words such as *place, house, street*.
	    *This is the street **where** I live.*

Omitting the relative	This is possible in defining object clauses.
	    He was a person everyone regarded as trustworthy.
	Sentences ending in a preposition or phrasal verb
	As outlined in *Who* and *whom* above, it is common to end a defining clause with a preposition or a phrasal verb.
	    *That's the house I used to live **in**.*
	    *I couldn't remember which station to **get off at**.*
	    *He's not someone who I really **get on with**.*

Omitting *which/who + be*	It is may be possible to reduce a verb phrase after *who/which* to an adjectival phrase in a defining clause, especially to define phrases such as *the only one, the last/first one*.
	    Jim was the only one of his platoon who had not been taken prisoner.
	    *Jim was the only one of his platoon **not taken prisoner**.*
	    *By 4.30, there was only one painting **not sold**.*

Which	**1** A non-defining clause can comment on the whole situation described in the main clause.
	    *There was nobody left on the train, **which made me suspicious**.*
	
	2 Phrases with *which*, such as *at which time/point, in which case, by which time, in which event* can be used in the same way.
	    *I watched the play until the end of the first act, **at which point** I felt I had seen enough.*
	    *A warning sign 'Overheat' may come on, **in which case** turn off the appliance at once.*

Clauses beginning with *what* and *whatever*	**1** *What* meaning *the thing* or *things which* can be used to start clauses.
	    *I can't believe **what you told me** yesterday.*
	    ***What you should do** is write a letter to the manager.*
	See Unit 14 Emphasis.

2 *Whatever, whoever, whichever* can be used in a similar way.
> *You can rely on Helen to do **whatever she can**.*
> ***Whoever arrives first** can turn on the heating.*

Non-finite clauses containing an -*ing* form

These are clauses without a main verb. The examples given here are non-defining. Note that the two clauses have the same subject.

1 Actions happening at the same time
> ***Waving their scarves and shouting**, the fans ran onto the pitch.*

2 One action happening before another
> ***Opening the letter**, she found that it contained a cheque for £1000.*
> This type of clause often explains the reason for something happening.
> ***Realising there was no one at home**, I left the parcel in the shed.*
> Both these types of sentence might begin with *on* or *upon*:
> *On opening the letter ...   Upon realising ...*

3 An event which is the result of another event
> *I didn't get wet, **having remembered to take my umbrella**.*

4 Where a passive construction might be expected, this is often shortened to a past participle.
> ***Having been abandoned** by his colleagues, the Minister was forced to resign.*
> ***Abandoned** by his colleagues, the Minister was forced to resign.*

Activities

1
Choose the most suitable words underlined.

a) What was the name of the person that/which bought your old car?
b) All the doors were open, that/which seemed rather odd.
c) I'll stay here till six, by that/which time Jane should have phoned.

d) Whatever/Whichever you do, don't press this red button.
e) This is the school which I used to go/I used to go to.
f) Driving carelessly/As he was driving carelessly, the police arrested David.
g) It seems odd that/what you should be here on holiday too.
h) This is Sophia, who/whom is taking over my job when I leave.
i) On the Sunday, that/which was my birthday, we went out for a meal.
j) The success of a shared holiday depends on who/whom you share it with.

2

Put *one* suitable word in each space.

a) Midway through the second half City scored their fourth goal, at *which* point United gave up completely.

b) There is one person to .... I owe more than I can say.

c) It was the kind of accident for .... nobody was really to blame.

d) .... leaves last should turn off the lights.

e) Mary was late yesterday, ... was unusual for her.

f) At 6.00, ... was an hour before the plane was due, thick fog descended.

g) I don't know .... told you that, but they were wrong.

h) The first time I saw you was .... you answered the door.

i) Mrs Brown was the first owner .... dog won three prizes in the same show.

j) I've just spoken to Sally, ... sends you her love.

3

Rewrite each sentence, starting as shown, so that the meaning stays the same. Omit any unnecessary relative pronouns.

a) The manager noticed I had dropped my purse and called after me.
Noticing *I had dropped my purse, the manager called after me.*

b) We were in a position which gave us no room for manoeuvre.
The position ....

c) I was really proud of that moment.
It was ....

d) I waited for him until 6.30 and then gave up.
I waited for him until 6.30, at ....

e) We suggested a lot of things, which were all rejected.
Everything ....

f) Jim used to be married to that girl.
That's the girl ....

g) If someone understands this book, they are cleverer than I am.
Anyone ....

h) A bumpy road led to the hotel.
The road which ....

i) Most people are in bed at that time.
It's a time ....

j) I won't tell you this again.
This ....

4

Rewrite each sentence so that it contains the word in capitals and so that the meaning stays the same.

a) I like Brenda, she's my kind of person.   THAT
Brenda is the kind of person that I like.

b) The whole summer was sunny and warm, for a change.   WHICH
....

c) Jean was the first person I asked for advice.   WHOSE
....

d) Not a single house in the street had escaped undamaged.   WHICH
....

e) Then I realised that I had left my wallet at home.   WHEN
....

f) I don't really approve of his proposal.   WHAT

....

g) It is an event I would rather forget.   WHICH

....

h) The police never caught the culprit.   WHO

....

i) I have read all of her books but one.   WHICH

....

j) The finder of treasure is entitled to part of its value.   WHOEVER

....

5

Decide whether it is possible to leave out the word or words underlined in each sentence.

a) It was the first car <u>that</u> I ever drove. (*possible*)
b) He was the first man <u>who</u> landed on the moon.
c) She was the first woman <u>who was</u> elected to parliament.
d) Harry isn't the kind of person <u>who</u> gets on with everyone.
e) In the whole book there was only one chapter <u>which</u> interested me.
f) There is only one Greek island <u>which</u> I haven't visited.
g) It's the long winters here <u>that</u> really depress most people.
h) Do you like the person <u>who</u> sits next to you in class?
i) The letter <u>that</u> arrived this morning contained bad news I'm afraid.
j) There is no one <u>whom</u> I would prefer to you as a co-driver.

6

Make one sentence from the sentences given, beginning as shown. Make any other necessary changes. Omit any unnecessary relative pronouns.

a) We eventually caught a train. It was one that stops at every station.
   The train (that/which) we eventually caught was
   one that stops at every station.
b) Carol slammed the door behind her. Her father had given her a car as a present. She drove off in it.
   Slamming ....
c) At the end of the street was a building. The street was crowded with shoppers. Tom had not noticed the building before.
   At the end of the street, ...
d) Some people have just moved in next door. They have the same surname as some other people. Those other people have just moved out.
   The people who have just moved in next door ....
e) I noticed that the door was open. I decided to go in. This turned out to be a mistake.
   Noticing ....
f) Everyone expects the Popular Party candidate to win the election. The candidate has been influenced by her advisers. She has announced that she will cut income tax by 10%.
   Influenced by her advisers, ...
g) I listened to George patiently until he started insulting me. At that point, I told him a few home truths. He didn't like it.
   I listened to George patiently until he started insulting me, ...

h) Pauline asked me a question. I had no reply to it.
   Pauline asked me ....

i) He rushed out of the room. He was shouting at the top of his voice.
   This was typical.
   Shouting ....

j) Some people wanted travel scholarships. The end of the week was the
   deadline. By then everyone had applied.
   By the end of the week, ...

7
Complete each
sentence with a
suitable word or
phrase.

a) I wasn't sure who *to address the* letter to, so I put 'The Manager'.

b) Most of the guests turned up two hours early, which ....
   by surprise.

c) Whoever .... to last was probably the person who
   murdered him.

d) The book I .... his birthday is one I enjoyed very much myself.

e) This cake was .... left on the plate, so I am eating it.

f) There's a chance that I may be late, in .... phone you.

g) Everyone admires her. She's just the kind of person .... up to.

h) No one knows who she is. She is the only member of the gang ....
   remained a secret.

i) After ten years with the firm, Brown was the only salesman ....
   promoted, so he decided to find another job.

j) This is the exact spot .... an accident two years ago.

8
Rewrite each
sentence so that it
contains the
word or words in
capitals, and so
that the meaning
stays the same.

a) The dog that chases our cat belongs to those people.   WHOSE
   Those are the people whose dog chases our cat.

b) I can't remember the last heavy rain.   WHEN IT
   ....

c) When she took up her new post, Professor Grant gave a party. ON

d) Do you get on with your next-door neighbour?   WHO
   ....

e) The person who told you you were clever was kidding you!   WHOEVER
   ....

f) I don't need anything else.   GOT

g) I was not familiar with that kind of computer.   WHICH
   ....

h) The police have no idea as to the whereabouts of the jewels.   WHERE
   ....

i) The most important thing is not to panic.   WHAT
   ....

j) I miss Jack more than anyone.   THAT
   ....

Unit 19 Verbs followed by *-ing* or infinitive

Explanations

This unit focuses on problem areas.

Verbs followed by either *-ing* or infinitive with *to*

1 *Can't bear, hate, like, love, prefer*
Like to usually refers to habitual preferences.
> We **like to** go out to lunch on Sunday.

Not like to means *think it wrong to*.
> I **don't like to** disturb colleagues at home.

2 *Attempt, begin, continue, intend, plan, propose, start*
There is no difference in meaning whether we use *-ing* or infinitive with *to*.
Intend, plan, and *propose* can be followed by *that* + clause. This may include *should*. See Unit 16 Reporting verbs.

3 *Forget, remember*
With *to* both verbs refer to an obligation.
> I **had to** phone the office but I **forgot to do** it.

With *-ing* both verbs refer to past events.
> I don't **remember learning** to walk.

Both can be followed by *that* + clause:
> I **remembered that I had to pay the phone bill.**

4 *Try*
With *to* this refers to something attempted, which might fail or succeed.
> I **tried to warn** him, but it was too late.

With *-ing* this refers to making an experiment, or to a new experience.
> Have you **tried windsurfing**? It's great!
> **Try taking** an aspirin. You'll feel better.

5 *Go on*
With *-ing* this refers to the continuing of an action.
> She **went on working** even though it was late.

With *to* this refers to the continuation of a speech.
> The Prime Minister **went on to praise** the Chancellor.

This means:
> The Prime Minister continued his speech by praising the Chancellor.

6 *Mean*

With the meaning *intend*, this is followed by *to*:

> *Sorry, I **meant to tell you** about the party.*

With *-ing*, and an impersonal subject, this refers to what is involved:

> *If we catch the early train, it will **mean getting up** at 6.00.*

That + clause is possible when meaning is being explained:

> *This **means that you have to report** to the police station.*

7 *Regret*

With *to* this refers to the speaker's regrets about what is going to be said. It often occurs in formal statements of this kind:

> *We **regret to inform you** that your application has been unsuccessful.*

With *-ing* this refers to a regret about the past.

> *I **regret saying that** to him.*

That + clause is also possible:

> *We **regret that we didn't tell her earlier.***

8 *Stop*

With *to* this refers to an intention.

> *Jane **stopped to check** the oil level in the engine.*

With *-ing* this refers to the ending of an activity.

> *The baby has **stopped waking up** during the night now.*

9 *Hear, see, watch*

When followed by infinitive without *to*, the action is complete.

> *We **watched all the cars cross** the finishing line.*

With *-ing*, the action is still in progress.

> *I **heard someone coming** up the stairs.*

Verbs with an object, followed by either *-ing* or infinitive with *to*

1 *Admit*

This can be used with or **without** *to* followed by *-ing*.

> *They **admitted (to) being** members of the gang.*

That + clause is also possible:

> *He **admitted that** he was wrong.*

2 *Allow, forbid, permit*

With an object and *to*:

> *The school **forbids students to smoke** in the classrooms.*

With an object *-ing* form:

> *The school does not **allow smoking.***

3 *Consider*

With an object and *to* this refers to an opinion:

> *She is **considered to be** the finest pianist of her generation.*

With *-ing* this means *think about*.

At one point I considered emigrating to Canada.
With *that* + clause it refers to an opinion:
We consider that she has behaved badly.

4 *Imagine*
With an object and *to*:
    I imagined the castle to be haunted.
With *-ing*: An object is also possible.
    I couldn't imagine (her) living in a place like that.
With *that* + clause it means *suppose*:
    I imagine that you'd like a cup of tea after your long journey!

5 *Require*
With an object and *to*:
    They required him to fill out a form.
With *-ing*:
    These letters require typing.

See Unit 7 for *needs doing*

Verbs normally followed by infinitive with *to*

1 Verbs marked * can also be followed by *that* + clause.
    *Agree, *appear, *arrange, attempt, ask, choose, dare, *decide, *demand, deserve, *expect, fail, grow, hasten, *happen, *hope, hurry, *learn, long, manage, neglect, offer, pay, *plan, *pledge, *pretend, *promise, refuse, *resolve, seek, *seem, struggle, *swear, *threaten, *vow, want, *wish

2 *Appear, (so) happen* and *seem* are only used impersonally with *that* + clause.
    It appears that I've made a mistake.
    It so happens that he is my brother!
    It seems that Mary is going to win.

3 *Want* can be used colloquially with *-ing*, like *need*:
    The car wants cleaning.

Verbs normally followed by *-ing*

1 Verbs marked * can also be followed by *that* + clause.
    *appreciate, avoid, contemplate, delay, *deny, detest, dislike, endure, enjoy, escape, excuse, face, *fancy, finish, involve, *mention, mind, miss, postpone, practise, *resent, risk, *suggest, burst out, it's no good/use, feel like, give up, keep on, leave off, put off, can't stand, spend/waste time

2 *Appreciate* is often followed by possessive + *-ing*
    I appreciate your trying to help.

3 See Unit 16 for *suggest*.

4   *Involve* has an impersonal subject.
Being an athlete involves *regular training.*

Verbs followed by infinitive without *to*

1   *Help* car. be used with or without *to*
I helped George (to)carry *the bags.*

2   *Make,* and expressions with *make.*
They **made me leave.**
We shall have to **make do.**
In the passive, *to* is used.
I **was made to** *leave.*

3   *Let* and expressions with *let.*
They didn't **let me leave.**
Let me go!

Verbs followed by an object and *to*

1   Verbs marked * can also be followed by *that* + clause.
*advise, assist, beg, bribe, command, dare, employ, enable, encourage, instruct, invite, lead, *order, *persuade, select, send, *teach, *tell, train, urge, *warn

2   See Unit 16 for *advise, order, persuade, tell, warn*

3   *Dare* can be used without *to* when there is no object. Compare:
They **dared him to jump.**
I didn't **dare (to) say** *anything.*
How **dare you speak** *like that to me!*

Activities

1
Choose the most suitable words underlined.

a) I never imagined the mountains to be/being so high!
b) Don't forget to wake me/waking me before you leave.

c) What do you mean to do/doing about the leaky pipes?
d) I regret to tell you/telling you that we cannot accept your offer.
e) Did you manage to find/finding the book you were looking for?
f) I tried taking/ to take that medicine you gave me but I couldn't swallow it.
g) We have postponed to tell/telling anyone the news until after Christmas.

h) Have you considered <u>to buy/buying</u> a microwave oven?

i) Sorry I'm late, I had to stop <u>to pick up/picking up</u> the children from school.

j) Margaret was slow at school, but she went on <u>to be/being</u> Prime Minister.

2

Rewrite each sentence, beginning as shown, so that the meaning stays the same.

a) I was made to study hard when I was at school.
They *made me study hard when I was at school.*

b) If I take the job I'll have to move to Paris.
Taking the job ....

c) It's very kind of you to give me a lift.
I appreciate ....

d) It might be a good idea to use honey instead of sugar.
Why don't you try ....

e) I'm quite happy to look after the baby for you.
I don't mind ....

f) I must see the manager!
I demand ....

g) 'Go on Jack, apply for the job,' said Sally.
Sally encouraged ....

h) You wouldn't know where the Hilton Hotel is, would you?
Do you happen ....

i) Parking is not permitted here.
You are ....

j) 'Shall I carry that bag for you, John?' said Pauline.
Pauline offered ....

3

Put one suitable word in each space.

a) It's too late to buy any food. We'll have to make *do* with what we've got.

b) I hardly .... ask how much it cost!

c) Have you ever .... taking a year off work?

d) I didn't like the town at first, but I .... to love it eventually.

e) What do you .... doing after this course has finished?

f) As soon as Sheila finished telling the joke, everyone burst out ....

g) Jim and I .... to meet at 6.00 but he didn't turn up.

h) It .... that we won't need to pay so much after all.

i) I can't wait for Saturday! I'm really .... to see you!

j) I can't .... getting up at 6.30 tomorrow morning!
I'll catch a later train.

4

Rewrite each sentence so that it included the word in capitals, and so that the meaning stays the same.

a) I'm sorry I didn't go to university.   **REGRET**
I regret not going/not having gone to university.

b) Winning the football pools meant we could buy a new car.   **ENABLED**
....

c) There is a risk that he will miss the plane if he waits.   **RISKS**
....

d) I believed you were the murderer because of this clue.   **LED**
....

e) Does using the hotel swimming pool cost extra?   PAY

....

f) I think that this is the right street.   APPEARS

....

g) Jean succeeded in finishing all her work on time.   MANAGED

....

h) They said they would like me to stay with them in Florida.   INVITED

....

i) Calling Jim is pointless, because his phone is out of order.   USE

....

j) It is compulsory for all students to leave a cash deposit.   REQUIRED

....

5

Put *one* suitable word in each space.

a) The government *hopes* to reduce inflation by strict control of the economy.
b) I couldn't .... actually living in a place like that!
c) The arrested man .... having been anywhere near the bank.
d) Carol .... the customs officer to ignore the gold bars in her bag.
e) Did you .... anyone waiting for me when you passed my office?
f) We .... to split the cost of all the bills.
g) I was .... to get to the station when I fell and injured my knee.
h) We strongly .... all clients to take out their own travel insurance.

i) I don't .... turning off the gas, now you mention it.
j) Margaret doesn't really .... to ask staff to work overtime on Friday.

6

Rewrite each sentence, beginning as shown, so that the meaning stays the same.

a) Is that the manager? I have a complaint about my room.
Is that the manager? I wish *to complain about my room.*
b) You waste time if you copy your work out again, don't do it.
Don't ....
c) I bet you wouldn't ask David to come with you to the party!
I dare ....
d) Brenda really hates staying in expensive hotels.
Brenda can't ....
e) 'Please don't leave me on my own,' Martin begged us.
Martin begged ....

f) If you work for this company, you have to travel a lot.
   Working for this company involves ....

g) Joe doesn't like it when people treat him like a child.
   Joe resents ....

h) You should go to the dentist's at once.
   Don't put ....

i) It was resolved that the matter would be brought up at the next meeting.
   They resolved ....

j) The police were told that the use of unnecessary force was forbidden.
   The police were instructed ....

7

Complete each
sentence with a
suitable word or
phrase.

a) Sorry, I *meant to tell you* I would be out, but I forgot.

b) If you really .... to your friends, why not phone them?

c) That's all for now. I .... hear from you soon!

d) If I take the new job, it .... working a lot harder!

e) Are you still tired? Or do .... going out for a meal?

f) I .... be standing outside the bank, and I saw the robbery take place.

g) Jane is .... be the most outstanding player in the team.

h) I wish you wouldn't .... complaining all the time!

i) .... suggest that I would take a bribe! I've never been so insulted!

j) We .... Helen carry her bags, but she said she could manage on her own.

113

Unit 20 Progress Test (Units 16, 17, 18, 19)

1
Put *one* suitable word in each space.

It now seems clear that one of (1) .... most pressing problems facing any large city at (2) .... end of (3) .... twentieth century, is that of water supply. While most cities were founded (4) .... because water was plentifully available, no one could have foreseen (5) .... demands put upon the water supply by the sprawling (6) .... of today. In many cases, cities are forced (7) .... bring water from many miles away, often to the detriment (8) .... the local environment, for water is not only a commodity needed by man for drinking and washing and industrial processes. Many lakes (9) .... once served (10) .... breeding grounds for wild birds now face (11) .... uncertain future. As neighbouring cities (12) .... greater and greater demands, (13) .... water level of such lakes falls lower and lower, thus depriving the birds of their habitat. And (14) .... apart from this environmental problem, there is the economic issue to consider. Who owns the water, and how much should (15) .... consumer pay for it? The next time you turn on the tap, it might be worth considering some of these problems, before you have wasted too much water.

2
Put *one* suitable word in each space.

a) I spoke to Helen yesterday, but she didn't .... the letter you sent her.
b) There is nobody for .... we feel greater respect.
c) My neighbours .... that they would call the police if I made any more noise.
d) We haven't got any sugar, so you'll have to make .... without.
e) Members of Parliament .... that the Prime Minister tell them the truth.
f) That's the couple .... house my sister bought.
g) When I feel really tired I just .... to get home and go to bed.
h) .... buys the wardrobe will have to arrange to pick it up themselves.
i) Why don't you .... phoning Directory Inquiries? They might know.
j) Do you .... going out for a pizza later on?

3
Put *a/an, the* or leave the space blank.

a) That's .... last time that I go to .... horror film.
b) In .... circumstances I would say he hasn't .... chance.
c) I'd like to buy .... piano .... one day but I haven't got .... money.
d) Could you give me .... hand to take .... rubbish downstairs?
e) .... girl I told you about is .... one on .... left.
f) .... address is: .... Park Hotel, 42 .... Castle Road, ... Dover.
g) Mary spent .... year and .... half working with .... sick people in .... Africa.
h) .... medicine .... doctor gave me makes me feel tired all .... day.
i) Dawson put .... ball in .... net early in .... second half but .... goal was disallowed.
j) Terry became .... teacher with .... best exam results in .... school.

4

Rewrite each
sentence,
beginning as
shown, so that
the meaning stays
the same.

a) 'Don't forget to give me a ring tomorrow, Peter,' said Wendy.
   Wendy reminded..

b) If we take the train, we'll have to change in Paris.
   If we take the train, it..

c) I would rather forget that experience.
   That's an..

d) You haven't seen my pen anywhere, have you?
   You don't..

e) 'Just make sure you avoid staying in the city centre, Mike,' said Ruth.
   Ruth warned Mike..

f) Everything I told you was true.
   I told you a lot of things, all..

g) Smoking is forbidden here.
   You are..

h) If anyone can eat this, they must be desperate!
   Anyone..

i) 'I think you'd better not come to work for a few days, Cathy.'
   I advised..

j) I used to work with that girl.
   That's a..

5

Choose the most
suitable word or
phrase.

a) My friends gave me a surprise party, ... was good of them.
   A) that   B) this   C) which   D) what

b) The inspector .... to say whether there were any suspects.
   A) refused   B) avoided   C) stopped   D) denied

c) I .... to say that your application has been unsuccessful.
   A) like   B) happen   C) regret   D) hope

d) Several people, ... voices could be clearly heard, were waiting outside.
   A) whose   B) their   C) of which   D) whom

e) I .... you'd like another cat, would you?
   A) reckon   B) suspect   C) don't know   D) don't suppose

f) The manager .... that all the customers should be searched.
   A) predicted   B) insisted   C) obliged   D) told

g) .... you should do now is take a long holiday.
   A) That   B) How   C) What   D) As

h) .... happens, I shall stand by you!
   A) Whatever   B) What   C) Which   D) That

i) Sarah congratulated .... passing my driving test.
   A) me   B) for   C) me on   D) me for

j) I left at 5.30, ... they were still arguing.
   A) at the time   B) all the time C) just in time   D) at which time

115

6

Rewrite each sentence so that it contains the word in capitals, and so that the meaning stays the same.

a) According to reports, the President is in poor health. REPORTED

....

b) Julia's inheritance meant that she could give up work. ENABLED

....

c) Stupidly, I left my umbrella at home. WHICH

....

d) We received a warning to stay at home. SHOULD

....

e) Nobody there knew the answer. WHO

....

f) You could easily become quite ill unless you give up smoking. BECOMING

....

g) Everyone cheered the Prime Minister's statement. WHAT

....

h) The decorators didn't make too much mess. MANAGED

....

i) Don't tell Tim under any circumstances. WHATEVER

....

j) It's pointless to worry about someone else's problems. THERE

....

7

Complete each sentence with a suitable word or phrase.

a) Everyone .... not to go out alone after dark, but I did.

b) I didn't know .... the parcel to, so I left it on the desk.

c) If you feel so tired every morning, why .... going to bed earlier!

d) The returning officer .... to the crowd that the Democratic candidate had won.

e) If I took a job like that, it .... earning less money.

f) I may not manage to catch that bus, ... I'll arrive about an hour later.

g) Jim is the last person .... robbing a bank! It's hard to believe.

h) I .... Jack do his homework, but he said he could do it himself.

i) This is the exact place .... the car broke down last week!

j) Do you still feel ill? Or .... coming shopping with me tomorrow?

8

Rewrite each sentence, beginning as shown, so that the meaning stays the same.

a) I apologised on realising that I had made a mistake.
Realising ....

b) I haven't been here before.
This ....

c) 'No, little Jimmy has got to make his own bed.'
His mother...

d) According to Valerie, she is a relation of mine.
Valerie claims ....

e) I don't know who she was, but she must have been strong.
Whoever ....

f) Did I tell her the news or not? I can't remember.
I can't ....

g) Does parking here cost anything?
Do I ....

h) Most people are on holiday at that time of the year.
It's the ....

i) I'm not going to tell you again.
This ....

j) I knew someone called John Smith who was a stockbroker.
The John Smith ....

9
Rewrite each sentence so that it contains the word in capitals, and so that the meaning stays the same.

a) When did you last have a haircut?   THE
....

b) The police officer obliged us to open the boot of the car.   MADE
....

c) After six months, Joe's search for a job was successful.   MANAGED
....

d) Jean was given permission by her boss to take a day off.   AGREED
....

e) It was foolish of you to drive so fast.   THING
....

f) Although Sue looked for the book, she couldn't find it.   LOOKING
....

g) All visitors to the town fall in love with it.   WHO
....

h) The headteacher said she would expel Tom next time.   THREATENED
....

i) I didn't expect to see you here!   LAST
....

j) Helen manages the bank across the street.   OF
....

10
Put *one* word in each space.

a) How much do you make .... week?

b) Could you do the washing up for me? I can't .... it just now.

c) There was nothing more .... I could do.

d) It is recommended that all luggage .... bear a personal label.

e) Is this the street .... you live in?

f) Half way through Ted's speech, everyone .... out laughing.

g) It is .... that more than a million people could benefit from the operation.

h) Charles is not the kind of person .... would help you.

i) If we don't lower the price, we .... losing the order.

j) We didn't .... tell the doctor she was wrong!

11

Rewrite each sentence, beginning as shown, so that the meaning stays the same.

a) We haven't seen one another for a long time.
   We stopped ....

b) It is the expense involved that bothers me.
   What ....

c) The weather was expected to be fine.
   We didn't ....

d) I don't know who did the washing up, but they didn't do it very well.
   Whoever ....

e) I'm sorry now that I didn't tell you the truth.
   Now I regret ....

f) Peter, this is my sister, Ann.
   Peter, let me ....

g) I couldn't pay for the meal as I had left my wallet at home.
   Having ....

h) Most people think Nigel is the best racing driver in the world.
   Nigel is considered ....

i) Janet came first, which surprised nobody.
   Nobody ....

j) They didn't let Graham take his dog to work with him.
   Graham was ....

12

Complete each sentence with a suitable word or phrase.

a) Are you spending your holiday .... mountains or by the sea?

b) I saw Harry arrive, but I don't remember .... leave.

c) It was a type of computer .... I was not familiar.

d) I wouldn't marry you even if you were .... world.

e) All my family were sitting in the front row, which .... nervous.

f) Then I noticed that Christine had a gun .... hand.

g) Sandra trained .... architect but ended up as a rock star.

h) .... in the capital that the army is about to take power, though this has been denied by government sources.

i) Anyone .... as wide as my children's are will know how difficult it is to find shoes.

j) Do you .... off the electric heater before we left?

Unit 21 Verbs followed by prepositions

Explanations

This unit focuses on a selection of verbs, including their adjectival forms. Many verbs have other uses followed by -ing or Infinitive (see Units 18,19). Passive uses with *by* are not included. See also Units 23, 24, 25.

Verbs followed by *in*	*absorbed in* something (especially *absorbed in her work/a book*) *confide in* someone *be engrossed in* something *implicate someone in* something *involve someone in* something *result in* something *specialise in* something *succeed in* something
Verbs followed by *for*	*account for* something *allow for* something (to take into consideration) *apologise for* something/someone (on their behalf: *Let me apologise for Jack.*) *blame* someone *for* something *care for* something/someone *cater for* something/someone *charge* someone *for* something (make them pay for it) *count for* something (especially: *I count for nothing in this company.*) *earmark* something *for* a particular use *pay for* someone/something
Verbs followed by *of*	*accuse* someone *of* something *convict* someone *of* something *remind* someone *of* something *suspect* someone *of* something
Verbs followed by *with*	*acquaint* someone *with* something *associate* something *with* someone *charge* someone *with* something *clutter with* something (especially passive: *The room was cluttered with boxes.*) *coincide with* something *collide with* something *comply with* something

concern *with* something (usually passive: *be concerned with*)
confront someone *with* something
confuse someone/something *with* someone/something
cram *with* something (especially passive: *be crammed with*)
deal *with* someone/something
discuss something *with* someone
face *with* something (especially passive: *be faced with*)
ingratiate oneself *with* someone
meet *with* something (especially: *meet with an accident*)
pack *with* something (especially passive: *be packed with*)
plead *with* someone
provide someone *with* something
tamper *with* something
trust someone *with* something

Verbs followed by *from*

bar someone *from* a place
benefit *from* something
derive something *from* something
deter someone *from* something
differ *from* something
distinguish one thing *from* another thing (also *distinguish between two things*)
distract someone *from* something
exempt someone *from* something
expel someone *from* a place
refrain *from* something
resign *from* something
result *from* something
stem *from* something
suffer *from* something
translate one language *from/into* another language

Verbs followed by *on*

base something *on* something
blame something *on* someone
centre something *on* something (usually passive: *be centred on*)
concentrate something *on* something
congratulate someone *on* something
decide *on* something
depend *on* someone/something
elaborate *on* something
impose *on* someone
insist *on* something/someone doing something
pride oneself *on* something

Verbs followed by *against*

insure something *against* something
protest *against* something

Verbs followed by *about*	*argue about* something *be concerned about* something (*be worried about*) *boast about* something *decide about* something *dream about* something *protest about* something
Verbs followed by *out*	*phase* something *out*
Verbs followed by *at*	*glance at* something *guess at* something *hint at* something *marvel at* something
Verbs followed by *to*	*answer to* something (especially: *answer to a description*) *appeal to* someone (*beg*) It *appeals to* me. (*I like the idea.*) *apply* oneself *to* something (*She applied herself to her studies.*) *apply to* something (*This rule doesn't apply to you.*) *attend to* something said/heard *attribute* something *to* someone *commit* oneself *to* something (especially passive: *be committed to*) *confess to* something *devote* oneself *to* something *prefer* one thing *to* another thing *react to* something *refer to* something (*This number refers to the next page.*) *refer* someone *to* someone (*The doctor referred me to a specialist.*) *be resigned to* something *resort to* something *see to* something (meaning *make sure it is done*) *subject* someone *to* something (stressed: *sub<u>ject</u>*) *succeed to* the throne *be used to* doing something

Activities

1

Choose the most suitable word underlined.

a) I discussed <u>with him/the matter with him</u> all afternoon.

b) We believe that our radio programmes should <u>cater to/cater for</u> all tastes.

c) The police tried to blame the accident <u>on Harry/for Harry</u>.

d) The Minister is resigned <u>to having to cancel/to have to cancel</u> the scheme.

e) Carol was sitting in a corner engrossed <u>in/with</u> checking the figures.

f) They accused Helen <u>of/with</u> stealing the gold bullion.

g) Several youths have been barred <u>from/to</u> the disco for rowdy behaviour.

121

h) The victim had been subjected <u>to/with</u> a vicious unprovoked attack.

i) The bus rolled down the slope and collided <u>with/into</u> a van.

j) Everything now depends <u>from/on</u> the weather tomorrow morning.

2

Complete each sentence with *one* suitable preposition.

a) I really prefer just about anything *to* watching television.

b) This year's conference coincided .... two other major conventions.

c) Is it possible to insure my bike .... theft?

d) The problem stems .... the government's lack of action.

e) When I asked Jean, she hinted .... the chance of a promotion for me.

f) Being rich doesn't count .... much on a desert island.

g) I pleaded .... John to change his mind, but he wouldn't listen.

h) I can't stand the way she is always boasting .... her wealthy parents.

i) My grandfather is always confusing Madonna .... Maradona.

j) Could you please refrain .... smoking in the lecture hall.

3

Put *one* word in each space. Each word is a form of a verb listed at the beginning of this unit.

a) The idea of marriage doesn't *appeal* to me.

b) We .... in finding Ann's house at the second attempt.

c) However poor I was I would not .... to stealing.

d) Have you .... for the wind speed in your calculations?

e) He confessed when he was .... with the evidence.

f) You need to .... yourself more to your work.

g) Alan .... himself on his punctuality.

h) I was .... from doing my work by the music.

i) I .... for breaking your electric drill.

j) Tina .... for everyone's lunch yesterday.

4

Rewrite each sentence so that it contains the word in capitals, and so that the meaning stays the same.

a) Peter always trusts me with his secrets.   IN
   Peter always confides in me.

b) A true story forms the basis of Mary's new novel.   ON
   ....

c) I don't understand the reference of this phrase.   TO
   ....

d) There were a lot of people on the bus.   WITH
   ....

e) You were in my dreams last night.   ABOUT
   ....

f) Danny was asked to leave the school for bad behaviour.   FROM
   ....

g) This house brings home to mind!   OF
   ....

h) Tina rewrote the French book in Spanish.   FROM
   ....

i) Christmas and roast turkey go together in my mind.   WITH
   ....

j) I think a rest would do you good.   FROM
   ....

5

Complete each sentence with *one* suitable preposition.

a) Dave's pockets were crammed <u>*with*</u> empty chocolate wrappers.

b) Everyone tried to blame Janet .... the mistake.

c) When I retired, I devoted myself .... improving my golf.

d) Tim was exempted .... military service because of his bad heart.

e) Mary specialises .... designing theatres and concert halls.

f) That creep! He is always trying to ingratiate himself .... the boss!

g) The Prime Minister refused to elaborate .... what he had said earlier.

h) I'm afraid that the parking regulations apply .... everyone, sir.

i) On its first voyage, the Titanic met .... disaster.

j) I'm really not used .... being treated like that!

6

Choose the most suitable word or phrase.

a) I would never have ....<u>C</u>..... Jim of being the culprit.
   A) accused   B) convicted   C) suspected   D) reminded

b) How did Sheila .... to the news of her award?
   A) react   B) answer   C) confess   D) appeal

c) Someone has been .... with the lock of the cash box.
   A) cluttering   B) dealing   C) tampering   D) matching

d) Don't worry about the lunch. I'll .... to it.
   A) succeed   B) apply   C) devote   D) see

e) More than two hundred police officers are .... in the investigation.
   A) absorbed   B) engrossed   C) specialised   D) involved

f) The trouble with Jean is that she is .... with sport!
   A) obsessed   B) packed   C) matched   D) dealt

g) Tony's parents decided that he couldn't be .... with money.
   A) acquainted   B) complied   C) trusted   D) met

h) Pauline and Helen .... on our staying for lunch.
   A) congratulated B) insisted   C) decided   D) concentrated

i) I am afraid that these regulations have to be .... with.
   A) complied   B) provided   C) faced   D) met

j) Our thoughts .... on our four missing colleagues.
   A) based   B) centred   C) imposed   D) depended

7
Rewrite each sentence so that it contains the word in capitals, and so that the meaning stays the same.

a) When he has to face a crisis, Tony panics. **FACED**
Faced with a crisis, Tony panics.

b) Collecting stamps gives me a lot of pleasure. **DERIVE**

c) The arrested man did not look the same as the wanted man. **ANSWER**

d) The facts of the case were familiar to the lawyer. **ACQUAINTED**

e) The deaths of over fifty people were caused by the storm. **RESULTED**

f) We have given winter equipment to all the soldiers. **PROVIDED**

g) We can only make a guess about the real truth. **GUESSED**

h) You haven't explained exactly how the money disappeared. **ACCOUNTED**

i) One of our philosophers is supposed to have said this. **ATTRIBUTED**

j) Brian is good at looking after the sick. **CARE**

8
Complete each sentence with *one* suitable preposition.

a) I wish you'd stop arguing *about* politics all the time.
b) Could you deal .... this problem, I'm rather busy.
c) The lights are designed to deter burglars .... approaching the house.
d) Your plan doesn't allow .... changes in the weather.
e) I would like to protest .... your treatment of the staff.
f) Damage to the building resulted .... an unusually high wind.
g) We really marvelled .... Helen's conjuring tricks.
h) I am not really concerned .... that side of the business.
i) The Minister is also implicated .... the scandal.
j) The company is committed .... raising salaries and improving conditions.

Unit 22 Prepositions following adjectives, and in prepositional phrases

Explanations

This unit focuses on a selection of expressions. See Vocabulary Units for more work in this area. Note that there may be other possible meanings for verbs and phrases given here, with different prepositions.

Prepositions following adjectives

1 Of   *afraid of, ashamed of, aware of, capable of, conscious of, fond of, full of, be good of (someone to do something), indicative of, irrespective of, jealous of*

2 About   *annoyed about, anxious about, certain about, excited about, pleased about, right about, sorry about, upset about, wrong about*

3 With   *angry with (a person), annoyed with (a person), bored with, commensurate with, connected with, be good at dealing with, happy with, incompatible with, obsessed with, pleased with, preoccupied with*

4 At   *angry at (a person), annoyed at (a person), be bad at, be good at, surprised at*

5 On   *keen on*

6 To   *addicted to, attentive to, grateful to, kind to, immune to, impervious to, indifferent to, liable to (likely to suffer from), married to, prone to*

7 By   *baffled by, bored by, detained by, distressed by, plagued by, shocked by, surprised by*

8 For   *early for, eligible for, famous for, late for, liable for (legally responsible), ready for, responsible for, sorry for*

9 In   *deficient in, experienced in, implicated in, interested in*

10 From   *absent from, derived from, different from, safe from, missing from*

Prepositions following nouns

1 On   *an authority on (expert), ban on, comment on, effect on, influence on, restriction on, tax on.*

2 To   *access to, an alternative to, an attitude to, an exception to, a solution to, a threat to, a witness to*

3 Over   *be in authority over, have control over, be in dispute over something*

4 With   *contrast with, be in dispute with someone, encounter with, link with, quarrel with, relationship with*

5 For   *admiration for, craving for, credit for, cure for, desire for, disregard for, provision for, recipe for, respect for, responsibility for, room for, sympathy for*

Expressions beginning with prepositions	**1** In	*in advance, in the balance, in all likelihood, in answer to, in any case, in charge of, in the charge of, in collaboration with, in comparison with, in comfort, in decline, in demand, in dispute, in distress, in the early stages, in earnest, in the end, be in favour of something, be in favour with someone, in fear of (being afraid of), in (good) condition, in harmony, in high spirits, in jeopardy, in one way or another, in practice, in recognition of, in response to, in short, in theory, in time, in trouble, in turn*

2 With *with the exception of, with intent to, with regard to, with a view to*

3 At *at any rate, at fault, at first sight, at the first/second attempt, at the end, at large*

4 On *on average, on approval, on a regular basis, on behalf of, on the contrary, on good terms, on loan, on the market (for sale), on (its) merits, on offer, on purpose, on the verge of*

5 Beyond *beyond belief, beyond a joke, beyond the shadow of a doubt*

6 By *by coincidence, by mistake, by the time, by rights, by surprise*

7 For *for fear of (because something might happen), for life, not for long, for the foreseeable future, for the time being*

8 Out of *out of breath, out of control, out of danger, out of doors, out of focus, out of luck, out of the ordinary, out of pocket, out of practice, out of all proportion, out of reach, out of stock, out of work*

9 Under *under age, under the circumstances, under control, under cover of, be under the impression that, under the influence of, under (a law), under an obligation, under pressure, under repair, under stress, under suspicion*

10 Without *without a chance, without delay, without exception, without a word*

11 Within *within the law, within reach*

12 After *after all*

Activities

1
Choose the most suitable words underlined.

a) Diane showed a complete disregard <u>for/with</u> her own safety.
b) I was totally baffled <u>by/of</u> Tim's behaviour.
c) For Romeo and Juliet it was love <u>at/with</u> first sight.
d) They wouldn't let me in the pub because I was <u>below/under</u> age.
e) Our house has been <u>in/on</u> the market for months.
f) You are perfectly capable <u>for/of</u> making your own bed, I would have thought!
g) We walked on tiptoe <u>for/from</u> fear of being discovered.
h) This is one of the exceptions <u>of/to</u> the rule.
i) I am surprised <u>at/by</u> you, forgetting your briefcase like that.
j) We met at the hotel completely <u>by/from</u> coincidence.

2

Rewrite each sentence so that it contains the word or words in capitals, and so that the meaning stays the same.

a) Please send the letter as soon as possible.   DELAY
   Please send the letter without delay.

b) You have to pay two months' rent before you move in.   ADVANCE
   ....

c) We get on very well with our next-door neighbours.   TERMS
   ....

d) Everybody wants Pauline as an after-dinner speaker.   DEMAND
   ....

e) I accidentally picked up the wrong suitcase at the airport.   MISTAKE
   ....

f) The whole team was in a happy mood.   SPIRITS
   ....

g) I realised I had said something wrong.   CONSCIOUS
   ....

h) You're not lucky today, I'm afraid.   OUT
   ....

i) You can't get to the village in winter because of the snow.   ACCESS
   ....

j) I don't want us to have a quarrel.   YOU
   ....

3

Put *one* suitable preposition in each space.

a) Helen had great admiration *for* her history teacher.
b) I'm afraid I'm not very good .... animals.
c) The favourite dropped out of the race .... the early stages.
d) I was .... the impression that you liked Indian food.
e) The minister stated that no real alternative .... the plan existed.
f) This town is famous .... its hand-woven carpets.
g) Your performance this term contrasts very favourably .... last term's.
h) Many young people become addicted .... drugs through ignorance.
i) Apparently a number of army officers were implicated .... the plot.
j) Carol doesn't have a very good relationship .... her mother.

4

Rewrite each sentence, beginning as shown, so that the meaning stays the same.

a) After trying twice, Ivan broke the record when he tried the third time.
   Ivan broke the record *at the third attempt.*...................

b) The meeting will probably be cancelled.
   In ....

c) Considering your position, we won't press charges.
   Under ....

d) Eventually you will be able to walk quite normally.
   In...

e) The students are living temporarily in a caravan.
   For the ....

f) I intend to discover the truth somehow or other.
   In one ....

g) The soldiers entered the castle while it was dark.
   Under ....

h) Speaking for my colleagues, I would like to thank you.
   On ....

i) I thought you had accepted.
   I was under ....

j) Everyone was exhausted apart from Sally.
   With ....

5

Choose the most suitable word or phrase.

a) It was very good ....D.... you to help Dave with his homework.
   A) for   B) to   C) with   D) of

b) Nothing .... the ordinary ever happens here.
   A) from   B) out of   C) about   D) within

c) The union and the management are in .... over working conditions.
   A) advance   B) practice   C) collaboration   D) dispute

d) After running up the stairs I was quite .... breath.
   A) out of   B) from   C) without   D) beyond

e) I'm afraid that this incident could put your career here ....
   A) beyond a joke   B) in jeopardy   C) in earnest   D) at fault

f) We are .... no obligation to change goods which were not purchased here.
   A) with   B) to   C) under   D) at

g) It seems to be your boss who is .... fault in this case.
   A) at   B) under   C) with   D) for

h) It's too late to phone Jill at work, at any ....
   A) case   B) time   C) situation   D) rate

i) Tina is an authority .... Byzantine architecture.
   A) for   B) on   C) with   D) in

j) I reckon Martin is .... of a nervous breakdown.
   A) in charge   B) under suspicion C) on the verge   D) indicative

6

Rewrite each sentence so that it contains the word in capitals, and so that the meaning stays the same.

a) I think this word comes from ancient Greek.   DERIVED
   I think this word is derived from ancient Greek.

b) I like to spend a lot of time in the open air.   DOORS
   ....

c) I don't think you mean what you say about helping me. EARNEST
   ....

d) Paul went to see the bank manager about getting a loan. VIEW
   ....

e) This miserable weather isn't funny any more!   JOKE
   ....

f) It's uncertain whether the band's tour will take place.   BALANCE

....

g) I wish I knew what to do about this problem.   SOLUTION

....

h) You can walk to the station easily from the hotel.   WITHIN

....

i) Karen received a medal for her services.   RECOGNITION

....

j) You have to pay your son's debts as he is under age.   LIABLE

....

7
Complete each
sentence with a
suitable word or
phrase.

a) Freddy wrote the book in __collaboration with__ three of his colleagues.
b) Mary suddenly left the room .... word.
c) I'm not in .... children leaving home at such an early age.
d) Goods are sent to you on .... for fourteen days before payment is due.
e) It took Sally a long time to find a job .... with her abilities.
f) Most of these photos are terrible, they are all out ....
g) The bridge is .... so we'll have to take the long way round.
h) What have you to say .... to the charges made against you?
i) That wasn't an accident, you did it on ....
j) The company asked Ann to work for them .... basis.

8
Put *one* word in
each space. Each
word is part of a
phrase listed at
the beginning of
this unit.

a) The police questioned each witness in ....
b) Sometimes I have an incredible .... for chocolate.
c) No one gave Tom .... for his discovery.
d) The jury must believe that the accused is guilty beyond the .... of a
   doubt.
e) Each plan should be judged on its own .... before we decide.
f) The programme is being shown again in .... to public interest.
g) Everyone was assigned a parking-space .... of whether they had a car.
h) Teachers are .... to back pain.
i) Who is in .... of checking the orders?
j) When some money went missing everyone in the bank was under ....

Unit 23 Phrasal verbs 1

Explanations

This unit (and Units 24 and 25) assume that a wide range of phrasal verbs, and their grammatical types, are already known. These units focus on multiple meaning, and other meanings of known phrasal verbs. Note that there may be other meanings for the verbs listed here.

Add up (make sense)
*His evidence just doesn't **add up.***

Ask after (inquire about)
*Jim was **asking after** you.*

Back down (yield in an argument)
*Sheila was right, so Paul had to **back down.***

Bargain for (take into acount)
*We hadn't **bargained for** there being so much traffic, and we missed the plane.*

Bear out (confirm the truth)
*Helen's alibi was **borne out** by her sister.*

Break down (lose control of the emotions)
*David **broke down** and wept when he heard the news.*

Break off (stop talking)
*He **broke off** to answer the phone.*

Break up (come to an end)
*The party finally **broke up** at 3.00am.*

Bring about (cause to happen)
*The crisis was **brought about** by Brenda's resignation.*

Bring off (succeed in doing something)
*The team tried for years to win the competition and they finally **brought** it **off**.*

Bring on (cause the onset of an illness)
*Sitting in the damp **brought on** his rheumatism.*
(cause trouble to happen to) oneself
*You have **brought** this **on/upon** yourself!*

Bring round (influence someone to your point of view)
*After much discussion, I **brought** the committee **round** to my point of view.*

Bring up (mention)
*I feel I ought to **bring up** another small matter.*

Call up (mobilise for military service)
*Mark was **called up** when the war broke out.*

Carry off (complete successfully – perhaps despite a problem)
*Jane had a difficult role to play, but she **carried** it **off**.*

Carry out (complete a plan)
*The attack was successfully **carried out**.*

Catch on (become popular – colloquial)
*This new hair style is beginning to **catch on**.*

Come about (happen)
*Let me explain how the situation **came about**.*

Come down to (be in the end a matter of)
*It all **comes down to** whether you are prepared to accept less money.*

Come in for (receive – especially *criticism, blame*)
*The government has **come in for** a lot of criticism over the decision.*

Come off (take place successfully)
*I'm afraid that deal didn't **come off** after all.*

Come out (appear)
*All the flowers have **come out**.*
*When the news **came out**, everyone was shocked.*
*My photos didn't **come out** very well.*

Come up (occur – usually *a problem* – colloquial)
*Look, something has **come up**, and I can't meet you.*

Come up against (meet a difficulty)
*We've **come up against** a bit of a problem.*

Come up to (equal – especially *expectations, standard*)
*The play didn't **come up to** expectations.*

Come up with (think of – especially *an answer, a plan, a solution*)
*We still haven't **come up with** a solution to the problem.*

Count on (rely on)
*Don't worry, you can **count on** me.*

Crop up (happen unexpectedly – colloquial)
*I can't come to your party, something has **cropped up**.*

Do away with (abolish – colloquial)
*Dog licences have been **done away with**.*
(murder – colloquial)
*What if they **do away with** the old man?*

Do up (decorate – colloquial)
*We are having our living room **done up**.*

Draw up (come to a stop)
*A white sports car **drew up** outside the door.*

Draw up (organise – especially *a document*)
*The contract is being **drawn up** at the moment.*

Drop in (pay a visit – colloquial)
***Drop in** any time you're passing.*

Drop off (fall asleep – colloquial)
*The baby has just **dropped off**.*

End up (finish in a certain way, or place)
*We **ended up** staying there for lunch.*
*The car **ended up** in a ditch.*

Face up to (have courage to deal with – especially *responsibilities*)
You have to face up to your responsibilities.
Fall about (show amusement – especially *laughing* – colloquial)
Everyone fell about when Jane told her joke.
Fall back on (use as a last resort)
If the worst comes to the worst, we've got our savings to fall back on.
Fall for (be deceived by – colloquial)
It was an unlikely story but he fell for it.
(fall in love with – colloquial)
I fell for you the moment I saw you.
Fall out with (quarrel with)
Peter has fallen out with his boss.
Fall through (fail to come to completion)
The plan fell through at the last minute.
Feel up to (feel capable of doing)
Old Mr Smith didn't feel up to walking all that way.
Follow up (act upon a suggestion)
Thanks for the information about that book. I'll follow it up.
(take more action)
We'll follow up this lesson next week.
Get across (be understood – especially *get an idea across*)
I had the feeling I wasn't getting across.
Get at (imply – about personal matters – colloquial)
What are you getting at exactly?
Get down (make to feel depressed – colloquial)
This cold weather really gets me down.
Get down to (begin to seriously deal with)
It's time we got down to some real work.
Get off with (avoid punishment)
They were lucky to get off with such light sentences.
Get on for (approach a certain age/time/number)
He must be getting on for seventy.
Get on (make progress – especially *in life*)
Sue is getting on very well in her new job.
Get over (be surprised)
I couldn't get over how well she looked.
Get over with (come to the end of something, usually unpleasant)
I'll be glad to get this awful business over with.
Get round to (find time to do – also *around*)
Sorry, but I haven't got round to fixing the tap yet.
Get up to (do something – usually bad when about children – colloquial)
The children are getting up to something in the garden.
What have you been getting up to lately?

Activities

1

Choose the most suitable words underlined.

a) Jim completely fell for my joke/story.

b) The conversation/meeting didn't break up until late.

c) It seems that we've come up against rather a tricky idea/problem.

d) It must be getting on for six o'clock/extremely well.

e) The witness's evidence bore out what Peter had said/as Peter said.

f) When David started speaking everyone fell about in laughter/laughing.

g) I really should get down to my homework/the weather.

h) Unfortunately my plan/suggestion didn't quite come off.

i) Mary's new novel doesn't come up to her usual expectation/standard.

j) Last night I dropped off at 11.30/from 11.30 until 7.00 this morning.

2

Rewrite each sentence so that it contains the word in capitals, and so that the meaning stays the same.

a) I don't think this record will ever be popular.   CATCH
I don't think this record will ever catch on.

b) A police car has just stopped outside.   UP
....

c) They didn't punish Karen, only gave her a warning.   GOT
....

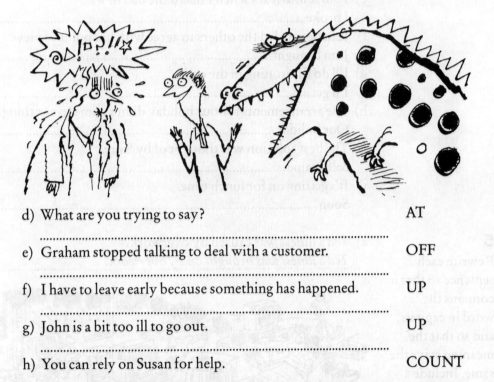

d) What are you trying to say?   AT
....

e) Graham stopped talking to deal with a customer.   OFF
....

f) I have to leave early because something has happened.   UP
....

g) John is a bit too ill to go out.   UP
....

h) You can rely on Susan for help.   COUNT
....

i) What sort of progress are you making in your new job?   GETTING
....

j) Because it was late, I had to walk home in the end.   UP
....

3

Put *one* suitable
word in each
space.

a) When I give an order I expect it to be *carried* out.

b) Getting up so early really gets me ....

c) It was a good idea, but I'm afraid it didn't quite .... off.

d) I'm afraid that your story doesn't really .... up.

e) I was so surprised when Harry got the job, I couldn't .... over it.

f) Terry's new book .... out next week.

g) Someone was .... after you in the club yesterday.

h) Just as I was .... off, there was a knock at the door.

i) Neil was too embarrassed to .... up the question of who would pay.

j) The police didn't .... up Bill's complaint about his neighbours.

4

Rewrite each
sentence,
beginning as
shown, so that
the meaning stays
the same.

a) A rather nasty problem has appeared.
We've come *up against a rather nasty problem.*

b) I'm doing more work than I bargained for.
I didn't expect ....

c) The sooner this job is over, the better.
Let's ....

d) Brenda doesn't get on with her next-door neighbour any more.
Brenda has ....

e) I burst into tears when I heard the bad news.
I broke ....

f) Jean persuaded the others to agree with her point of view.
Jean brought...

g) I'll do the ironing in the end.
I'll get...

h) The arrangements for our holiday didn't come to anything.
Our holiday...

i) The best solution was thought of by Sally.
Sally came...

j) It's getting on for lunch time.
Soon...

5

Rewrite each
sentence so that it
contains the
word in capitals,
and so that the
meaning stays the
same. Include a
phrasal verb in
your answer.

a) Ted's illness was caused by overwork.   ON
Ted's illness was brought on by overwork.

b) Carol has trouble communicating her ideas to others.   ACROSS

....

c) Some men are coming to decorate our bedroom.   DONE

....

d) How exactly did this situation happen in the first place?   COME

....

e) What happened confirmed the truth of Jack's prediction.   BORNE

....

f) This could be a vital clue so you should investigate it.   UP

....

g) Let's give this business our serious attention.   GET

....

h) It was a simple trick, but the teacher was taken in by it.   FOR

....

i) They laid most of the blame on Margaret.   FOR

....

j) Our lawyers are working on the agreement at the moment.   UP

....

6

Choose the most suitable word or phrase.

a) The meeting didn't ....B.... until late.
   A) end up   B) break up   C) come about   D) fall through

b) In the end it all .... a question of trust.
   A) gets round to   B) adds up to   C) feels up to   D) comes down to

c) The hotel didn't .... my expectations.
   A) come up to   B) get up to   C) come down to   D) get down to

d) At first Tim insisted he was right, but then began to ....
   A) back down   B) follow up   C) drop off   D) break up

e) It's no good pretending, you've got to .... reality.
   A) bargain for   B) come up against   C) face up to   D) get down to

f) What were you two .... just now in the garden?
   A) bringing about   B) getting up to   C) coming up with
   D) getting round to

g) You should always have an alternative plan to ....
   A) bring about   B) ask after   C) feel up to   D) fall back on

h) When they .... , I had to report to the nearest barracks.
   A) called me up   B) asked after me   C) asked me after   D) called up me

i) The school examination for eleven-year-olds was .... some years ago.
   A) followed up   B) drawn up   C) carried out
   D) done away with

j) When I took over the business I got more than I ....
   A) asked after   B) bargained for   C) drew up   D) came in for

Unit 24 Phrasal Verbs 2

Explanations

This unit (and Units 23 and 25) assume that a wide range of phrasal verbs, and their grammatical types, are already known. These units focus on multiple meaning, and alternative ways of expressing meanings of phrasal verbs. Note that there may be other meanings for the verbs listed here.

Give away (betray)

His false identity papers gave him away.

Give off (send off a smell – liquid or gas)

The cheese had begun to give off a strange smell.

Give out (be exhausted)

When our money gave out we had to borrow.

Give over (abandon, devote)

The rest of the time was given over to playing cards.

(stop – colloquial)

Why don't you give over! You're getting on my nerves!

Give up (surrender)

The escaped prisoner gave herself up.

(believed to be dead or lost)

After ten days the ship was given up for lost.

Go back on (break a promise)

The management has gone back on its promise.

Go in for (make a habit of)

I don't go in for that kind of thing.

(enter a competition)

Are you thinking of going in for the race?

Go off (become bad – food)

This milk has gone off.

Go on (happen – usually negative)

Something funny is going on.

Go round (be enough)

There weren't enough life-jackets to go round.

Go through with (complete a promise or plan – usually unwillingly)

When it came to actually stealing the money, Nora couldn't go through with it.

Grow on (become more liked – colloquial)

This new record is growing on me.

Hang onto (keep – colloquial)

I think we should hang onto the car until next year.

Have it in for (be deliberately unkind to someone – also as *have got*)

My teacher has (got) it in for me.

Have it out with (express feelings so as to settle a problem)
*I put up with the problem for a while but in the end I **had it out with** her.*
Have someone on (deceive – colloquial)
*I don't believe you. You're **having me on**.*
Hit it off (get on well with – colloquial)
*Mark and Sarah really **hit it off** at the party.*
Hit upon/on (discover by chance – often *an idea*)
*They **hit upon** the solution quite by chance.*
Hold out (offer – especially with *hope*)
*We don't **hold out** much hope that the price will fall.*
Hold up (delay)
*Sorry I'm late, I was **held up** in the traffic.*
(use as an example – ie *a model of good behaviour*)
*Jack was always **held up** as an example to me.*
Hold with (agree with – an idea)
*I don't **hold with** the idea of using force.*
Keep up (continue)
*Well done! **Keep up** the good work!*
Lay down (state a rule – especially *lay down the law*)
*The company has **laid down** strict procedures for this kind of situation.*
Let down (disappoint, break a promise)
*Sorry to **let** you **down**, but I can't give you a lift today.*
Let in on (allow to be part of a secret)
*We haven't **let** Tina **in on** the plans yet.*
Let off (excuse from punishment)
*As Dave was young, the judge **let** him **off** with a fine.*
Let on (inform about a secret – colloquial)
*We're planning a surprise for Helen, but don't **let on**.*
(not) Live down (suffer a loss of reputation)
*If City lose, they'll never **live it down**.*
Live up to (reach an expected standard)
*The play quite **lived up to** my expectations.*
Look into (investigate)
*The police have promised to **look into** the problem.*
Look on (consider)
*We **look on** this town as our real home.*
Look someone up (visit when in the area)
*If you're passing through Athens, **look me up**.*
Make for (result in)
*The power steering **makes for** easier parking.*
Make off with (run away with)
*The thief **made off with** a valuable necklace.*
Make out (pretend)
*Tim **made out** that he hadn't seen the No Smoking sign.*

(manage to see or understand)

*I couldn't quite **make out** what the notice said.*

Make someone out (understand someone's behaviour)

*Janet is really odd. I can't **make her out**.*

Make up (invent)

*I think you **made up** the whole story!*

Make up for (compensate for)

*Our success **makes up for** all the hard times.*

Miss out (fail to include)

*You have **missed out** a word here.*

(lose a chance – colloquial)

*Five people got promoted, but I **missed out** again.*

Own up (confess – colloquial)

*None of the children would **own up** to breaking the window.*

Pack in (stop an activity – colloquial)

*John has **packed in** his job.*

Pay back (take revenge – colloquial)

*She **paid** him **back** for all his insults.*

Pick up (improve – colloquial)

*The weather seems to be **picking up**.*

Pin someone down (force to give a clear statement)

*I asked Jim to name a suitable day, but I couldn't **pin him down**.*

Play up (behave or work badly)

*The car is **playing up** again. It won't start.*

Point out (draw attention to a fact)

*I **pointed out** that I would be on holiday anyway.*

Pull off (manage to succeed)

*It was a tricky plan, but we **pulled** it **off**.*

Push on (continue with some effort – colloquial)

*Let's **push on** and try to reach the coast by tonight.*

Put across (communicate ideas)

*Harry is clever but he can't **put** his ideas **across**.*

Put down to (explain the cause of)

*Diane's poor performance was **put down to** nerves.*

Put in for (apply for a job)

*Sue has **put in for** a teaching job.*

Put oneself out (take trouble – to help someone)

*Please don't **put yourself out** making a meal. A sandwich will do.*

Put off (discourage, upset)

*The crowd **put** the gymnast **off**, and he fell.*

Put up (offer accommodation)

*We can **put** you **up** for a few days.*

Put up with (tolerate, bear)

*I can't **put up with** all this noise!*

Activities

1

Choose the most suitable words underlined.

a) Richard and I have never really hit <u>it/ourselves</u> off.
b) The manager promised to look into <u>my request/the matter</u>.
c) I am afraid I don't hold with <u>this kind of thing/people like you</u>.
d) Hang onto the tickets, <u>they might fall/we'll need them later</u>.
e) The team couldn't keep up <u>the pressure/the score</u> in the second half.
f) This'll go off unless you <u>put it in the fridge/close the window</u>.
g) I think <u>the second paragraph/a great opportunity</u> has been missed out.
h) Most of the meeting was given over <u>in the end/to Tom's report</u>.
i) Stephen eventually <u>confessed/owned up</u> to sixteen murders.
j) Something odd is going on <u>behind my back/tomorrow afternoon</u>.

2

Rewrite each sentence, beginning as shown, so that the meaning stays the same.

a) Gerry has applied for the job of financial director.
   Gerry has put *in for the job of financial director.*
b) Our teacher used Sophia as an example of a good student.
   Our teacher held ....
c) I'm not much interested in sports.
   I don't really go ....
d) Terry was rude but Anne got her revenge on him.
   Anne paid ....
e) You can stay with us for a week.
   We can ....
f) The police only warned Sally because it was her first offence.
   Sally was let ....
g) Sue drew attention to the flaw in the plan.
   Sue pointed ....
h) The plain clothes policeman's boots showed he was a policeman.
   The plain clothes policeman was given ....
i) We can say that hard work was what caused Jill's success.
   Jill's success can ....
j) Brenda never takes the trouble to help anyone.
   Brenda never puts ....

3

Put *one* suitable word in each space.

a) We can't watch that programme if the television is *playing* up again.
b) This novel is beginning to .... on me.
c) It is quite clearly .... down that only amateurs can take part.
d) Sales were slow to start with, but now they're .... up.
e) I don't want to .... you off, but this type of plane has crashed quite often.
f) Two members of the gang eventually .... themselves up.
g) We .... out that we had forgotten Jane's birthday, though it wasn't true.
h) There should be enough plates to .... round.
i) What does that notice say? I can't .... it out.
j) Hilary told me to .... her up the next time I was in London.

4

Rewrite each sentence so that it contains the word in capitals and so that the meaning stays the same.

a) You have broken your word.
   You have gone back on your word.   GONE
   ....

b) I can't bear your constant complaining.   WITH
   ....

c) The box smelled faintly of fish.   GAVE
   ....

d) I couldn't make Julie give a definite answer.   PIN
   ....

e) I think that my boss is prejudiced against me.   IT
   ....

f) The holiday wasn't as good as we expected.   LIVE
   ....

g) Martin promised to babysit but didn't show up.   LET
   ....

h) We don't expect that the missing climbers have survived.   HOLD
   ....

i) You get a smoother shave with Razacream foam.   MAKES
   ....

j) You're kidding!   ON
   ....

5

Complete each sentence with a suitable word or phrase.

a) In the end we hit ....*upon a solution*............ to the problem by chance.

b) Helen manages to put .... view very successfully in meetings.

c) The Foreign Secretary was looked .... the Prime Minister's successor.

d) Mary planned to murder her husband, but when the moment came she couldn't go ....

e) I hope that this holiday will .... all the weekends we have had to work.

f) Why don't you .... in! You're being really annoying!

g) Our in-laws didn't really .... off when we invited them all round.

h) No one has .... to writing graffiti on the wall.

i) Don't tell Dave about it. We shouldn't .... on the plan.

j) Shirley never .... for anyone. She is totally selfish.

6
Rewrite each sentence so that it contains the word in capitals, and so that the meaning stays the same.

a) It was a risky robbery, but the thieves managed it.   PULLED
It was a risky robbery, but the thieves pulled it off.

b) In the end I just didn't have any strength left.   GAVE
....

c) Eventually I aired my grievances with my boss.   OUT
....

d) Is there enough juice for everyone?   GO
....

e) Have you decided to enter the poster competition?   GO
....

f) Don't worry, I won't tell anyone.   ON
....

g) The smell of drains stopped me eating my breakfast.   PUT
....

h) Alan is a strange person. I can't understand his character.   MAKE
....

i) If I lose the race my reputation will suffer.   LIVE
....

j) Pauline isn't one of the people who knows the secret.   ON
....

Unit 25 Phrasal Verbs 3

Explanations

This unit (and Units 23 and 24) assume that a wide range of phrasal verbs, and their grammatical types, are already known. These units focus on multiple meaning, and alternative ways of expressing meanings of phrasal verbs. Note that there may be other meanings for the verbs listed here.

Rip off (charge too much – colloquial)
*You paid £50? They really **ripped** you **off**!*
Run down (criticise)
*She's always **running down** her husband.*
(lose power, allow to decline)
*I think the batteries are **running down**.*
Run into (meet)
*Guess who I **ran into** at the supermarket!*
Run to (have enough money)
*I don't think we can **run to** a holiday abroad this year.*
Run over (check – also *run through*)
*Let's **run over** the plan once more.*
Run up (a bill – let a bill get longer without paying)
*I **ran up** a huge telephone bill at the hotel.*
Run up against (encounter – usually *a problem*)
*We've **run up against** a slight problem.*
See someone off (go to station, airport, etc to say goodbye to someone)
*I went to the station to **see them off**.*
See through (realise the truth about)
*I **saw through** his intentions at once.*
Send up (make fun of by imitating)
*Jean is always **sending up** the French teacher.*
Set about (start working)
*We must **set about** re-organising the office.*
Set in (establish itself – especially weather)
*I think this rain has **set in** for the day.*
Set out (give in detail in writing)
*This document **sets out** all the Union demands.*
(arrange)
*I've **set out** the refreshments in the hall.*
(start an action)
*Sue **set out** to write a biography but it became a novel.*
Set up (establish)
*An inquiry into the accident has been **set up**.*

Set (up)on (attack)

    *We were **set upon** by a gang of hooligans.*

Sink in (realise slowly – colloquial, intransitive)

    *Slowly the realisation that I had won began to **sink in**.*

Slip up (make a mistake – colloquial)

    *Someone **slipped up** and my application was lost.*

Sort out (find a solution – colloquial)

    *Don't worry, Mary will **sort out** your problem.*

Stand by (keep to *an agreement*)

    *The company agreed to **stand by** its original commitment.*

Stand for (represent – initials)

    *e.g. **stands for** exempli gratia, it's Latin.*

    (tolerate)

    *I will not **stand for** this kind of behaviour in my house!*

Stand in for (take the place of)

    *Carol has kindly agreed to **stand in for** Graham at the monthly meeting.*

Stand up to (resist, bear stress)

    *The engine won't **stand up to** the strain.*

Step down (resign – colloquial)

    *The Chairman has **stepped down** after criticism from shareholders.*

Step up (increase)

    *Production at the Leeds plant has been **stepped up**.*

Stick up for (defend – especially *yourself, your rights* – colloquial)

    *You must learn to **stick up for** yourself.*

Take in (deceive)

    *Don't be **taken in** by her apparent shyness.*

Take (it) out on (make someone else suffer because of one's own sufferings)

    *I know you are unhappy, but don't **take it out on** me!*

Take off (imitate – colloquial)

    *Dave **takes off** the Prime Minister really well.*

Take on (acquire a new characteristic)

    *My grandmother has **taken on** a new lease of life since her operation.*

    (do something extra)

    *She has **taken on** too much with a full-time job as well.*

Take out (*insurance* – sign an insurance agreement)

    *Ann has **taken out** life insurance.*

Take over (gain control of)

    *The army tried to **take over** the country.*

Take to someone (develop a liking for)

    *You'll soon **take to** your new boss, I'm sure.*

Take up (*time* – occupy time)

    *The meeting **took up** a whole morning.*

Talk out of or into (dissuade from, persuade into)

    *Paul **talked me into** going skiing, against my better judgement.*

Tell off (scold – colloquial)
> *Our teacher **told** us **off** for being late.*

Tie in with (be in agreement with)
> *I'm afraid your party doesn't quite **tie in with** our arrangements.*

Track down (trace the whereabouts of)
> *The police **tracked down** the killer and arrested him.*

Try out (test – *a machine*)
> *Let's **try out** the new washing machine.*

Turn down (reject an offer)
> *Another company offered me a job but I **turned** them **down.***

Turn out (happen to be in the end)
> *He **turned out** to be an old friend of Helen's.*

(come to a meeting or to form a crowd)
> *Thousands of fans **turned out** to welcome the team.*

Turn up (be discovered by chance)
> *Don't worry about that missing book, it's bound to **turn up** sooner or later.*

(arrive – often unexpectedly)
> *Not many people **turned up** for the lesson.*

Wear off (lose effect – especially *a drug*)
> *These painkillers **wear off** after about two hours.*

Work out (calculate – also *work out at* for specific amounts)
> *The hotel bill **worked out** at over £500.*

Activities

1

Choose the most suitable words underlined.

a) Tom managed to run up <u>an account/a bill</u> at the supermarket.
b) <u>In the end/Initially</u> I set out to prove that such a voyage was possible.
c) If he treated me like that I wouldn't stand for <u>him/it</u>.
d) The government should set up <u>a committee/a minister</u> to sort the matter out.
e) Both teams stepped up <u>the pace/the rate</u> in the second half.
f) The dog didn't take to <u>its new owner/liking me</u>.
g) <u>The news/The prize</u> hasn't really sunk in yet.
h) I <u>told her off/told off her</u> for leaving the office unlocked.
i) After a week on the ice the expedition ran into <u>difficulties/potholes</u>.
j) They really rip <u>the bill/you</u> off in this restaurant!

2

Rewrite each sentence so that it contains the word in capitals, and so that the meaning stays the same.

a) The Foreign Secretary has been forced to resign.   DOWN
The Foreign Secretary has been forced to step down.
....

b) The treaty explains the terms of the agreement to reduce nuclear arms.   OUT
....

c) I need someone to take my place at the ceremony.   IN
....

d) In the end it was quite a sunny day after all.   OUT

....

e) Don't be deceived by his long words!   IN

....

f) Members of the audience started making fun of the speaker.   UP

....

g) We still haven't managed to locate that missing file.   DOWN

....

h) Janet persuaded me not to sell my house.   OUT

....

i) It looks as if someone has made a mistake.   UP

....

j) I can't afford such expensive clothes on my salary.   TO

....

3

Put a suitable word or phrase in each space, so that the sentence contains a phrasal verb.

a) The exact total *worked out* at just over £750.
b) What awful weather! It looks as if the rain has .... for the day.
c) Don't be so passive! .... for yourself.
d) I don't think Sam will be able to .... to the pressure of the job.
e) I can't help you. You'll have to .... the problem yourself.
f) Even if you are miserable, there's no need to .... on me!
g) It seemed like a good plan, but when we .... out it didn't work.
h) I'm going to the airport to .... some friends who are going to Japan.
i) What exactly do the letters BBC .... for?
j) Don't worry about the missing dog. It will .... up when it gets hungry!

4

Rewrite each sentence, beginning as shown, so that the meaning stays the same.

a) Brian takes off the French teacher really well.
Brian does *a very good imitation of the French teacher.*
b) Tina saw through Peter's plan at once.
Tina realised ....

c) The effect of these pills wears off after three hours.
The effect of these pills only ....
d) Her face had taken on a strange expression.
She had a ....
e) Harry swore he would stand by his promise.
Harry swore that he would not go...
f) The terms of the agreement are set out in this document.
This document gives ....

145

g) The full truth is only just beginning to sink in.
   I am only just beginning to...
h) Sally turned down Philip's marriage proposal.
   Sally didn't ....
i) Sue talked me into acting in this play.
   Sue persuaded ....
j) Tony stood in for me at the meeting.
   Tony took...

5

Rewrite each sentence so that it contains the word in capitals, and so that the meaning stays the same. Each sentence should contain a phrasal verb.

a) Stop criticising everybody!   DOWN
   Stop running everybody down! ....
b) Terry has just insured her life.   OUT
   ....
c) In the end it was discovered that Joe was the thief.   OUT
   ....
d) I need a calculator to arrive at the total.   OUT
   ....
e) I met your friend David the other day.   INTO
   ....
f) I think you've been overcharged, old son!   OFF
   ....
g) I think we should increase the pressure on her to resign.   UP
   ....
h) I won't allow swearing in my classroom!   FOR
   ....
i) The company was bought up by a large multinational.   OVER
   ....
j) Your story is different from the facts.   WITH
   ....

6

Put *one* word in each space.

a) The government has allowed the coal industry to run *down.*
b) Robert was set .... by two masked men and robbed.
c) Why didn't you stick .... for me instead of saying nothing?
d) Let's run .... the details of the arrangements just once more.
e) Most of my time is taken .... with answering the phone.
f) I've run .... against a number of difficulties in this area.
g) The buffet was set .... on a number of low tables.
h) Hundreds of people turned .... in the rain to see the prince.
i) No one expected the government to stand .... the agreement.
j) On the following day, teams of local people set .... clearing up the damage.

Unit 26 Progress Test
(Units 21, 22, 23, 24, 25)

1

Put *one* suitable word in each space.

Unlikely as it may seem, there has now been expert confirmation that wild pumas and lynxes are (1) .... large in parts of Britain, rather than being the figments (2) .... some wild imaginations. Previous sightings (3) .... such large jungle cats had been put down (4) .... exaggeration. (5) .... all, the argument went, some people are prone (6) .... seeing flying saucers and Loch Ness monsters, particularly when (7) .... the influence of one drink too many. Some newspapers were suspected (8) .... having made (9) .... stories such as that of the Beast of Exmoor, an animal which is responsible (10) .... the deaths of hundreds of sheep over the past ten years. But experts have now come (11) .... with proof that such stories were (12) .... earnest after all. The animals are (13) .... all likelihood pets which have escaped (14) .... small zoos, or been abandoned (15) .... their owners. Because the keeping (16) .... such animals is severely restricted (17) .... the Dangerous Wild Animals Act of 1976, owners of unlicensed animals might not report an escape (18) .... fear of prosecution. Britain's only surviving native feline species, the wild cat, is confined (19) .... Scotland. After examining hair samples, experts now say that the Beast of Exmoor in the South of England is (20) .... the shadow of a doubt a puma or lynx, both of which animals are normally native to the Middle East and Asia.

2

Put *one* suitable word in each space.

a) My cousin George is obsessed .... keeping fit.
b) Many frozen foods are deficient .... vitamins.
c) They say that there is an exception .... every rule.
d) It was very good .... Sue to drive us to the airport.
e) Breaking his leg a second time put Peter's football career .... jeopardy.
f) Don't worry, the whole situation is .... control.
g) The same rule applies, irrespective .... how much you have paid.
h) With complete disregard .... her own safety, Ann jumped into the sea to rescue the dog.
i) I'm afraid you are not eligible .... a pension until you are 65.
j) There were no ripe apples .... reach, so I moved the ladder.

3

Rewrite each sentence, starting as shown, so that the meaning stays the same.

a) You think I am someone else.
   You are confusing ....
b) Gary is proud of the fact that he is never late.
   Gary prides ....
c) On this ship passengers cannot get onto the bridge.
   Passengers have no ....

d) This should work, theoretically.
In ....

e) What is the difference between nuclear fission and nuclear fusion?
How exactly does ....

f) We cannot solve this problem.
There ....

g) On his way home Terry had an unfortunate accident.
Terry met ....

h) The result was just as you predicted.
You were ....

i) An electrical failure was said to be the cause of the fire.
They blamed ....

j) Lately I have thought of nothing but work.
I have been rather ....

4

Choose the most suitable word or phrase.

a) If this plan .... off, I promise you you'll get the credit for it.
   A) lets   B) goes   C) comes   D) gets

b) I just couldn't .... over how well the team played!
   A) get   B) turn   C) make   D) put

c) The policeman .... me off with a warning as it was Christmas.
   A) sent   B) gave   C) let   D) set

d) Please don't .... yourself out. A sandwich will do.
   A) let   B) take   C) leave   D) put

e) I hope there are enough glasses to .... round.
   A) drink   B) set   C) go   D) lay

f) It's time you .... about organising your revision programme.
   A) got   B) set   C) took   D) put

g) Tony has .... for the same trick that I did.
   A) fallen   B) stood   C) made   D) looked

h) I can't quite .... out what the sign says.
   A) make   B) read   C) get   D) carry

i) Half the meeting was .... over to reading the minutes.
   A) taken   B) left   C) got   D) given

j) We have .... up a huge bill at the grocer's across the road.
   A) set   B) run   C) ended   D) paid

5

Put one suitable word in each space.

a) It looks as if the front door lock has been .... with.

b) The people were protesting .... the closure of two local factories.

c) The captured bank robber .... the bank manager in the robbery.

d) We all .... at the way Kathy did so well in her exams.

e) The hotel .... me £14 for phone calls I had not made.

f) Charles is always .... about how much money he earns.

g) The new television channel tries to .... for all tastes.

h) I couldn't .... from laughing at the president's remark.

i) Could you .... on what you said? We need to know more details.

j) I think that you would both .... from a few days holiday.

6

Rewrite each sentence so that it contains the word in capitals, and so that the meaning stays the same.

a) What exactly do the letters AM and PM mean? STAND

....

b) It's all a matter of money, in the end. COMES

....

c) We had to stop building when there was no more money. GAVE

....

d) Carol pretended that she hadn't understood my request. MADE

....

e) His smooth manner didn't deceive us. TAKEN

....

f) I have decided to ask my solicitor to prepare my will. DRAWN

....

g) How is the decorating going? GETTING

....

h) What exactly is happening? GOING

....

i) The total came to just under £4000. WORKED

....

j) I haven't realised what it means yet. SUNK

....

7

Complete each sentence with a suitable word or phrase.

a) Don't mention the missing money to George. I'll .... with him in the morning.

b) Dawn was given a medal .... of her services to the government.

c) I must .... Paul. I am sure he didn't mean what he said.

d) You are under .... to order any more books unless you wish to.

e) The collision .... in the death of a 64-year-old woman passenger.

f) Everyone turned up, ... of Jack, who was ill.

g) I'm sorry. I was under .... that this seat was free.

h) If I were you I'd have the brakes .... to before you cause an accident.

i) They sent us the goods on .... for three weeks, but then we had to pay for them.

j) When I saw the house it .... of the one I grew up in.

8

Put *one* suitable word in each space.

a) It's safe to hide here. We won't give you ....

b) My mum told me .... for coming home late from school.

c) Sorry I'm late. Something cropped .... at the office.

d) You can rely on her. She won't let you ....

e) Nick was taken to court but he got ....

f) It was surprising how quickly that fashion caught ....

g) Don't worry. I'll sort it ....

h) I don't really hit it .... with my new boss.

i) Don't eat that sausage. I think it's gone ....

j) She'll come round when the anaesthetic wears ....

9

Rewrite each sentence, beginning as shown, so that the meaning stays the same.

a) Wendy's speciality is heart surgery.
Wendy specialises ....

b) In the end we walked to the railway station.
We ended ....

c) There was a collision on the motorway between a bus and a lorry.
A bus and a lorry ....

d) Don't make me suffer because of your problems!
Don't take ....

e) Martin left the committee after arguing with the chairperson.
Martin resigned ....

f) The Mountain Rescue Team is pessimistic about the missing climbers.
The Mountain Rescue Team doesn't hold ....

g) Sally persuaded me not to sell my car.
Sally talked ....

h) A true story is the basis of the novel.
The novel is ....

i) Yesterday I met your brother at the shops.
I ran ....

j) They said the accident was Mary's fault.
They blamed ....

10

Complete each sentence with a suitable word or phrase.

a) Julie's parents were very tolerant in .... with her friends' parents.

b) Boris played badly, and said he was .... practice.

c) Be sensible! You have to .... to the facts, occasionally!

d) The psychiatrist told Jack to have more .... over his emotions.

e) Most of the members were in .... postponing the meeting for a week.

f) I'm afraid that book is out .... at the moment but we can order it for you.

g) Guess who .... up at our party last night? Your ex-boyfriend, Harry.

h) Ian was on .... of giving up, when he found what he was looking for.

i) Diana's prize .... for all her earlier disappointments.

j) We started saving with a .... buying a house.

11

Rewrite each sentence so that it contains the word in capitals, and so that the meaning stays the same.

a) Many customs restrictions within the EC have been abolished. AWAY
....

b) The manager promised to have the goods delivered at once. DELAY
....

c) This situation is really not funny! BEYOND
....

d) What are you implying? AT
....

e) Joe gets on very well with his mother-in-law.   TERMS

....

f) These rainy Monday mornings make me feel miserable.   GET

....

g) I would like to thank you from all the staff.   BEHALF

....

h) How can you bear to work with all this noise?   UP

....

i) There is nothing strange about this.   OUT

....

j) Ellen has been unemployed for six months.   OUT

....

12

Choose the most suitable word or phrase.

a) Gerry isn't fat. ...., he's quite skinny.
   A) In any case   B) By rights   C) In practice   D) On the contrary

b) A huge crowd .... in the pouring rain to cheer the president.
   A) turned out   B) held up   C) saw off   D) dropped in

c) This machinery will have been .... by the end of the decade.
   A) broken down   B) set out   C) phased out   D) made off with

d) Fiona decided not to .... the exam in December.
   A) take on   B) go in for   C) get round to   D) make for

e) We hadn't .... for such heavy traffic, and we were delayed.
   A) expected   B) bargained   C) calculated   D) supposed

f) Whatever Jean .... to do, she finishes.
   A) gets on   B) sees to   C) sets out   D) looks for

g) This conservation project looks promising, but it's still ....
   A) in the early stages B) in advance   C) under stress   D) at first sight

h) Has Tony's new book .... yet?
   A) published   B) come out   C) developed   D) drawn up

i) The smell of the kippers cooking .... my breakfast.
   A) put me off   B) came up against C) gave off   D) held up

j) Derek was .... from military service on health grounds.
   A) ejected   B) barred   C) earmarked   D) exempted

Unit 27 Text features 1

Explanations

There are many features of texts which help the reader understand how the information in the text is organised. A selection of features is highlighted here and in Unit 28. Note that the organisation of texts varies according to the type of text.

Reference words

1 *This, that, it*
Within the text, words may refer to ideas already mentioned, or point forward. Pronouns such as *it, this, that, these, those* are very common in this role.
*In the end, the government decided that relief supplies and medical aid could be sent by road. **This** turned out to be more difficult than was expected, however.*

2 *Such*
This has the effect of *like this:*
***Such** action turned out to be more difficult than was expected, however.*

Text Organisers

This term covers a wide range of words and phrases which make text easier to understand. A selection is given here.

1 Adding a point
*There was **also** the weather to be considered.*
***As well as** the obvious dangers, there was the weather to be considered.*
***In addition to** the obvious dangers, there was the weather to be considered.*
***Not only** were there the obvious dangers, **but** there was **also** the weather to be considered.*

2 Contrast
*The identity of the attacker is known to the police. **However**, no name has been released.*
***Although** the name of the attacker is known to the police, no name has been released.*
***While** the name of the attacker is known to the police, no name has been released.*
***Despite the fact that** the name of the attacker is known to the police, no name has been released.*
*The name of the attacker is known to the police. It has **nevertheless/none the less/still** not been released.*
*The name of the attacker is known to the police, **but/yet** no name has been released.*

3 Logical relations
The government does not intend to cause any further provocation.
***As a result/Accordingly/Thus/Hence**, all troops have been withdrawn.*
*The employers have promised to investigate these complaints, and we **in turn** have agreed to end the strike.*

| Collocations | This refers to groups of words which go together. See the Words and Phrases section for work on these. |

Problems with plurals

Some words which end in -s are singular:
the news a means
In adjectival phrases involving numbers, nouns are singular:
a three-mile walk a ten-year-old child

Activities

1

Put *one* word in each space.

Practice in this unit is with texts which have single words missing. See Units 28 and 29 for other kinds of practice. Note that the activities are not simply a test of the points made in this unit.

Starting your (1) .... business could be the way to achieving financial independence, or (2) .... could just as well land you in debt for the rest of your life. That, at (3) ...., is the view of Charles and Brenda Leggat, a Scottish couple, who last week saw (4) .... fish farm business put into the hands of the receiver. 'We started the business in 1985 when (5) .... was being encouraged by the banks to borrow money. (6) .... the time we were sure that we could make (7) .... into a going concern,' said Charles Leggat, a farmer from (8) .... Highlands, 'and the banks lent us more or less (9) .... we asked for. Their people analysed the proposals we put (10) ...., and they agreed that it would be a highly profitable business.' Sure (11) ...., within five years the Leggats were exporting trout and salmon products to hotels (12) .... over Europe, and employed over fifty staff. But with the advent (13) .... the recession, they began to lose ground as orders dried up. 'The awful thing (14) ....,' said Brenda Leggat, 'that now the business has been valued by the banks at a fraction of its true worth. If they had left us to work our way out of our difficulties I am sure that we could have gone back into profit. (15) .... it is, we have been left (16) .... a livelihood, and the banks have not recovered (17) .... they lent us.' The Leggats both felt that their banks had not treated (18) .... fairly. 'They were falling over (19) .... to lend us the money, but they have done very little to keep the business going, and fifty local people (20) .... work.' A spokesman for the main bank concerned, the National Caledonian, refused to comment.

2

Put *one* word in each space.

Recently there have been doubts about the proper functioning of the English legal system, after several well-publicised cases in (1) .... police evidence was eventually shown to be suspect, but (2) .... after the wrongful conviction of the accused. In several of (3) .... cases, the crimes involved acts of terrorism, and the police were (4) .... considerable pressure to discover (5) .... had been responsible. Although this in no way excuses the actions of police officers (6) .... may have falsified evidence, or suppressed evidence which worked against their case, (7) .... underlines the ways (8) .... which publicity in the press and on television exercises an enormous influence, (9) .... the supposed guarantees under the law designed to prevent a jury from becoming unduly influenced. The specific details of a criminal case are not discussed in the press before a case reaches the courts, and the names of those involved (10) .... often withheld. (11) ...., as many recent murder trials make clear, the press all too often reaches its (12) .... verdict to suit its taste for sensationalism and members of the police might be accused of enlisting the aid of the press by 'leaking' details of a prosecution. Unfortunately, far too (13) .... press reports of court cases examine the evidence (14) .... the defence in the same spirit as (15) .... for the prosecution. And a verdict of guilty simply seems to confirm that all those details of defence evidence are (16) .... 'true'. (17) .... is also the assumption that if a case has reached the courts, then the police have sufficient evidence, and that therefore the establishing of a guilty verdict is just a (18) .... of course. Ironically, there is (19) .... a well-established tradition of investigative journalism which is devoted to setting right miscarriages of justice, and in (20) .... such investigations carried out by newspapers and television programmes have led to the overturning of convictions, often when innocent parties have spent ten years or more behind bars.

3

Put *one* word in each space.

Very few popular spectator sports today remain amateur in (1) .... sense. In the past, even in cases (2) .... payments to players or athletes was forbidden, many sports tolerated (3) .... became known as 'shamateurism'. This (4) .... that payments were made in the (5) .... of expenses, or in some extreme cases, simply made illegally. More (6) .... sport has become, in effect, a branch of the entertainment and advertising industry, and the top performers in sports (7) .... as golf, tennis, football and track athletics can expect to become very rich. (8) .... in itself worries some people. Where is the old Olympic ideal, they say, and hasn't the urge to win been transformed into mere greed for money? But (9) .... fact is that sport has become more and more professional in the wider sense, (10) .... only requiring total dedication from aspiring champions, (11) .... also requiring expensive facilities, training and medical advice. (12) .... is just no longer possible (13) .... combine a career in sport with a career elsewhere. And besides, many would argue that top champions deserve large prizes. After all, (14) .... shouldn't they be adequately rewarded for reaching the top of their profession? Perhaps most criticism is levelled (15) .... two abuses: (16) .... taking of performance-enhancing drugs, and the sheer lack of entertainment in many team games, (17) .... the need to win has effectively stifled all sense of flair. Both, (18) .... a sense, are forms of cheating, and both are difficult to define. (19) .... every banned substance, there is another legal one which can also be said to be a 'drug'; and where is the dividing line (20) .... negative tactics and clever strategy?

4
Put *one* word in each space.

The new scheme for training teachers envisages a radical departure from the previous system. The old division of training courses into periods of theoretical study dealing with (1) .... subjects as sociology and psychology, and teaching practice, will largely disappear. Trainees will instead be attached to schools for most of their course, and learn the skills of classroom teaching through practical experience. They will be supervised by practising teachers, rather (2) ...., as formerly, supervised by educationalists who no (3) .... actually teach. These changes seek to answer the complaints of trainees (4) ...., who tend to feel that they have acquired (5) .... little practical knowledge, and of schools, who frequently report that new teachers (6) .... basic classroom abilities. (7) ...., there are some obvious objections to (8) .... a scheme. (9) .... of all, it places a heavy burden onto the shoulders of teachers who already complain of being overworked, and of having too many administrative tasks. Secondly it runs the risk of going (10) .... far from one extreme to (11) .... , and of creating a breed of teachers (12) .... plenty of superficial classroom skill, but no theoretical understanding of wider educational issues. There are (13) .... some voices raised in protest at (14) .... they see as an attempt by the government to cut back the role of training colleges as places where new ideas can be developed and put into practice. However, it may (15) .... be that changes in education are best pioneered in the schools themselves, to develop from the grass roots, as it (16) ...., rather than being imposed from above. (17) .... the success of the new scheme, it throws into even more urgent relief the unavoidable fact that education in the Britain has yet to firmly decide (18) .... it should be teaching, (19) .... it should be teaching it, and (20) .... best to organise its schools.

5
Put *one* word in each space.

Last summer we had two Italian students to stay. It was a (1) .... of exchange, with our two children off to Rome this summer, giving me, incidentally, an interlude of peace in (2) .... to write this column, among other things. But back to the two Italians, two charming girls (3) .... English was a revelation to everyone in our family. I am not going to say that it was perfect or anything (4) .... that, simply that (5) .... used expressions that have either long ago died out in these islands, (6) .... are greeted when used with blank incomprehension. (7) .... example, when a day or two after their arrival Lucia made some coffee and handed it to my neighbour (who had come round to see (8) .... her husband kept popping over to brush up his Italian), she unmistakably said 'Here you are'. The shock was (9) .... great that we both nearly fell off our chairs. (10) .... the benefit of foreign readers, or for anyone who has just returned from a monastery or a (11) .... years on Mars I should explain that this now quaint English expression has long (12) .... been replaced by the transatlantic 'There you go', an utterance which threw me into considerable confusion (13) .... first used by hairdressers, waitresses and barmen. I kept gazing (14) .... my shoulder nervously looking out for (15) ....

it was that had gone, or wondered whether they were telling me I should beat a hasty retreat. The two girls also surprised us by asking intelligible questions (16) .... of making vague statements which were (17) .... to be taken as questions. And they had retained that ancient habit of addressing strangers by (18) .... surnames, preceded by a Mr or Mrs, as in 'Good morning, Mrs Scott', rather than greeting me at the door on arrival with a 'Hello, Gloria, and have a nice day'. All in (19) .... , they were a delight, although I am sorry to report that by the time they left, they had absorbed (20) .... passes as the English language hereabouts, and had plunged downhill towards unintelligibility. Oh well, there you go, I suppose.

6

Put *one* word in each space.

The idea of a castle as being a kind of fortified home was a concept introduced into England by the Normans.(1) .... the Norman conquest, all castles in the old Anglo-Saxon kingdom had been (2) .... of a system of state defences, (3) .... than the private possessions of great lords. Rochester Castle in Kent is a good (4) .... of a Norman fortification, the original castle having been built there after 1066. (5) .... excavation has not located the precise site of this castle, it is assumed to have stood (6) .... the river outside the city walls, and to have consisted (7) .... a mound of earth surrounded by a walled area. This type of castle later became (8) .... as the 'motte and bailey' castle. The mound and the walls were defended by ditches, banks and towers. This first castle was probably the (9) .... besieged by William the Conqueror's son, Rufus, after his accession to the throne in 1087. At this (10) .... Rufus was obliged to suppress the supporters of his elder brother Robert, the Duke of Normandy, whom many (11) .... have preferred (12) .... king of a still unified kingdom of Normandy and England. Rochester Castle became a focus for the revolt and was defended by Bishop Odo. Eventually the defenders were (13) .... to surrender, and were expelled from their English possessions. The present castle (14) .... thought to date from after the siege, and was built by Gundulf, Bishop of Rochester, (15) .... a site within the city walls. He was obliged to build the castle at his own (16) .... as a way of paying off a debt of £100 to the king. The king had (17) .... this sum of money as payment for confirming the cathedral of Rochester in its possession of land near Buckingham. The new castle was built on cathedral (18) .... in the south-west corner of the old Roman city of Rochester, and (19) .... the remains of the Roman walls for its foundations on the side facing the river. The old castle was (20) .... retained as an outer defence, although this has not been definitely proved.

Unit 28 Text features 2

Explanations

Organisers

Some texts include a signal for a series of points which will follow. These points are introduced by sequencing phrases.

*There are **a number of ways** in which the government could act.*
First of all …, Next …, Finally …
The first point … Last but not least …

Some phrases signal that a related phrase is going to appear, as in the contrast between *one* and *another*.

It is quite impossible to carry out this policy.
For one thing …
and for another …
and besides

Modifying words and phrases

1 Intensifying a point
 *It is **more than** likely that the plan will fail.*
 *A clear result looks **more and more** uncertain.*
 *This point has been made **over and over again**.*

2 Giving an opinion
 *The second course of action is **undoubtedly** preferable.*

3 Modifying an opinion or a number
 *It is **almost/nearly** impossible to believe …*
 *There is **hardly any** doubt …*
 *It is **largely/mainly** a matter of getting down to basics.*
 *In **many/some ways/respects** this is a good idea.*
 *There were twenty **or so** cars stopped at the toll booth.*

4 Making assertions
 *It is **simply/just** not true that …*
 *This is **mere** play-acting on the part of the minister.*
 *This is **merely** the last in a series of grievous blows …*
 *The **sheer** idiocy of the plan almost beggars belief …*
 *The audience was plunged into **utter** despair …*
 *The whole plan is **utterly** wrong …*
 *The minister was **literally** speechless …*

 'Literally' here emphasises that the word following has a direct rather than a metaphorical meaning ie the minister had really lost his or her voice, rather than meaning 'not knowing what to say'.

157

5   Giving examples
    *Critics of the scheme, **such as** Professor Benson …*
    ***This is an example of** government interference …*
    ***For example,** passengers who have heavy luggage …*
    ***In the case of** Mrs Golding, there was no such guarantee.*

6   Linking cause and effect
    These words and phrases refer to a previous explanation of causes.
    *Innocent shoppers may **in this way** be led into a spiral of debt.*
    *A tired driver may **thus** fail to fail to judge distances correctly.*

7   Summarising
    ***All in all,** this is a car I would thoroughly recommend.*

8   *That* meaning *the one*
    This is often signalled by a phrase which includes a comparison.
    *The worst earthquake in the area was **that** of 1962.*

Activities

Practice in this unit is with texts which have single words or phrases missing.
Four choices are given. See Units 27 and 29 for other kinds of practice.

1

Choose the most
suitable word or
phrase for each
space.

What can the average Briton do to create a home environment which is green
and friendly? Well, (1) .... bear in mind that (2) .... half the average
home's energy bill is spent on heating rooms, but (3) .... a typical house
loses nearly half its heat through the walls and roof. So (4) .... number one
is to ensure that your house is adequately insulated. Get advice (5) ....
double glazing, and loft insulation. The next most important point to consider
is (6) .... of waste. Packaging and wrapping is an obvious (7) ....
Try to use economy size boxes, and re-use containers (8) .... glass jars and
plastic cartons instead of wrapping food in foil or plastic. Take bottles to bottle-
banks, and only shop in supermarkets which use environment-friendly
packaging. (9) .... people are simply refusing to buy goods packed in
wasteful plastic. The garden too is an area where waste can be recycled. Start a
compost heap using old food scraps and garden weeds (10) .... putting
them in the dustbin. And it is surprising (11) .... can be done with some
other things we usually throw away. For example, try papering your bedroom
with pictures from magazines. The third problem area is (12) .... water.
This is becoming a more and more precious commodity, (13) .... save as
much as you can. Flushing the toilet accounts for a third of all household water
use, so don't flush wastefully, if you are only getting rid of a tissue, for example.
Take a shower instead of a bath, and don't keep the water running while you
wash, or clean your teeth. And don't use a hosepipe to wash your car or water
the garden. (14) .... banned in some areas (15) .... when there are
water shortages. Try putting some in a bucket instead.

1	A) the first point	B) one could hardly	C) first of all	D) what is to
2	A) the	B) over	C) one and a	D) in
3	A) similarly	B) at the same time	C) nevertheless	D) besides
4	A) the	B) all of	C) with this	D) point
5	A) from	B) for	C) with	D) about
6	A) that	B) instead	C) in spite	D) still
7	A) one	B) example	C) task	D) advantage
8	A) with	B) as	C) such as	D) or
9	A) More and more	B) All	C) Increasing	D) The
10	A) before	B) despite	C) if	D) instead of
11	A) what	B) the following	C) it	D) this
12	A) thus	B) merely	C) use of	D) again
13	A) as	B) so	C) why	D) which is to
14	A) It is	B) While	C) These are	D) Even
15	A) in any case	B) except	C) often	D) merely

2

Choose the most suitable word or phrase for each space.

The relationship between the British royal family and the popular press is curious, to say the least. (1) .... the press has yet to realise that the royals are indeed the goose that lays the golden egg. Royal scandals and royal divorces (2) .... tasteless photographs and supported by the worst kind of journalistic excess have proved to be (3) .... the thing for raising newspaper circulations. The same papers that oozed sentimentality over royal weddings, and drooled over idealised princesses, later went out of their way to hound various royals into separation or divorce. Every photograph became a contribution to (4) .... new rumour; (5) .... private telephone conversations were printed on the front page. (6).............. the press has yet to realise is that (7) .... intrusions into the privacy of members of the royal family have also helped to create an atmosphere (8) .... the very existence of the monarchy has been called into question. The prestige of the royal family has (9) .... suffered. And how could this not be (10) .... when their lives have been turned into some absurd soap opera? (11) .... the press feeds the illusion that the characters on television, those awful creeps in 'East Enders' and 'Neighbours', are somehow 'real people', so it has reduced the royal family to the status of a series of cardboard characters. And if you are secretly thinking, 'Well, that's what they are, (12) ....,' perhaps you are just another victim of the illusion. (13) .... real issues still to be debated about the role, and indeed the survival, of the royal family, issues to which the popular press has (14) .... contributed. If the monarchy should lose its constitutional role, the press will be largely to blame. And (15) .... it will then have lost one of its main circulation boosters, and it will have killed off its golden goose for good.

1	A) First of all	B) In many respects	C) Nevertheless	D) A reader of
2	A) illustrated with	B) showing	C) having taken	D) provide
3	A) made	B) merely	C) more than	D) just

4	A) this	B) some	C) create	D) feed
5	A) even	B) in	C) their	D) despite the fact that
6	A) So	B) In fact	C) What	D) Thus
7	A) what	B) no	C) such	D) all
8	A) and so	B) in which	C) whenever	D) if rarely
9	A) undoubtedly	B) been	C) utterly	D) not
10	A) the point	B) the one	C) the last	D) the case
11	A) For example	B) Just as	C) Like	D) What
12	A) all in all	B) at the end	C) moreover	D) anyway
13	A) If they are	B) What are the	C) There are	D) They create the
14	A) merely	B) hardly	C) utterly	D) extremely
15	A) thus	B) literally	C) ironically	D) if

3

Choose the most suitable word or phrase for each space.

If you feel like something just a little different in the way of a skiing holiday, why not try heli-skiing in Canada? The last person I suggested (1) ...., answered predictably, 'What the hell is that?' It's quite simple (2) .... Not only do you have to travel by helicopter to the ski lodge, which (3) .... the one I visited was (4) .... buried in the Rocky Mountains, and is inaccessible by road during the winter months, (5) .... flying is also the only means of getting to the slopes. So (6) .... the familiar queue at the ski-lift, you radio for a helicopter. As it sets down to pick you up, just make sure the blast of air from the rotors doesn't blow away your hat and coat, and then off (7) .... Somewhere in the snowy wastes the helicopter will deposit you and a dozen (8) .... onto a slope of virgin snow. The appeal is meant to be that it is a far cry from the busy slopes of Europe and (9) .... American ski resorts. You are fifty miles from the nearest town, and there is nothing resembling a ski-lift or cable car, so you have to (10) .... on legs, skis and the helicopter. You might see the occasional mountain-goat or grizzly bear, but there won't be hordes of people all dressed (11) .... There are one or two (12) .... however, apart from the cost of flying all the way to Canada. Your friendly helicopter pilot might just put you down in a fifteen-foot snow drift. Your guide might forget where the snow neatly disguises a hundred-foot drop, or might warn you too late. (13) .... is the freezing weather, which might ground your helicopter and leave you stranded in the wilderness. (14) ...., though, the whole point is the adventure, and the exhilaration of skiing in open country, on fresh powdery snow. So if the idea attracts you, and you have about £4000 to spend on a week's holiday, and the skiing ability (15) .... with the conditions, it might be just the thing for you.

1	A) going	B) this to	C) this	D) they went
2	A) really	B) skiing	C) surely	D) basic principle
3	A) just like	B) quite near	C) in the case of	D) unlike
4	A) undoubtedly	B) literally	C) thoroughly	D) utterly
5	A) helicopter	B) and of course	C) despite the fact that	D) but

6	A) you join	B) line up in	C) in spite of	D) instead of
7	A) you go	B) your clothes	C) it is	D) the mountain
8	A) down	B) others	C) else	D) or so
9	A) quite handy for	B) the	C) substitutes	D) most other
10	A) keep going	B) rely	C) exist	D) go for miles
11	A) up	B) there	C) the same	D) at the very least
12	A) expenses	B) disadvantages	C) other points	D) people
13	A) Another problem	B) What remains	C) One example	D) And that
14	A) Last of all	B) Although	C) Finally	D) In the end
15	A) to cope	B) and you agree	C) appropriate	D) joined

Unit 29 Text features 3

Explanations

Tests may include proof-reading activities, focused on spelling, punctuation and checking whether words have been omitted or extra words included.

Words commonly mis-spelled

1 Common errors

Learners can benefit by making lists of the words they most frequently mis-spell. The words listed here are spelled correctly.

accommodation, address, advertisement, beginning, committee, conscience, curiosity, disappear, disappointed, embarrassed, faithfully, favourite, forbidden, government, guarantee, immediately, independent, jealous, journey, manufacture, marriage, medicine, necessary, pollution, prefer, preferred, pronunciation, quiet, quite, receive, recommend, responsibility, separate, sincerely, successful, truly, unconscious, unfortunately, unnecessary, writing

Note the following US English spelling and GB English equivalents:

US	GB	US	GB	US	GB
center	*centre*	*honor*	*honour*	*math*	*maths*
check	*cheque (bank order)*	*jeweler*	*jeweller*	*practice(v)*	*practise(v)*
color	*colour*	*license(n)*	*licence(n)*	*story*	*storey (floor)*
dialed	*dialled*	*marvelous*	*marvellous*	*traveled*	*travelled*

2 Words with similar spelling but different meanings.

altogether	This means 'completely'.
all together	This describes a group of things or people in one place.
effect	verb: bring about, make. noun: result
affect	have an effect on
lose	verb: fail to have or find
loose	adjective: not tight
specially	for a special purpose
especially	particularly
stationery	paper, envelopes, etc (collective noun)
stationary	not moving (used formally of vehicles)
principle	general truth or standard
principal	head of college or school

3 Words with the same pronunciation but different spelling and meaning. This is a selection, as there are many of these:

allowed– aloud	*hair–hare*	*practice(n)–practise(v)*	*their–there*
bear–bare	*pear–pair*	*stair–stare*	*weather–whether*
fair–fare	*piece–peace*		

Punctuation

1 Apostrophes

Apostrophes are used to indicate letters omitted, possession and plurals of letters and figures:

Letters omitted: *It's warm today.*

Possession: *Jack's car, the players' entrance, the people's decision*

Possessive *its* does not have an apostrophe.

Plurals: *There are two l's in 'specially'. Are these 7's or 3's?*

2 Colons and semi-colons

Colons introduce examples, lists, and statements which give in detail what has been stated in general.

> *There were two possible courses of action: borrowing from the bank, or asking for more time to find the money elsewhere.*

Semi-colons divide parts of long sentences or long phrases in a list; it is usually possible to divide one sentence into shorter ones, so that semi-colons are unnecessary.

Activities

Practice in this unit is with proof reading. See Units 27 and 28 for other kinds of practice.

1

In most lines of this text, there is either a spelling or punctuation error. For each line, write the correctly spelled word, or show the correct punctuation, in the space beside the text. Indicate correct lines with a tick. Three examples are given.

It is an accepted part of everyday nostalgia to assume	0 ✓
that in the passed food was somehow better than it is today.	0 past
The fruit and vegetables were more naturaly grown and this	0 naturally
was not seen as an extra bonus which added ten per sent on to	1
the price. Most food was fresh, not frozen, and you had the	2
chance to examine it to see weather you wanted it. When you	3
went shopping you could ask for exactly what peace of meat you	4
wanted and see the butcher cutting, it instead of finding it	5
ready-wrapped in plastic. And your local tradesman soon got to	6
know what you wanted, and provided it for you: otherwise they	7
would have gone out of businness. Of course, unless we invent	8
time-travell we shall never know whether this is all true.	9
Survivors from those distant days naturally tend to dislike	10
todays convenience foods, and to prefer the Good Old Days	11
when a joint of beef filled the oven, produced thick red juce	12
instead of water when cooked, and cost the same as a can of	13
Coke. What is always forgoten is that then as now the quality	14
of your food dependent very much upon who you were,	15
how well-off you happened to be, and where you lived.	16
Shopping then demanded considerable skill, and shopper's had	17
to be able to tell the fresh from the not so fresh. Their was	18
no sell-by date to act as a guide. If you were hard up; then	19
frozen meat and canned foods' would have been on the menu,	20
just as they are today.	

2

In most lines of this text, there is either a spelling or punctuation error. For each line, write the correctly spelled word, or show the correct punctuation, in the space beside the text. Indicate correct lines with a tick. Three examples are given.

The common cold, as it is technicaly known, still resists the	0 technically
efforts of science to control and cure it, and has given rise to a	0 ✓
rich popular mythology. As the name sugests, the assumption	0 suggests
is that you catch a cold because you go out in the cold or get wet.	1
As we now that a cold is a virus, and that we actually catch it	2
from being in contact with others' , this is not strictly true.	3
Shakeing hands with people, kissing them or just being in the	4
same room, can pass on the virus. It is now generally beleived	5
that cold viruses; and there is more than one type, are always	6
present in the throat, but only become active when the bodys	7
resistence to infection is lowered. The activated cold virus then	8
attacks the membranes in the nose and throat, who's tissues	9
become weakened and thus suseptible to infection by types of	10
bacteria which are generally also present in the body.	11
Sudden chilling, or getting soked to the skin, promote	12
conditions in nose and throat membranes that permitt the cold	13
virus to invade the body, although some individuals seem to be	14
resistant to this. Just being out in the cold is not enough, and	15
studys conducted in wartime among troops living in the open	16
found that the incidence of colds' was no greater. As far as	17
prevention and cure are concerned, nearly everyone has there	18
own favourite remedy. Doctors have been unable to produse an	19
affective vaccine against colds, although strong claims have been	20
made for vitamin C in tablet form as both a preventative measure	
and an aid to recovery.	

3

In most lines of this text, there is either a spelling or punctuation error. For each line, write the correctly spelled word, or show the correct punctuation, in the space beside the text. Indicate correct lines with a tick. Three examples are given.

A river in the west of England, made famous by the best-seller	0 ✓
'Tarka the Otter' has, once again become safe for otters after ten	0 Otter', has
years of what had been thought a loosing battle against pollution	0 losing
from chemicals. The River Torridge in North Devon was the	1
setting for Henry Williamsons book, the success of which has	2
led to the arae calling itself Tarka Country, and becoming a	3
popular tourist spot. Since 1927 when the book was writen,	4
however the human population of the area has increased	5
three-fold, and increased use of pestisides and fertilizers	6
had lead to the river being declared 'dead' in the early nineteen	7
eighty's. Otters are shy creatures and the river provides them	8
with numerous places to hide along the river vallies, and the	9
fear was that they had been elliminated because of the clearing	10
away of undergrowth and trees, and the affects of chemicals on	11
their breeding capabilities, nor to mention otter hunting, though	12
this has now ceased. However, a number of projects desined to	13
cleanse the river area seems to have born fruit, despite a	14
pesimistic announcement earlier this year. The Tarka Project,	15

which includes local councils and environmental groups, now	16
says that the otter poppulation is healthy and thriving. Signs of	17
otter habitation have been found in a number of places, and more	18
and more sitings of otters have been recorded. When	19
Williamson's book was published the otter was widespred	20

throughout the country, but North Devon is now one of the few
remaining areas where otters live naturally.

4

In most lines of
this text there is
one unnecessary
word. It is either
incorrect
grammatically, or
does not fit the
sense of the text.
For each line write
the unnecessary
word in the space
beside the text.
Tick each correct
line.

Letter 1. Can I add some comments to your to debate about the — 0 to
value of television? Your readers may find that some of my — 0 ✓
views reflect exactly of their own experience in this matter. — 0 of
First of all, I heartily agree with your reader Mrs Goldwood who — 1
she wrote that she has decided to abandon her television set. Like — 2
her I am retired out, and was finding it more and more difficult — 3
to pay back the licence fee, and so six months ago I decided that — 4
enough was enough, and sent the set back to the rental company. — 5
I can assure Mrs Goldwood that she will not miss it. I too was — 6
also something of a devotee of soap operas, at least I enjoyed — 7
following the storyline in some episodes of them, but I have since — 8
discovered that there are equally interesting serials on the radio. — 9
I think that she will also find herself reading more, and at times — 10
least with books you can choose what a kind of story you want to — 11
follow, instead of being at the mercy of the programme for — 12
planners. I am sure that my other readers can confirm that life — 13
after The Box is richer and more rewarding.

Letter 2. Was I alone in detecting that the note of superiority in — 14
the letter from Mr Hackett about giving up television? What is — 15
a lot of fuss about nothing. Mr Hackett seems not to think that if — 16
you have a television you have to look at it. Surely not it is a — 17
question of choosing programmes carefully enough, and turning — 18
off when there is nothing worth it watching. As for the licence — 19
fee, I myself am not well-off, and so I have always bought — 20
licence stamps at the post office when I collect my pension.
That way you can spread the cost of the licence out over the
whole year.

5

In most lines of this text there is one unnecessary word. It is either incorrect grammatically, or does not fit the sense of the text. For each line write the unnecessary word in the space beside the text. Tick each correct line.

The term 'drugs' covers many of kinds of chemical substance	0 of
which they are absorbed by the body, the majority being	0 they
medicines designed to cure illnesses. They are manufactured	0 ✓
from a variety of sources which include animal and products,	1
plants and minerals. In the recent years it has become possible	2
to synthesise in the laboratory many drugs which previously	3
obtained from plants and animal products. A small number of	4
drugs can become addictive if taken excessively, as that is either	5
too frequently, or in doses larger than they recommended for	6
medical to use. Drugs intended as painkillers, or drugs with a	7
hypnotic effect are used as sleeping pills, can both become	8
addictive if abused. It is important to make emphasise the fact	9
that it is the abuse of drugs which has once become a widespread	10
social problem in many societies, and not that the drug itself	11
may have many of beneficial effects when used medically. This is	12
why many drugs are obtainable only through prescription from	13
a doctor. Some people would argue that if addiction to drugs	14
involves both psychological and social factors, since those are	15
people who become addicts may do so as in order to find some	16
relief from personal or social inadequacies. This argument	17
implies that it is somehow the addict's fault if not he or she	18
becomes addicted, and this is it to ignore the powerful physical	19
effects of many drugs. Although temporary the effects of	20
well-being may be obtained, these effects soon wear off and lead	
to severe physical discomfort, which can only then be relieved	
by a further dose of the drug.	

6

In most lines of this text there is one unnecessary word. It is either incorrect grammatically, or does not fit the sense of the text. For each line write the unnecessary word in the space beside the text. Tick each correct line.

A study into family of health conducted in California comes	0 of
up with some interesting conclusions, though these might not be	0 ✓
acceptable to everybody. The main conclusion is so that for a	0 so
family to remain healthy, both the relationship between husband	1
and wife plays a major role. The family perhaps surprising	2
aspect of this research, however, is that statistically the	3
healthy family is as optimistic, church-going, and led by a	4
traditional male. And perhaps not so much surprisingly, what	5
promotes the health of the husband and does not necessarily	6
promote the health of the wife too, and vice versa. For	7
example, when it comes to expressing emotions, thus it is	8
generally assumed that giving up an outlet to feelings is healthy.	9
But according to the study, there may be benefits for one party	10
but not for the other. If the wife talks to more than the husband	11
does in these situations and gives him feelings of guilt, then he	12
is likely to become a depressed, whereas if the wife lets the	13
husband dominate on the argument, then she in turn will be the	14

one of whose mental state will suffer. The study also found that   15
when men dominate in the domestic arguments, they often end up 16
trying to avoid from the real issue, or become silent and   17
withdrawn. This has the effect of making the wife feel anxious   18
and depressed. As a person's mental state there is closely linked 19
to their physical as well being, it is clear that the dynamics of   20
family relationships help to determine health in general.

Unit 30 Progress Test (Units 1 to 29)

1

Put *one* suitable word in each space.

The port of Dover in South Eastern England is the (1) .... sight that greets many visitors from Europe as they approach Britain from the continent of Europe. The famous White Cliffs loom through the mist, the ferry noses into the harbour, and the passengers clutching their duty-free drinks file through Customs. Or at least that is the way it all (2) .... to be. Two significant changes (3) .... dealt a heavy blow to a local economy already reeling under the force of the depression, with unemployment levels in East Kent higher than (4) .... in Scotland and Wales. The first instrument of change has (5) .... in the pipeline, as it were, for some (6) .... now. It is the Channel Tunnel, which threatens to transform Dover from a port handling a fifth of Britain's foreign trade with over fifteen million ferry passengers, to a small coastal town. (7) .... the bulk of the cross-Channel traffic should eventually use the tunnel, then Dover will be (8) .... with an inevitable decline over the next decade. (9) .... the tunnel provided 8000 (10) .... during construction, this was only temporary, and over the years (11) .... the tunnel project began, ferry companies and related service industries have been shedding jobs in an effort to emerge (12) .... competitive as possible for the smaller market which was to come. The (13) .... major blow was the opening of Europe's internal frontiers at the beginning of 1993. Dover Customs (14) .... work for 800 customs officers, (15) .... to mention the hundreds of jobs involved in customs broking, storage and transport. In a one-industry town (16) .... as Dover, such changes have spelled economic disaster for scores of small companies, many of (17) .... employees are under 30, skilled in the use of computers and at (18) .... half of whom speak one or more foreign languages. Hopefully Dover will recover, (19) .... many other British towns (20) .... have seen the end of traditional industries in recent years. Just for now, though, the local unemployed face a gloomy future, and talk around here of 'the light at the end of the tunnel' is understandably not very popular.

2

Complete each sentence with a suitable word or phrase.

a) If you .... using my calculator, I'd like it back later, please.

b) Strange .... seem, the winter can be drier than the summer.

c) The lighting works automatically. We .... turn it on.

d) You are awful! You .... told me you were having a party!

e) There is nobody for .... I feel more respect than Mrs Giles.

f) But for your help, ... unable to finish the work on time.

g) Susan .... on making us a cup of tea, even though we had to leave.

h) I should .... David would know better.

i) I'd rather .... bring your dog in here, if you don't mind.

j) Our teacher didn't arrive until the .... end of the lesson.

3

Rewrite each sentence, beginning as shown, so that the meaning stays the same.

a) Who owns this umbrella?
Who does..

b) I had only just arrived home when the phone rang.
Hardly ....

c) Don't under any circumstances press this red button.
Whatever you...

d) Someone has just stolen John's car.
John ....

e) Please wait here, and I'll see if the doctor is free.
If you'll...

f) You can stay with us for a few days.
We ....

g) Apparently her ex-husband was a terrible gambler.
Her ex-husband is...

h) I would rather not think about it.
That's ....

i) Tony knew what the answer was after reading the book.
By the time ....

j) What would you do if you won the football pools?
Supposing..

4

Rewrite each sentence so that it contains the word in capitals, and so that the meaning stays the same.

a) Our MP demanded a police investigation.   SHOULD
....

b) I think a change would do you good.   FROM
....

c) My passport needs renewing.   GET
....

d) Nobody there had heard of Miss Rutherford.   WHO
....

e) I shouldn't think Carol will want to come.   WHETHER
....

f) There is something on your mind, isn't there?   ABOUT
....

g) The film wasn't as good as we expected.   COME
....

h) I'm afraid it just isn't possible for you to see her.   QUITE
....

i) Is there any news of the missing jewels?   ABOUT
....

j) I suppose you are Peter's brother.   MUST
....

5
Put *one* suitable word in each space.

a) Your sister .... be really annoying, you know!
b) The cracks in the beams resulted .... the collapse of the ceiling.
c) The block of flats was built .... money lent by the local authority.
d) In the middle of the ceremony, Tom .... out laughing.
e) Have you insured the car .... fire?
f) I wish grandfather .... be here to see all the children.
g) I wouldn't be surprised if Mary .... come first after all.
h) .... this really be the right address? The house is for sale.
i) The spokesperson refused to elaborate .... the plans any further.
j) If you .... see Judith, would you give her my love?

6
Complete each sentence with a suitable word or phrase.

a) It's high time .... about the potholes in this road.
b) That was a silly thing to do! You .... done it!
c) If you .... make so much noise, can you go outside?
d) Paul said it was accidental, but I'm sure he did it ....
e) We were so surprised when Brian turned up, we couldn't .... over it.
f) Thanks for .... to phone Joe. I would have forgotten otherwise.
g) The postman couldn't make out .... was addressed to, so he took it back.
h) If I took the job in Wales, it .... my moving to Cardiff.
i) Keep the plan a secret from Andy. We don't want to .... on it.
j) You don't .... seen my glasses anywhere, do you?

7
Choose the most suitable word or phrase.

a) No sooner had we left the house, ... it started snowing.
   A) and   B) than   C) when   D) that
b) Can you .... to it that no one uses this entrance?
   A) ensure   B) guarantee   C) assure   D) see
c) Several cars, ... owners had parked them under the trees, were damaged.
   A) their   B) of which   C) whom   D) whose
d) It was very good .... you to give up so much of your time.
   A) of   B) for   C) with   D) to
e) The play was not .... what we had expected.
   A) just   B) absolutely   C) at all   D) very
f) We had to get a bank loan when the money finally ....
   A) gave in   B) gave off   C) gave over   D) gave out
g) The minister .... to say whether all the coal mines would be closed.
   A) refused   B) avoided   C) denied   D) bothered
h) When Helen agreed to run the school play, she got more than she ....
   A) came down to   B) bargained for   C) faced up to   D) got round to
i) At the end of the match the players were .... exhausted.
   A) solely   B) utterly   C) actually   D) merely
j) .... you should do first is make a list of all the things you have to do.
   A) That   B) What   C) As   D) If

8

Rewrite each
sentence,
beginning as
shown, so that
the meaning stays
the same.

a) I am not to be disturbed under any circumstances.
   Under ....

b) It's a long time since I read such a good article.
   I ....

c) You will eventually appreciate what I am getting at.
   In ....

d) Everyone said that the accident had been Carol's fault.
   Carol ....

e) I'd rather you didn't go.
   I'd prefer ....

f) They'll arrive soon.
   It ....

g) Let's go home at the end of the second act.
   As soon as ....

h) This will be the group's first concert in the USA.
   This will be the first time ....

i) There is a rumour that you stole it.
   It ....

j) Fancy you and I meeting in the middle of Africa like this!
   It's really odd ....

9

Rewrite each
sentence so that it
contains the
word in capitals,
and so that the
meaning stays the
same.

a) I can't find the answer without a calculator.   OUT
   ....

b) Although it's expensive, it's a good hotel.   IF
   ....

c) I didn't expect to see Tim there!   LAST
   ....

d) Everyone who spoke to the victim is a suspect.   UNDER
   ....

e) This is none of your business!   DOESN'T
   ....

f) I should really be going now.   TIME
   ....

g) Foolishly, I paid all the money before collecting the goods.   WHICH
   ....

h) Robert had no idea of his next move.   DO
   ....

i) It was only when I checked that I noticed the tyre was flat.   DID
   ....

j) Please inform the relevant authorities at once.   DELAY
   ....

10

Complete each sentence with a suitable word or phrase.

a) It's ....we last went roller-skating.
b) Don't be silly! It ....Sally you saw. She's in Scotland.
c) But for your help I ....the prize.
d) It's after twelve. It's time you ....in bed.
e) By the end of this year, we ....each other for half a century!
f) It didn't rain, so we ....taken the umbrella after all.
g) Never before ....such heavy snow in April.
h) Be that ...., your behaviour is still unacceptable.
i) If you'd told me you were ill, I .... the chemist's for you.
j) I have known I would become world champion ever since I .... racing.

11

Rewrite each sentence, beginning as shown, so that the meaning stays the same.

a) If the government did resign, I think they would win the election.
   Were ....
b) It's a pity we didn't meet a long time ago!
   I wish ....
c) This problem cannot be solved instantly.
   There is ....
d) My friends persuaded me to go to the party in fancy dress.
   My friends talked...
e) The painting is thought to have been stolen by one of the attendants.
   One of the attendants ....
f) Only when I got home did I realise I had left the parcel behind.
   It was not...
g) In the end Pauline phoned the insurance company.
   What ....
h) The garden party won't take place if the weather stays bad.
   Unless...
i) We moved into this house thirty years ago today.
   It's ....
j) I wouldn't eat too many of those, if I were you.
   You'd ....

12

Complete each sentence with a suitable word or phrase.

a) It's by ....certain that the plan will be adopted.
b) If anyone calls, say I'm out, no matter ....
c) Try ...., I just couldn't get the car started.
d) How kind of you! But you really ....brought me a present.
e) Philip agreed to rob the bank, but then found he couldn't go .... it.
f) Not until I looked at my watch ....how much time had passed.
g) George gave the police three accounts of the accident, ...was true.
h) Ann strongly ....taken the money.
i) Do you ....coming out for a walk later?
j) Harry didn't seem the .... worried by what the policeman said.

1 Leisure Activities

1
Choose the most suitable word for each space.

According to a magazine article I read recently, we (1) .... live in an age of increasing leisure. Not only are more and more people reaching (2) .... age with their taste for enjoyment and even adventure relatively (3) .... but the working week is becoming shorter and the opportunities for (4)..........are becoming greater and greater all the time. Not to mention the fact that people (5) .... to spend less time travelling to work or may even be working from home. What I can't understand, however, is who these people are. As far as I can (6) .... the whole thing is another one of (7) .... journalistic fictions. I admit that there are a lot of retired people (8) ...., but I am not sure that all of them are dashing about learning hang-gliding or sailing single-handed (9) .... the world. My own parents seem to (10)............ most of their time gazing at the television. And as for the shorter working week, I wish someone (11) .... remind my company about it. I seem to be working longer and longer hours (12) .... the time. The little leisure time I have is eaten into by sitting in traffic jams or waiting for trains to (13)....... up at rain-swept platforms. I haven't noticed any dramatic improvements in my (14) .... either, but perhaps I just have to wait until I get my (15) ....

1) A) presently	B) at the moment	C) now	D) at this time
2) A) retirement	B) their	C) later	D) third
3) A) present	B) survived	C) free	D) intact
4) A) this	B) longer	C) leisure	D) people
5) A) use	B) tend	C) have	D) demand
6) A) concern	B) imagine	C) expect	D) tell
7) A) the	B) those	C) these	D) some
8) A) in our days	B) in these times	C) nowadays	D) now and again
9) A) round	B) over	C) through	D) into
10) A) have	B) use	C) the	D) spend
11) A) would	B) to	C) had	D) might
12) A) at	B) for	C) take	D) all
13) A) keep	B) line	C) show	D) set
14) A) cost of living	B) lifestyle	C) lifeline	D) livelihood
15) A) pension	B) retirement	C) insurance	D) salary

2
Choose the most appropriate word or phrase underlined.

a) Last week well over a thousand people <u>took place in/took part in</u> our local round-the-city marathon.

b) This kind of race doesn't <u>appeal to me/amuse me</u> personally.

c) I'm not really <u>cut out for/made out for</u> long distance running.

d) I know that running has a very <u>beneficial/positive</u> effect.

e) I don't mind watching other people <u>gasping /panting</u> for breath.

f) But I'd rather be a spectator than <u>an actor/a participant</u>.

g) This year I was persuaded to run to <u>earn/raise</u> money for charity.

h) Friends and colleagues agreed to <u>sponsor/support</u> me, and pay for each mile I completed.

i) I ended up among the <u>strugglers/stragglers</u>.

j) But I managed to <u>catch up with/run into</u> my grandmother who finished first in her age group.

3
Choose two items from the list for each activity.

> rod flippers rehearsal horse easel lens roller rucksack
> choir spanner bait mask tripod model compass bars

a) Gymnastics ....
b) Skin Diving ....
c) Fishing ....
d) Walking ....
e) Photography ....
f) Do-It-Yourself ....
g) Music ....
h) Painting ....

4
Complete each sentence with a word formed from the word in capitals.

a) The new leisure centre doesn't quite come up to my .... EXPECT
b) There was a bare .... of people at the youth club. HAND
c) Helen's solo crossing of the Pacific was a .... feat. REMARK
d) We .... go to the pub before lunch on Sunday. VARY
e) All the runners, with the .... of Mark, were exhausted. EXCEPT
f) Our club has just purchased new sports .... EQUIP
g) Our city has some open spaces, but they are not very .... ACCESS
h) Is it possible to .... between a hobby and an interest? DISTINCT
i) Nowadays .... numbers of people are taking up jogging. INCREASE
j) Leisure habits won't change much in the .... future. SEE

5
Choose the most suitable word or phrase.

a) One .... adults takes physical exercise at least once a week.
  A) from four   B) in four   C) at four   D) with four

b) Mary lost one running shoe, but won the race despite this ....
  A) awkwardness B) disaster   C) handicap   D) feat

c) The .... of the museum showed the school party round.
  A) guard   B) curator   C) principal D) exhibitor

d) I still play golf occasionally, just to keep my .... in.
  A) eye   B) arm   C) foot   D) hand

e) Robert is completely .... in his new book on photography.
  A) absorbed   B) interested C) disappointed D) occupied

f) Our local youth club tries to .... for all interests.
  A) equip   B) apply   C) organise   D) cater

g) Next year I hope to .... my ambition of climbing Mont Blanc.
  A) complete   B) follow   C) realise   D) impose

h) Pauline managed to win the car rally at the first ....
  A) attempt   B) try   C) rate   D) entry

i) The attendance at our local music society meetings is very low ....
  A) practically B) commonly   C) by percentage D) on average

j) When I have some free time I tend to do nothing .... laze about.
  A) only   B) but   C) and   D) like

6

Complete each sentence a) to j) with one of the endings 1) to 10).

a) As far as I'm concerned, there is no comparison ....
b) Now that I have two mornings a week free I have acquired ....
c) To be perfectly honest I don't find ....
d) The performance of the company last year surpassed ....
e) I'm afraid that this plan doesn't really allow ....
f) Mr Potts says that he will devote ....
g) I'm afraid I can't come out to lunch, I'm up to ....
h) Members are asked to return the form irrespective of ....
i) The manager later gave us ....
j) I know her face but unfortunately her name ....

1) .... an assurance that we would not be disturbed again.
2) .... collecting stamps a particularly interesting activity.
3) .... my eyes in work just at the moment.
4) .... for the effects of possible variations in the climate.
5) .... escapes me just at present.
6) .... between amateur and professional sport.
7) .... the rest of his life if necessary to uncovering the truth.
8) .... our expectations in every respect.
9) .... whether they expect to attend the annual dinner.
10) .... a taste for strolling along the sea-front for an hour or two.

7

Complete each sentence with a word from the list. Use each word once only.

board draw lap referee runner-up dive fan oar round whistle

a) While I was rowing across the lake I lost one ....
b) Neither team deserved to lose and the match ended in a ....
c) Ruth was well out in front by the end of the fifth ....
d) After the rugby match David was attacked by an angry ....
e) Brian impressed everyone with his .... into the pool.
f) Our gym teacher used to make us stop by blowing a ....
g) During the chess game Carol knocked all the pieces off the ....
h) Our team was knocked out of the competition in the second ....
i) During the match one of the spectators offered the .... his glasses.
j) Denise won the race and her sister was ....

8

Put *one* word in each space.

It is now generally recognised that stress is a major (1) .... of heart disease, and contributes to many (2) .... illnesses. Stress is increased by factors (3) .... as worry, overwork and lack of exercise or relaxation. For (4)........ is just as important from a psychological point of (5) .... to relax as it is to take physical exercise. Relaxing (6) .... not necessarily mean just lazing about and (7) .... nothing. Above all, there should be some freedom (8) .... the tensions of everyday life, and this may mean getting out of the house and forgetting (9) .... both domestic and professional worries. Some people can do (10) .... most easily through sport, though others may (11) .... such activities just as seriously as anything (12) .... in life and build (13) .... their stress levels accordingly. Professional sportsmen and women suffer high levels of stress. (14) .... some environmental factors such as noise, light or (15) .... colour may affect stress levels, it is generally advisable to have a (16) .... of scene if you wish to wind down after a trying day. The benefits of a weekend away, (17) .... to mention an annual holiday, are considerable, and although there are some individuals who thrive on stress, and (18) .... to need its stimulus, for most of us over-working or over-involvement in domestic problems (19) .... to a feeling of exhaustion, and can (20) .... on severe depression.

2 Travel and Movement

1
Choose the most suitable word for each space.

In most capital cities, which were built (1) .... before the heyday of the private car, there is rarely enough (2) .... for moving traffic, and certainly not enough for parked (3) .... Buses move slowly because of the volume of (4) .... thus encouraging more commuters to abandon public (5) .... Banning traffic from some areas may help, but such a (6) .... may not actually diminish the number of cars coming into the city. What has happened in effect is that the (7) .... of the private car have become the number one priority, and the older functions of the city centre as meeting (8) .... and focus for social life have been lost. The new city cannot (9) .... without a series of ring roads. Giant car parks are its new palaces and cathedrals. During the working hours of the day, there is the constant (10) .... of traffic, but at night the centre is almost empty, apart from a few homeless in doorways. Most people have (11) .... back to the suburbs, and very few of those who live in the centre have cars, for often there is nowhere to park them. The old city, with its narrow streets, may still retain a lively (12) .... but that may be because it exists as an island, where no cars are (13) .... Unless the local authorities have not yet plucked up the courage to (14) .... most traffic from the streets, in which case the city centre is (15) .... by day, and a gigantic car park by night.

1) A) far   B) long   C) much   D) even
2) A) area   B) roads   C) space   D) speed
3) A) vehicles   B) pedestrians   C) drivers   D) areas
4) A) this   B) noise   C) congestion   D) traffic
5) A) means   B) transport   C) order   D) restrictions
6) A) area   B) issue   C) solution   D) way
7) A) numbers   B) needs   C) car parks   D) uses
8) A) people   B) others   C) place   D) this
9) A) build   B) survive   C) plan   D) construct
10) A) din   B) amount   C) parking   D) filling

11) A) parked   B) left   C) commuted   D) got
12) A) activity   B) role   C) air   D) population
13) A) going   B) permitted   C) banned   D) entering
14) A) leave   B) direct   C) ban   D) regulate
15) A) surrounded   B) sparse   C) congested   D) deserted

2

Choose the most suitable word underlined.

a) We managed to complete our journey <u>ahead of/in front of</u> schedule.
b) On our way to York, we <u>divided/broke</u> our journey in Peterborough.
c) As I wasn't coming back by train, I asked for a <u>single/simple</u> ticket.
d) The two coaches collided, but luckily no one was <u>injured/wounded</u>.
e) We drove to the town centre and stopped at the library <u>in the way/on the way</u>.
f) My car skidded off the road and <u>crashed/hit</u> a tree.
g) The train was packed, and there was standing <u>place/room</u> only.
h) When her bike hit the rock, Jane was thrown over the <u>handlebars/saddle</u>.
i) The police accused Donald of breaking the speed <u>limit/restriction</u>.
j) My plane arrived in Paris <u>dead/way</u> on time.

3

Complete each sentence with one of the words given. Use each word once only.

book change direct hail pick bring come grind hitch set

a) Jim walked down the street trying to .... a taxi, but none would stop.
b) We heard the old bus slowly .... to a halt outside.
c) Fifty extra policemen were called in to ....the traffic outside the stadium.
d) The mayor promised to ....the new buses into operation without delay.
e) My old car takes quite a long time to .... up speed.
f) The school bus always used to ....the children down opposite the church.
g) When her car broke down, Julie had to .... a ride to the nearest phone.
h) When I went to .... a ticket to Athens, I found that the flight was full.
i) This car is an automatic, so you don't have to .... gear all the time.
j) As our ship rounded the headland, we watched the town .... into view.

4

Choose the most suitable word or phrase.

a) The horse stopped suddenly and its rider was .... to the ground.
   A) dropped   B) flung   C) launched   D) tripped
b) After its engine failed, the small boat .... with the current.
   A) waved   B) tossed   C) hastened   D) drifted
c) The only means of .... to the station is through a dark subway.
   A) arrival   B) admission   C) access   D) approaching
d) When I enquired about the times of trains, I was given a ....
   A) schedule   B) programme   C) itinerary   D) timetable
e) I suddenly noticed that the runaway bus was hurtling .... me!
   A) over   B) nearby   C) towards   D) without
f) The plane's engines cut out, but it .... in to land safely.
   A) floated   B) glided   C) swept   D) fluttered
g) There are roadworks at Junction 63 and long .... are expected.
   A) delays   B) halts   C) intervals   D) pauses

h) The next train at platform three .... at Gatwick Airport only.

    A) arrives   B) terminates   C) calls   D) alights

i) I was running low on petrol so started looking for a filling ....

    A) station   B) garage   C) stop   D) area

j) Only a mechanic could appreciate the true .... of the damage to the car.

    A) extent   B) rate   C) amount   D) affect

5

Complete each sentence with one of the words given. Use each word once only.

> boat   fence   legs   run   walk   crossroads   foot   pace   stride   way

a) John took the loss of his job in his ....

b) After a hard day's work in the garden I was on my last ....

c) Our relationship somehow got off on the wrong ....

d) As far as this year's championship is concerned, United have missed the ....

e) There are people from every .... of life in our local drama club.

f) Laura found it hard to keep .... with the changes in her company.

g) I am sure that in the long .... this decision will prove to be the best.

h) It's time you stopped sitting on the .... and made a decision.

i) Choosing to work in Africa turned out to be a .... in Helen's life.

j) If you want to be a rock singer, my boy, I will not stand in your ....

6

Rewrite each sentence using an expression based on the words or expressions from exercise 5.

a) It is too late for me now.

b) This is an important moment of change in my career.

c) I won't stop you doing what you want to do.

d) I managed to cope with the bad news.

e) My salary isn't keeping up with inflation.

f) I feel extremely tired.

g) I haven't decided which side to support yet.

h) The problems are the same for all employees here.

i) Things went badly between my boss and myself from the beginning.

j) I'll be better off in the end.

7

Replace the words underlined in each sentence with a form of one of the words given. It may be necessary to use a plural or a particular tense form.

> accelerate   ascend   collide   dismount   fasten
> alight   board   disembark   endanger   reverse

a) Ann <u>got off her horse</u> and picked up her riding hat.

b) As the plane <u>went faster</u> down the runway, David began to sweat nervously.

c) Without realising it, Jim <u>drove backwards</u> into a lamp post.

d) In thick fog, the two ships <u>ran into each other</u> outside the harbour.

e) Passengers who wish to <u>get off</u> at Hove should travel in the front two coaches.

f) Please <u>do up</u> your safety belt before we begin the journey.

g) All visitors to the ship must <u>get off</u> immediately as we are about to sail.

h) The captain refused to <u>put at risk</u> the safety of the other members of the crew.

i) The balloon <u>rose up</u> gracefully into the summer sky.

j) The sooner the passengers <u>get on</u> the aircraft, the sooner it can take off.

8

Match each person with one of the comments. Use each comment once only.

hitch hiker	conductor	passenger	driver	traffic warden
commuter	steward	passer-by	pedestrian	rambler

a) I love wandering through the countryside along deserted footpaths.

b) I'll bring you your drink in just a minute, madam.

c) I've been waiting all morning at this roundabout for someone to stop.

d) I was just walking down the street opposite the bank when I saw it happen.

e) I've spent the last half an hour looking for a spot. It's hopeless.

f) I'll ring the bell for you, love, when it's time to get off.

g) The sign clearly says two hours only and you've been here all day.

h) It's just impossible getting across the road here. We need a subway.

i) Do you think you could go a little more slowly, I'm a bit nervous.

j) This train is late every morning. It has been for years.

3 News Events

1

Choose the most suitable word for each space.

Reports that the government is about to (1) .... the go ahead to plans for the building of a new runway at London's Gatwick airport have angered (2) .... residents and raised (3) .... of increased noise and exhaust pollution. The (4) .... plans also include permission for additional night flights and will (5) .... the compulsory purchase of farmland, as well as the demolition of a number of private homes. (6) .... to sources close to the Ministry of Transport, the government is known to be (7) .... by the increasing volume of traffic at London Heathrow, where there are no plans for further runways in the foreseeable (8) .... Gatwick is widely regarded (9) .... a better prospect for expansion than London's third airport, Stansted, which still suffers from poor transport links. A spokesperson for the Keep Gatwick Quiet association, (10) .... up of local people, accused the government of going back (11) .... promises made before the General Election. 'We were told then that the airport authority had no intention of building another runway, and we believe that the government has a duty to (12) .... by its pledges.' (13) .... figures in the government are also believed to be concerned at the news, although the Prime Minister, interviewed last night, is (14) .... as saying that reports were 'misleading'. However, he would not give an (15) .... that plans for building a runway had definitely been rejected.

1) A) have	B) make	C) give	D) perform
2) A) airline	B) local	C) particular	D) with
3) A) money	B) views	C) percentages	D) fears
4) A) controversial	B) debatable	C) notorious	D) undecided
5) A) involve	B) request	C) assume	D) need
6) A) Next	B) Up	C) According	D) Used
7) A) pleased	B) concerned	C) divided	D) important

8) A) years   B) events   C) time   D) future
9) A) and   B) for   C) because   D) as
10) A) made   B) woken   C) taken   D) formed
11) A) from   B) to   C) on   D) with
12) A) perform   B) act   C) vote   D) stand
13) A) Protuberant   B) Prominent   C) Prevalent   D) Petulant
14) A) known   B) believed   C) quoted   D) written
15) A) estimate   B) objection   C) assurance   D) inquiry

2

Choose the most suitable word underlined.

a) The two men, disguised/transformed as security guards, overpowered staff at the bank and escaped with £150 000.

b) The pilot was the one/sole survivor of the crash.

c) The fire extensively/widely damaged the 500-year-old building.

d) Mr Johnson was taken to Maidstone General Hospital where his condition was described as 'critical/perilous'.

e) The cause/reason of the accident is not known.

f) A woman and a man were later detained/arrested for questioning.

g) The findings/results of the committee are due for publication this week.

h) The government has agreed that the problem must be removed/tackled at once.

i) Miss Herbert is an authoritarian/expert on air pollution.

j) A police spokesperson admitted that detectives were baffled/upset by Mr Day's disappearance, but were hoping to come up with an explanation.

3

Complete each sentence with one of the words given.

| conditions evidence knowledge place responsibility |
| confidence incident opinion prospect verge |

a) With Smith out injured, there is little .... of City reaching the next round.

b) After heavy rain, ... during the race were hazardous.

c) It is common .... that Douglas intends to retire at the end of the season.

d) Two French and two English forwards were involved in an ugly .... just before half-time.

e) Miss Schmidt easily secured her .... in the next round with a confident display of power tennis.

f) The final day begins with the Australian team on the .... of victory.

g) Whether Alberto was offside is a matter of ...., in my view.

h) I have every .... that Jack Wood is the man to lead our team to victory.

i) There is no concrete .... that anyone in the team has taken drugs.

j) The club has disclaimed .... for the damage, blaming it on supporters from London.

4

Complete each sentence a) to j) with one of the endings 1) to 10).

a) The union is drawing up ....

b) The managing director said that recent events had put ....

c) No one holds out ....

d) He went on to say that the company prided ....

e) Both sides have agreed to meet on a regular ....

f) The union has since challenged. ....
g) Others believe that both sides would jump at the ....
h) It is unlikely that the union will moderate ....
i) The management stated that the problem had been exaggerated out of ....
j) The minister said that he put himself at the ....

1) .... basis from now on, he added.
2) .... all proportion, and that an agreement was close.
3) .... a strain upon everyone employed by the company.
4) .... its demand for a shorter working week.
5) .... the figures given to the press by the financial director.
6) .... new proposals to put to the employers.
7) .... disposal of both sides in the dispute.
8) .... itself on its good relations with all its employees.
9) .... chance to resume negotiations without delay.
10) .... much hope for the success of the discussions.

5
Choose the most suitable word or phrase.

a) Mrs Dawson was given the award in .... of her services to the hospital.
   A) spite   B) recognition   C) charge   D) sight of
b) The Prime Minister made no .... to the incident in his speech.
   A) reference   B) mention   C) impression   D) gesture
c) Police believe there is a .... between the two crimes.
   A) joint   B) chain   C) link   D) connector
d) The spokesperson would not .... any further on such a sensitive matter.
   A) hint   B) quote   C) disclose   D) elaborate
e) The chairman's announcement was followed by a .... debate.
   A) warm   B) heated   C) hot   D) boiling
f) There is .... in the press that the couple will soon get divorced.
   A) speculation   B) rumour   C) news   D) indication
g) Harrison has been .... in his criticism of the present government.
   A) outlandish   B) outspoken   C) outlying   D) outright
h) The journalist refused to .... the source of his information.
   A) disclose   B) expose   C) enclose   D) propose
i) Many trains have been cancelled, and long .... are expected.
   A) distances   B) postponements   C) timetables   D) delays
j) The problem has been .... about by the increase in global warming.
   A) thought   B) brought   C) written   D) caused

6
Replace the words underlined in each sentence with one of the words or phrases given.

| argue that there should be   have no intention   raised fears   brought about |
| it is common knowledge   regarded as   explained the cause as |
| little prospect of success   say for certain   have every confidence |

a) I <u>am not thinking</u> of resigning at the moment.
b) <u>Everybody is aware</u> that Smith has a criminal record.
c) I <u>am quite sure</u> that enough money will be collected to save the Zoo.

d) We all know what <u>caused</u> the closure of the factory.

e) The report has <u>made people afraid</u> that others may be at risk from the disease.

f) Jane is <u>thought to be</u> the best high-jumper in Britain at present.

g) We shall try hard, although there is <u>not much chance of winning</u>.

h) A hospital spokesperson refused to <u>confirm</u> that the injured man had been shot.

i) Some conservationists <u>advocate</u> an immediate ban on hunting.

j) Commenting on the week-end travel chaos, British Rail <u>attributed this to</u> a combination of snow and high winds.

7

In each headline, replace the word or words underlined with one of the 'headline' words given.

> bid   clash   held   quits   toll   boost   cleared   looms   set   vows

a) Miners' union <u>promises</u> fight over local pay deals.

b) Change to school funding aims to <u>increase</u> teacher numbers.

c) Newspapers and union <u>going</u> to clash over pay claim.

d) Man <u>found innocent</u> in bank robbery case.

e) British <u>attempt</u> to aid refugees turned down.

f) Jackson <u>resigns</u> in government reshuffle.

g) Woman <u>arrested</u> by police after pub shooting.

h) <u>Number of people killed</u> rises to 6.

i) Rail strike <u>approaches.</u>

j) Ministers <u>in disagreement</u> over pay rises.

8

Match each news extract with a headline from 7.

a) ..... after efforts to end the ordeal of over a thousand boat-people had been rejected by the government. A spokesperson for Oxfam later accused.......

b) ..... by which men at pits in some parts of the Midlands would receive additional payments for overtime working. This, they said, was not.....

c) ..... unless the government intervenes, which is unlikely at this stage. Services most likely to be hit at first would include some Inter-City links from......

d) ..... pointed out that the Minister had been one of the first to propose a pay-freeze earlier in the year, and asked whether this abrupt turnaround.....

e) ..... left the court accompanied by cheering relatives and friends. This brings to three the number of similar cases recently dismissed by the courts for...

f) ..... and accused them of blackmail. He asked them to bear in mind that with advertising much reduced as a result of the recession, circulations were.....

g) ..... thanked the Prime Minister for his support, but regretted that under the circumstances he had been left with no alternative. Other sources,however..

h) ..... Jean Noakley, 49, of no fixed address. Police later released the description of a man who they believe could help them with their inquiries. He is.....

i) ..... by which head teachers would control their own budgets. At present the most serious shortages in London and the South East are in maths, physics and.......

j) ..... was said to be in a serious condition. This latest accident adds to the growing criticism that the crash barriers on the M25 are not adequate and that..........

4 Places

1

Choose the most suitable word for each space.

When I first arrived here to take up my new job, I stayed in a hotel, but I soon started looking for some permanent (1) .... The first flat I (2) .... over was in (3) .... , and was obviously extremely damp in winter. Quite apart from the fact that the only (4) .... was of a brick wall. Then I had a look at a small flat in a modern (5) .... It had a (6) .... space and a garden, but the (7) .... was far too high for me. I didn't want to (8) .... up in a tiny place, so I answered an ad for house-sharing. The house was in a quiet (9) .... , and as soon as I saw it I fell in love with it. There was a high overgrown (10) .... around the front garden, and (11) .... to park cars in the drive. The room to (12) .... looked out (13) .... the back garden, and had a big bay window. Although it meant (14) .... the kitchen and living room, I did have my own bathroom, really just a shower and washbasin (15) .... into what must have once been a cupboard.

1) A) home	B) accommodation	C) house	D) landlords
2) A) passed	B) viewed	C) came	D) looked
3) A) an attic	B) a basement	C) a cave	D) a bedsit
4) A) view	B) entrance	C) distance	D) bathroom
5) A) tower	B) department	C) block	D) square
6) A) living	B) breathing	C) working	D) parking
7) A) lift	B) roof	C) area	D) rent
8) A) end	B) live	C) shut	D) pay
9) A) surroundings	B) neighbourhood	C) context	D) premises
10) A) fence	B) bush	C) hedge	D) lawn
11) A) room	B) permission	C) areas	D) place
12) A) let	B) myself	C) pay	D) luckily
13) A) in	B) over	C) at	D) for
14) A) without	B) in	C) sharing	D) having
15) A) poured	B) crowded	C) cluttered	D) crammed

2

Complete each description with one of the words given.

> architecture desert pond scenery summit
> castle estuary range site valley

a) One advantage of travelling by train is that you can forget about traffic jams and crowded roads, and sit back and admire the ....

b) Many buildings in this part of the town date from the seventeenth and eighteenth centuries, and include fine examples of the .... of those periods.

c) We began climbing the narrow path before dawn, and when we reached the .... , the plain below was still shrouded in mist.

d) From this point on, the landscape becomes increasingly bare, until the rocky slopes give way to the rolling dunes of the ....

e) My eye followed the course of the river, winding down through its green .... towards the distant town of Woodchester.

f) At the bottom of the garden, almost hidden by overhanging trees, was a round .... , which proved on closer inspection to be full of lilies and croaking frogs.

g) It was this section of the battlements, close to the Great Tower, which was undermined in the siege of 1286, when the .... was captured by Duke Alfonso.

h) At the end of the village, take the track on the right just past the petrol station. The .... of the temple lies 3 km to the east of the village. Only the first 2 km are passable for cars.

i) Further along the coast many diving and wading birds nest in the .... of the River Bourne, mainly in the marshes to the west of the railway bridge.

j) The island is divided by a .... of mountains running approximately north to south, the highest of which is Mount Ash, 3230 metres.

3

Choose the most appropriate word underlined.

a) The couple had their photo taken on the <u>steps/stairs</u> outside the church.

b) We had to put up a <u>fence/a hedge</u> to stop the dog getting out.

c) I still haven't found <u>accommodations/lodgings</u> for this term yet.

d) Jim keeps his lawnmower in a <u>shed/shack</u> at the bottom of the garden.

e) Before the advent of the railways, goods were often transported by <u>canal/channel.</u>

f) They are going to put up a ten-<u>floor/storey</u> building opposite my house.

g) Groups with guides should go to the side <u>access/entrance</u>.

h) The children playing in the garden made a beautiful <u>scene/scenery</u>.

i) As I was crossing the street, I dropped my ice cream on the <u>floor/ground</u>.

j) It was an old house, with exposed oak <u>beams/logs</u> in all the rooms.

4

Complete each sentence with a word or compound word formed from two of the words given. Words may be used more than once. Some words may not be useful.

| bed | bus | fire | green | home | lady | place | shelter | station |
| bridge | fall | foot | head | house | land | path | sit | water |

a) That'll be the .... She's calling to collect the rent.

b) Although our house has central heating, there's a .... in the living room.

c) The river then comes to a .... over a hundred metres high.

d) We grow tomatoes in a .... in the garden.

e) I live in a tiny .... because I can't afford a flat.

f) The lighthouse is built at the end of the .... above the sea.

g) As soon as I saw smoke coming from the window, I called the ....

h) Follow this .... until you come to the wood, then turn left.

i) We waited at the stop in the rain, sitting in the ....

j) I crossed the railway line by going over the ....

5
Choose the most suitable word or phrase.

a) The area was neglected and soon turned into an overcrowded ....
   A) suburb   B) slum   C) quarter   D) estate

b) The explosion shattered hundreds of .... of glass in the building.
   A) windows   B) fragments   C) sheets   D) panes

c) From the cliff top it was a/an .... drop to the beach below.
   A) sheer   B) straight   C) upright   D) erect

d) The old cottage had bow windows and a .... roof.
   A) plaited   B) straw   C) woven   D) thatched

e) The city takes its water supply from a nearby ....
   A) tanker   B) pond   C) reservoir   D) sewer

f) When my parents retired they bought a tiny .... in the country.
   A) bungalow   B) mansion   C) shack   D) barn

g) The car skidded off the road and fell into a .... full of muddy water.
   A) lake   B) gutter   C) ditch   D) puddle

h) The pointed .... of the church could be seen from miles away.
   A) dome   B) building   C) summit   D) steeple

i) A tall building like this requires very deep ....
   A) roots   B) foundations C) basis   D) establishment

j) The house possesses extensive .... with gardens, tennis-courts and an orchard.
   A) grounds   B) property   C) fields   D) surroundings

6
Complete each sentence with the most suitable word given.

bay horizon pass slope strait cliff landscape plain spring tide

a) This water comes from a .... near the bottom of the mountain.
b) The hills could be seen faintly outlined against the ....
c) The ship won't be able to sail until the .... comes in.
d) There was a rocky .... rising a hundred feet above the beach.
e) The two islands are divided by a narrow ....
f) There is only one .... through the mountains.
g) Many small boats could be seen moored in the wide curving ....
h) The children amused themselves by rolling down the grassy ....
i) The whole .... had turned white after the overnight fall of snow.
j) At the foot of the mountains was a wide well-cultivated ....

7
In these sentences the meaning of the words underlined is used as a metaphor or in an idiomatic sense. Match each sentence with one of the explanations below.

a) We have had a <u>flood</u> of applications.
b) John <u>towered</u> above his opponent.
c) Paul is still <u>sitting on the fence</u>.
d) Both presidents are due to attend a <u>summit</u> meeting.
e) The crowd was <u>streaming</u> out of the stadium.
f) I was completely <u>floored</u> by the question.
g) We expect output to <u>peak</u> at around £150 000 a month.
h) I've decided to <u>channel</u> all my energy into writing poetry.
i) Harry has been <u>grounded</u> by the airline.
j) I think that <u>the tide has now turned</u>.

1) One for national leaders.
2) He hasn't made a decision one way or the other.
3) To reach the highest point.
4) A very large number.
5) The worst point has passed.
6) Moving rapidly in large numbers.
7) He was much taller.
8) He is not allowed to fly.
9) Puzzled or defeated by.
10) To guide everything into one direction.

8

Complete each sentence a) to j) with one of the endings 1) to 10).

a) I paused at the top of the stairs on the ....
b) The walls of the bathroom were covered in ....
c) I chained my bike to the ....
d) There was a clock on the ....
e) I left my umbrella in the ....
f) After the storm we had to replace several ....
g) We stored our old books upstairs in the ....
h) I decided to oil the front door ....
i) There was no heat coming from the ....
j) You should try to remember to wipe your feet on the ....

1) .... railings at the front of the house.
2) .... hinges, which were rather rusty.
3) .... loft, in case we needed them again.
4) .... mantelpiece over the fireplace.
5) .... landing and wondered which was my room.
6) .... doormat outside the back door.
7) .... slates which had fallen off the roof.
8) .... radiator under the window.
9) .... tiles with a pattern of fruit and flowers.
10) .... porch and opened the front door.

5 Media and Advertising

1

Choose the most suitable word for each space.

After more than fifty years of television, it might seem only obvious to conclude that it is here to (1) .... There have been many objections to it during this time, of course, and (2) .... a variety of grounds. Did it cause eye-strain? Was the (3) .... bombarding us with radioactivity? Did the advertisements (4) .... subliminal messages, persuading us to buy more or vote Republican? Did children turn to violence through watching it, either because so (5) .... programmes taught them how to shoot, rob, and kill, or because they had to do something to counteract the hours they had (6) .... glued to the tiny screen? Or did it simply create a vast passive (7) ...., drugged by glamorous serials and inane situation (8) ....? On the other hand did it increase anxiety by sensationalising the news (or the news which was (9) .... by suitable pictures) and filling our living rooms with war, famine and political unrest? (10) .... in all, television proved to be the all-purpose scapegoat for the second half of the century, (11) .... for everything, but above all, eagerly watched. For no (12) .... how much we despised it, feared it, were bored by it, or felt that it took us away from the old paradise of family conversation and hobbies (13) .... as collecting stamps, we never turned it off. We (14) .... staring at the screen, aware that our own tiny (15) .... was in it if we looked carefully.

1) A) long	B) stay	C) exist	D) be
2) A) with	B) over	C) by	D) on
3) A) screen	B) danger	C) machine	D) reason
4) A) contain	B) of	C) take	D) having
5) A) that	B) far	C) many	D) what
6) A) almost	B) spent	C) quite	D) madly
7) A) programme	B) personality	C) audience	D) tense
8) A) comedies	B) programmes	C) perhaps	D) consequently
9) A) taken	B) presented	C) capable	D) accompanied
10) A) Taken	B) All	C) Somewhat	D) Thus
11) A) broadcasting	B) looking	C) blamed	D) ready
12) A) one	B) matter	C) difference	D) reason
13) A) known	B) even	C) described	D) such
14) A) refused	B) received	C) turned	D) kept
15) A) fault	B) reflection	C) situation	D) consciousness

2

Choose the most suitable word underlined.

a) Before the attack, planes dropped <u>brochures/leaflets</u> warning people to take cover.
b) We do not have the book in stock. It is <u>off the shelf/out of print</u>.
c) *Words* is the official <u>journal/magazine</u> of the Linguistics Association.
d) The *Sunday News* has the highest <u>circulation/output</u> of any newspaper in Britain.
e) They are bringing out Sue's book in a new <u>edition/publication</u> soon.
f) Are books subject to <u>banning/censorship</u> in your country?
g) Ted is in charge of the <u>stationary/stationery</u> cupboard in the office.
h) This page looks very crowded and I don't like the <u>outline/layout</u>.
i) Mass circulation newspapers usually specialise in <u>rumour/sensational</u> stories.
j) Don't include all the details. Just write a <u>summary/version</u> of what happened.

3

Match each word given with one of the descriptions.

---

an abbreviation   a draft   a manual   a royalty   a sponsor
a circular   an editorial   a preface   a rumour   a viewer

---

a) An article stating the policy of a newspaper.
b) Unofficial news which may have no basis in fact.
c) The introduction to a book written by the author.
d) A company which pays for a broadcast in return for advertising.
e) The payment made to an author for the number of books sold.

f) A book containing instructions for doing or using something.

g) The first version of a piece of writing.

h) A shorter way of writing a common phrase.

i) A leaflet delivered free to a large number of people.

j) A person who watches television.

4

Complete each sentence with one of the words given. Use each word once only.

> ban   claim   forecast   market   publish
> broadcast   cover   launch   publicise   tune in

a) Over a hundred journalists will .... the royal wedding next week.

b) The government has decided to .... the sale of this book.

c) Our company finds it difficult to .... products in that part of the world.

d) Don't forget to .... at this time next week for part two of the programme.

e) Both articles .... that the economy will recover by the end of the year.

f) Make sure you .... the rock concert well in advance.

g) The BBC intends to .... more programmes in Russian soon.

h) Both newspapers .... to be the first to have learned the news.

i) The company has decided to .... only paperbacks from now on.

j) We are going to .... the new product at a press conference next week.

5

Choose the most suitable word or phrase.

a) The journalist refused to disclose his .... to the judge.
   A) information   B) source   C) sponsor   D) article

b) Most people .... ice-cream with the summer.
   A) link   B) image   C) associate   D) remind

c) Mary hurriedly .... the message on a scrap of paper.
   A) jotted down   B) wrote up   C) scribbled away D) dashed off

d) The captain recorded all the details of the voyage in the ....
   A) tape recorder   B) notebook   C) handbook   D) log

e) If you can't pick up the BBC in the summer, try a different ....
   A) wavelength   B) broadcast   C) transmission   D) satellite

f) Some people feel that television should give less .... to sport.
   A) programmes   B) coverage   C) concern   D) involvement

g) If you can't find what you want in this chapter, look it up in the ....
   A) reference   B) index   C) catalogue   D) directory

h) This article will be continued in our next ....
   A) publication   B) page   C) issue   D) serial

i) Sally paid no attention, as she was completely .... in her book.
   A) engrossed   B) distracted   C) concentrated   D) dominated

j) Here is a report from our political ....
   A) journalist   B) editorial   C) correspondent D) bulletin

6

Complete each sentence, using one of the words given.

| fiction illiterate literature outline shorthand |
| gist illegible manuscript prose unprintable |

a) The first chapter is based on fact, but the rest of the book is complete ....

b) David was unable to read the postcard because the writing was ....

c) I understood the .... of the article, but I didn't read it in detail.

d) Brenda's comments were so insulting they were ....

e) Bill had decided to study French .... at university.

f) I managed to make notes of the speech in ....

g) Old Mrs Brown never went to school and is ....

h) Some people feel that Davis's .... is better than his poetry.

i) Sheila left the .... of her novel on a train by mistake.

j) Just tell me the .... of the story, don't go into too much detail.

7

Match the parts in a) to j) with the wholes in 1) to 10).

a) keyboard	1) serial
b) spine	2) library
c) episode	3) set
d) entry	4) book
e) editorial	5) notepad
f) character	6) newspaper
g) reference book	7) novel
h) sheet	8) word-processor
i) semi-colon	9) punctuation
j) screen	10) index

8

Complete each sentence with one of the words given. Use each word once only.

| broadcast bulletin coverage forecast media |
| brochure campaign edition manual novel |

a) Read the instruction .... before using your new word-processor.

b) *David Copperfield* is an autobiographical ....

c) What did it say on the weather ....?

d) This is a party political .... on behalf of the Always Right Party.

e) What time is the next news ....?

f) This channel doesn't have very good sports ....

g) A first .... of this book is worth a fortune.

h) The mass .... in most countries are dominated by advertising.

i) When does our new advertising .... begin?

j) I spent all of yesterday evening looking at this holiday ....

6 The Natural World

1

Choose the most suitable word for each space.

Whenever we read about the natural world nowadays, it is generally to be (1) .... dire predictions about its imminent destruction. Some scientists go so (2) .... as to assert that from now on, the world can no longer be called 'natural', insofar as future processes of weather, (3) ...., and all the interactions of plant and animal life will no longer carry on in their time-honoured way, unaffected by (4) .... There will never be such a thing as 'natural weather' again, say such writers, only weather (5) .... by global warming. It is hard to know whether to believe such (6) .... of doom, possibly because what they are saying seems too terrible to be (7) .... There are other equally influential scientists who argue that climate, for example, has changed many times over the (8) .... , and that what we are experiencing now may simply be part of an endless cycle of change, rather than a disaster on a global (9) .... One cannot help wondering whether these attempts to wish the problem away (10) .... underline the extent to which western industrialised countries are to blame for upsetting the world's (11) .... It is not our fault, they seem to be saying, because everything is all right, really! One certain (12) .... which is chilling in its implications, is that there is no longer anywhere on the earth's (13) .... , whether in the depths of the oceans or in the polar wastes, which is not (14) .... by polluted air or (15) .... with empty cans and bottles. Now we are having to come to terms with understanding just what that means, and it is far from easy.

1) A) made	B) given	C) told	D) granted
2) A) much	B) often	C) really	D) far
3) A) change	B) atmosphere	C) climate	D) even
4) A) beings	B) man	C) people	D) humans
5) A) built	B) manufactured	C) affected	D) organised
6) A) prophets	B) champions	C) warriors	D) giants
7) A) stopped	B) true	C) guessed	D) here
8) A) top	B) again	C) centuries	D) world
9) A) sense	B) form	C) scale	D) existence
10) A) simply	B) to	C) that	D) or
11) A) future	B) ecology	C) balance	D) population
12) A) fact	B) must	C) fault	D) and
13) A) planet	B) atmosphere	C) anywhere	D) surface
14) A) full	B) stained	C) breathing	D) only
15) A) even	B) recycled	C) littered	D) bothered

2

Choose the most suitable word underlined.

a) Could you close the window? There's a bit of a <u>current/draught</u>.

b) I'm soaked, I got caught in a <u>downpour/torrent</u>.

c) You'd better do some work in the garden, it's full of <u>herbs/weeds</u>.

d) The roads were packed with holidaymakers heading for the <u>coast/shore</u>.

e) I feel hungry. Could you <u>peel/skin</u> an apple for me?

f) Don't be afraid of the monkey, it's quite <u>tame/trained</u>.

g) That's an unusual dog. What <u>breed/race</u> is it?

h) Our country has many natural <u>resources/sources</u>.

i) Before you put those roses in a vase, cut the <u>stems/twigs</u> a bit.

j) We've had a very good <u>crop/production</u> of apples this year.

3

Match the words listed to the creature which which they are associated. Do not repeat the same word more than once.

nine lives	blind	flock	hole	ivory	lead	night	spray	kitten
tusks	bark	cheese	purr	honey	kennel	mane	paw	stable	trap
wing	bite	cub	hive	hoof	lamb	net	saddle	sting	trunk	wool

a) horse ....
b) bee ....
c) lion ....
d) mosquito ....
e) dog ....
f) sheep ....
g) elephant ....
h) mouse ....
i) bat ....
j) cat ....

4

Complete each sentence with one of the words given.

animal	domesticated	environmental	health	rare
artificial	endangered	extinct	pedigree	wild

a) Michael breeds .... cocker spaniels as a hobby.
b) We should make a distinction between wild and .... animals.
c) Some farms have stopped using .... fertilizers.
d) Many species of wildlife could become .... if left unprotected.
e) The gardens contain many kinds of .... plants.
f) Some vegetarians object to eating .... products of any kind.
g) The dolphin is one of many .... species.
h) More and more of my friends are eating so-called .... foods.
i) People are becoming more concerned about .... matters.
j) We're going up the mountainside to look for .... strawberries.

5

Choose the most suitable word or phrase.

a) We believe that these animals could be saved if our plan were ....
   A) adopted   B) taken up   C) practised   D) exploited
b) Local people are concerned about pollution from .... oil wells.
   A) maritime   B) sea-going   C) off-shore   D) coastline
c) Through my binoculars, I watched a tiger stalking its ....
   A) nourishment   B) adversary   C) culprit   D) prey
d) The .... from a nearby tree were scratching against the window.
   A) trunks   B) boughs   C) barks   D) twigs
e) Our city is very bare and doesn't have enough .... , I'm afraid.
   A) green   B) evergreens   C) greenness   D) greenery
f) The match had to be cancelled because of the severe ....
   A) ice   B) frost   C) snow   D) freezing
g) This spray is suitable for dealing with all garden ....
   A) pests   B) plagues   C) outbreaks   D) swarms
h) I was woken up by the sound of sheep .... in the meadow.
   A) neighing   B) crowing   C) bleating   D) croaking

i) My dog is a .... He's a cross between an alsatian and a setter.
    A) mongrel   B) mix-up   C) breed   D) transplant

j) As Jane came up the path, I could hear her feet crunching on the ....
    A) lawn   B) kerb   C) gravel   D) slates

6

Use a word from the list to complete each phrase. Do not use a word more than once.

| nest   pack   troop   shoal   swarm   flock   flight   herd |

a) a .... of sheep.   e) a .... of wolves
b) a .... of cattle   f) a .... of monkeys
c) a .... of bees   g) an ants' ....
d) a .... of fish   h) a .... of sparrows

7

Match each word or phrase a) to j) with one of the explanations 1) to 10).

a) a gale   1) a small river
b) a reptile   2) a place where a wild animal sleeps
c) a rainbow   3) a period when there is a shortage of water
d) a lair   4) a very strong wind
e) a drought   5) an animal which feeds its young with its own milk
f) a stream   6) a wild plant not wanted in the garden
g) an insect   7) a crawling animal such as a snake or lizard
h) a rodent   8) a small creature with no bones and six legs
i) a weed   9) an arch of colours that appears in the sky
j) a mammal   10) a small animal with very strong teeth

8

Choose the most appropriate word underlined.

a) Last year this tree was struck by lightning/thunder/a storm.
b) I like spring best, when the apple trees are in blooming/blossom/flowers.
c) Something must be done to protect wild/wilderness/wildlife.
d) When I want to relax, I go for a walk in the countryside/the nature/the outside.
e) In this part of the country, the earth/the land/the soil is quite expensive.
f) Suddenly we saw a ship appear on the atmosphere/horizon/sky. We were saved!
g) Most animals will attack you to protect their babies/litters/young.
h) Julia recently discovered a new category/make/species of fruit-fly.
i) We got soaked to the skin in the torrential drizzle/downpour/snow.
j) While I was eating cherries I accidentally swallowed a nut/pip/stone.

7 Education and Work

1

Choose the most suitable word given for each space in the text.

Have you ever asked yourself what you are working for? If you have ever had the time to (1) .... this taboo question, or put it to others in moments of weakness or confidentiality, you (2) .... well have heard some or all of the (3) .... It's the money of course, some say with a smile, as if explaining something to a small child. Or it's the satisfaction of (4) .... well done, the sense of achievement behind the clinching of an important (5) .... I worked as a bus conductor once, and I can't say I (6) .... the same as I staggered along the swaying gangway trying to (7) .... out tickets without falling over into someone's lap. It's the company of other people perhaps, but if that is the (8) .... , what about farmers? Is it the conversation in the farmyard that keeps them captivated by the job? Work is power and a sense of status say those (9) .... have either attained these elusive goals, or feel aggrieved that nobody has yet recognised their leadership (10) .... Or we can blame it all on someone else, the family or the taxman. I suspect, and I say this under my (11).............., that most of us work rather as Mr Micawber lived, hoping for something to (12) .... up. We'll win the pools, and tell the boss what we really think. We'll scrape together the (13) .... and open that little shop we always dreamed of, or go (14) .... the world, or spend more time in the garden. One day we'll get that (15).............we deserve, but until then at least we have something to do. And we are so busy doing it that we won't have time to wonder why.

1) A) propose	B) meditate	C) consider	D) launch
2) A) might	B) can	C) will	D) should
3) A) below	B) rest	C) following	D) latter
4) A) a work	B) a job	C) a task	D) an effort
5) A) deal	B) position	C) job	D) engagement
6) A) enjoyed	B) wished	C) hoped	D) felt
7) A) make	B) turn	C) issue	D) give
8) A) one	B) case	C) question	D) former
9) A) people	B) must	C) who	D) to
10) A) qualities	B) status	C) property	D) requirements
11) A) oath	B) suspicion	C) breath	D) pressure
12) A) move	B) turn	C) ease	D) end
13) A) resources	B) opportunities	C) rest	D) money
14) A) round	B) over	C) into	D) to
15) A) ambition	B) station	C) vocation	D) promotion

2

Choose the most appropriate word or words underlined.

a) The bookmaker was discussing the binding/odds/printing with a client.

b) Jim is a real craftsman and works on a boat/with his hands/for a low salary.

c) I had to call a plumber because my room was blacked out/flooded/cracked.

d) If you are selling your house, you'll need an advocate/a barrister/a solicitor.

e) Peter is an undertaker and goes to funerals/the stock exchange/the factory.

f) If you are an accountant you have to be good at figures/numbers/totals.

g) Sue is a lecturer at the local institute/secondary school/university.

h) We were married by my uncle, who was the local father/official/vicar.

i) If you're passing the vet's, could you collect my carpet/cat/licence?

j) Helen doesn't work for a company, she's freelance/liberated/unattached.

3

Complete each sentence with one of the words given. Use each word once only.

agent	competitor	executive	industrialist	producer
client	dealer	foreman	labourer	trainee

a) Nowadays you often find that the top .... in a company is a woman.

b) If you have any problems with your work, talk to the ....

c) 'Happy Chips' is the number one .... of potato crisps in the country.

d) I'm starting next week as a .... chef in a large hotel.

e) Our company is the .... for several large insurance companies.

f) David was not content until he had become a rich ....

g) Our firm is quite a long way ahead of our nearest ....

h) With mechanisation it is difficult to find work as an unskilled ....

i) I have been working as a used car .... for the past six months.

j) A company should make every .... feel important.

4
Choose the most suitable word or phrase given.

a) We're very busy this week. Can you work ....?

A) extra time   B) supplementary time   C) overtime   D) double time

b) I succeeded in my job through sheer hard ....

A) work   B) labour   C) industry   D) effort

c) Catherine works for a/an .... engineering company.

A) main   B) forefront   C) outgoing   D) leading

d) I'm thinking of changing my job because there are few .... of promotion.

A) prospects   B) opportunities   C) chances   D) sources

e) Bill has a real .... for looking after handicapped children.

A) career   B) post   C) inspiration   D) vocation

f) Ruth is looking for a new .... at the moment.

A) vacancy   B) appointment   C) condition   D) employment

g) I am well-qualified and have completed a .... in graphic design.

A) lesson   B) curriculum   C) course   D) timetable

h) In our company I am afraid there is very little .... to work hard.

A) inspiration   B) advantage   C) gain   D) motivation

i) The government is building a nuclear power .... not far from here.

A) works   B) factory   C) station   D) industry

j) It's not very interesting work, but at least it's a .... job.

A) regular   B) continuous   C) firm   D) steady

5
Complete each sentence with a word or compound word formed from the word in capitals.

a) Jack built his own boat in a .... in his garden. WORK

b) I don't have a job, so I'm living on............... benefit. EMPLOY

c) We can't .... with these low prices. COMPETITOR

d) Many pupils at............. school have already chosen a career. SECOND

e) This used to be a rural area but it has become .... INDUSTRY

f) .... in our factories is falling because of absenteeism. PRODUCE

g) You won't be paid much as a/an .... worker. SKILL

h) The government is encouraging............... in heavy industry. INVEST

i) Jim is very disorganised and not very .... BUSINESS

j) We would like details of your .... on this form. QUALIFY

6
Use one of the words given to identify the place in each sentence.

> factory garage market restaurant shop
> farm library office school university

a) Shop-floor personnel are required to wear protective clothing at all times.

b) Please proceed to registration after assembly.

c) Reference material should be returned to the check-out desk.
d) The yield per acre is up more than fifteen per cent.
e) Reservations can be accepted for groups of up to ten.
f) This seminar is compulsory and the essay will be part of your final assessment.
g) Profit margins on such retail items are minimal.
h) Dismantling of stalls is the responsibility of stall-holders.
i) One of your tasks will be to overhaul the filing system.
j) Change the filters and top up the battery.

7

Complete each sentence a) to j) with one of the endings 1) to 10).

a) Workers in the mining industry have decided to come out in ....
b) Union representatives pointed ....
c) The employers claim that working ....
d) Mr Johnson added that the decision ....
e) It is claimed that government privatisation plans mean that at least ....
f) The two sides have now reached ....
g) The minister said that the dispute ....
h) The meeting agreed that a vote ....
i) Nobody is yet certain whether or not ....
j) The arbitration service recommended that ....

1) .... to go on strike had not been taken lightly.
2) .... a thousand workers will become redundant.
3) .... shift workers should receive an increase of 6%.
4) .... out that industrial action was inevitable unless the management agreed.
5) .... the train-drivers' go-slow will disrupt commuter services.
6) .... agreement that there will be no more stoppages.
7) .... was not between the unions and the government.
8) .... sympathy with the train-drivers from tomorrow.
9) .... should be taken on whether to stop picketing the factory.
10) .... conditions have improved over the last two years.

8

Match the descriptions a) to j) with the explanations 1) to 10).

a) Jane was headhunted by a multinational company.
b) Pam is at the end of her tether.
c) Mary's assistant was given the sack.
d) Jean really has her nose to the grindstone.
e) Sue was given a golden handshake.
f) Helen took on a new secretary.
g) Ann is on the go all day.
h) Brenda was overlooked.
i) Judith has made good.
j) Pauline's boss keeps her on her toes.

1) She is always busy.
2) She doesn't have the chance to become complacent.
3) She's working hard.

4) She didn't get promoted.
5) She was offered a better job.
6) She has become successful.
7) She was dismissed.
8) She received a cash bonus on leaving her job.
9) She has run out of patience.
10) She gave someone a job.

8 Business and Money

1

Choose the most suitable word for each space.

Someone once described the age we live in as that of a vanishing world, one in which the familiar is constantly disappearing for ever and technological change is often difficult to (1) .... with. So it should come as no surprise to most of us to hear that yet another part of everyday life is (2) .... to go for ever. Still, when I read recently that within the next decade money as we (3) .... it will probably cease to exist in technologically advanced countries, I had to read the article twice to make sure it wasn't April 1st. (4) .... to Professor Gerry Montague of the Institute for Economic Reform, the familiar (5) .... and banknotes will soon be replaced entirely by credit cards of various kinds. And the shop of the future (the 'retail outlet' as Prof. Montague puts it) will be (6) .... directly to the network of banking computers. The assistant will simply key in your bank account code number and the (7) .... you have spent, and thank you politely. You won't have to dig deep in your (8) .... for change or pretend at the pub that you have left your money at home. You may not even have a number for your (9) .... as such, as the computer may by then be able to read your handprint. So no more credit card frauds (10) .... But I am afraid that I shall (11) .... money. I have felt strongly attached to it, ever since I received my first pocket money when I was five, and kept it in a money-box. Even if my credit card of the future will be able to tell me exactly how much (12) .... power I have left in the computer files, even if it lights up and plays a happy (or sad) tune at the same time, nothing will be able to replace the sheer pleasure I gained from (13) .... the coins in my money-box. Not to (14) .... the other obvious problems which will be caused by (15) .... of real money - like how to start a football match, for example!

1) A) keep B) manage C) cope D) survive
2) A) about B) almost C) ready D) tending
3) A) earn B) know C) use D) need
4) A) Thanks B) Contrary C) According D) Accustomed
5) A) banks B) coins C) change D) pence
6) A) taken B) alone C) responsible D) linked
7) A) money B) charge C) cost D) amount
8) A) pockets B) wallet C) cheque book D) cash
9) A) wealth B) savings C) account D) payment

196

10) A) arrested	B) either	C) stolen	D) however
11) A) miss	B) spend	C) waste	D) borrow
12) A) more	B) financial	C) economical	D) spending
13) A) rattling	B) withdrawing	C) estimating	D) throwing
14) A) tell	B) confront	C) guess	D) mention
15) A) a shortage	B) an expense	C) an absence	D) a replacement

2

In each sentence choose one or more appropriate words.

a) Harry gains/gets/makes over £20 000 a year.

b) Mary was awarded a grant/scholarship/subsidy to study child psychology.

c) How much did you give/pay/take for your new car?

d) Their house fetched/produced/sold for a lot more than they expected.

e) I'm going to the bank to get out/remove/withdraw the money for the rent.

f) The manager disappeared with the receipts/takings/wages from the concert.

g) By the time Kate retired she was a fortunate/prosperous/wealthy businesswoman.

h) We had a good holiday but it was rather costly/expensive/valuable.

i) We would appreciate it if you would close/settle/pay your bill as soon as possible.

j) Unfortunately the old painting I found turned out to be priceless/valueless/worthless.

3

Complete each sentence with one of the words given.

> account company enterprise market price
> claim currency figures payment venture

a) John became rich by playing the stock ....

b) We have decided to turn our business into a limited ....

c) This government believes firmly in the value of free ....

d) I am interested in buying the property, but I find the .... too high.

e) I am saving money to make the down .... on a new car.

f) We put in an insurance .... after our house was damaged in a storm.

g) Everyone was impressed with the sales .... for the new product.

h) Margaret lost a lot of money in an unwise business ....

i) I keep most of my money in a savings ....

j) Our company receives a lot of payments in foreign ....

4

Match each sentence a) to j) with a sentence from 1) to 10) which has a similar meaning.

a) We have to haggle.

b) We have a nice little nest-egg.

c) We have high expenditure.

d) We get in free.

e) We are in debt.

f) We are very thrifty.

g) We are paid on commission.

h) We want a rise.

i) We lend money.

j) We have a high income.

1) We spend a lot.

2) We don't waste money.

3) We let people borrow from us.

4) We earn according to what we sell.

5) We argue about the price.

6) We earn a lot.

7) We don't have to pay.

8) We need higher wages.

9) We owe money.

10) We have some savings.

5

Choose the most suitable word or phrase.

a) I inherited £10 000 in my uncle's ....
   A) legacy   B) inheritance C) will   D) testament

b) The .... price is always lower than the retail price.
   A) wholesale   B) bargaining C) cut   D) budget

c) I still have three more .... to pay on my motorbike.
   A) shares   B) donations   C) instalments D) contributions

d) We had to give the customs official a .... not to inspect our suitcases.
   A) fee   B) reward   C) bonus   D) bribe

e) After my business failed, I was declared .... by the court.
   A) profitless   B) bankrupt   C) insignificant D) uneconomical

f) As soon as you buy a car, it starts falling in ....
   A) cost   B) worth   C) value   D) price

g) A multinational company has made a/an .... to take over our firm.
   A) bid   B) venture   C) investment D) estimate

h) We demanded pay rises to take account of the .... of inflation.
   A) figures   B) percentage C) price   D) rate

i) Things are going well. In fact, business is ....
   A) soaring   B) booming   C) leaping   D) rolling

j) I .... you don't make as much profit this year!
   A) assure   B) challenge C) bet   D) doubt

6

Replace the words underlined by one of the words given.

| agenda | chair | expense | handle | takings |
| bargain | charge | fortune | income | unavailable |

a) Sheila made a <u>lot of money</u> selling used cars.

b) When Mark took his new job, his <u>earnings</u> nearly doubled.

c) The <u>cost</u> of moving house was another problem for us.

d) We need someone else to <u>be in charge of</u> the meeting.

e) I am afraid this product is temporarily <u>out of stock</u>.

f) We usually count the <u>money we have made</u> when the shop closes.

g) Do you like my new dress? It was a <u>very good price</u>.

h) We don't <u>deal with</u> goods of that kind in this company.

i) Don't forget to draw up the <u>list of items to be discussed</u> for the next meeting.

j) We make no <u>request for payment</u> for delivery in the London area.

7

Replace the phrase underlined in each sentence with one of the phrases given. Do not use any phrase more than once.

challenged the figures	financial means	make a wise investment
come into a fortune	free of charge	on easy terms
commercially viable	in credit	on expenses	on the market

a) We've decided to put our house <u>up for sale</u>.

b) Jean has <u>inherited a lot of money</u>.

c) At the meeting Peter <u>said he thought the amounts were wrong.</u>

d) No one believes that the shop will ever be <u>a business success</u>.

e) I am <u>the possessor of a healthy balance</u> at the bank.

f) Sue and Jane went to S America <u>with everything paid for by their company</u>.

g) We don't believe you have the <u>money</u> to take over this company.

h) All employees can stay at the hotel <u>without paying</u>.

i) We bought our new electric cooker <u>by instalments</u>.

j) Harry became rich after he managed to <u>put his money in the right place</u>.

8

In each sentence, replace one or more words with one of the words given, so that the sentence has an opposite meaning.

> appreciate hard up prosperous rise wasteful
> dear make purchase squander worthless

a) The precious stones our company mines are now known to be priceless.

b) Nigel cannot get used to being an unsuccessful businessman.

c) The company has decided the sell the premises in East Road.

d) I like living in this part of town. Of course, it's very cheap!

e) Jim inherited £20 000 and managed to save it all.

f) We were poor when I was young and my father was very thrifty.

g) At the moment house values tend to go down in this area.

h) The workers were given a cut in wages when the takeover was announced.

i) Nobody thought that the company would lose a lot of money.

j) Richard's family is incredibly well-off.

9 People and Relationships

1

Choose the most suitable word for each space.

If cartoons are anything to go by, then the attitude of the British towards the family, and of British men towards the (1) .... sex, has not changed much recently, despite (2) .... to shame people into admitting their prejudices. The mother-in-law, frequently of horrific (3) .... , and usually either about to visit, or being somehow driven from the house, is still a favourite butt of this kind of (4) .... Marriage itself has been reduced to the skinny male, dominated by a massive female who habitually lies in (5) .... with the rolling pin behind the door for the return of her drunken (6) ....
Children are rarely shown other than as screaming infants, or else as ill-favoured urchins who (7) .... all their time being objectionable or asking for money. The old are simply (8) .... as comic characters. The problem is, how do such cartoons relate to the way people truly see each other? Does a joke always (9) .... some grain of truth, however much we may dislike to admit it? (10) .... other words, is life really a series of mother-in-law jokes? Or do jokes have a life of their own, with a (11) .... of stereotypes we can recognise, (12) .... the Englishman with his umbrella and bowler hat, or the Frenchman with his striped jumper and beret? According to this (13) .... of thinking, we laugh at the stereotype, although we know really that it does not represent real life. Personally, I feel that many of these cartoon prejudices have outlived their usefulness, if they ever had (14) .... They may give us a chance to laugh at situations we know we should not be laughing at, but it seems more (15) .... that they strengthen our prejudices.

1) A) other	B) problematic	C) opposite	D) taboo
2) A) attempts	B) trying	C) of	D) often
3) A) sight	B) view	C) appearance	D) dress
4) A) person	B) type	C) category	D) humour
5) A) bed	B) wait	C) the way	D) the end
6) A) spouse	B) opposite	C) colleague	D) groom
7) A) waste	B) spend	C) take	D) pass
8) A) seen	B) such	C) enough	D) notorious
9) A) suppose	B) achieve	C) imply	D) contain
10) A) With	B) As	C) From	D) In
11) A) one	B) set	C) life	D) base
12) A) as	B) example	C) like	D) take
13) A) way	B) in spite	C) approach	D) subject
14) A) this	B) one	C) any	D) been
15) A) so	B) interesting	C) over	D) likely

2
Choose the most suitable word underlined.

a) Let me introduce you to my <u>betrothed/engaged/fiancée.</u> We're getting married next month.

b) Jim is just a/an <u>acquaintance/colleague/figure</u> I met on holiday.

c) The playground was full of <u>infants/juveniles/toddlers</u> running about and falling over.

d) As I am officially a/an <u>alien/outsider/stranger</u> I have to register with the police.

e) Local people are campaigning for better facilities for the <u>aged/ancient/elder</u> .

f) Our <u>ancestors/descendants/predecessors</u> are all buried in the local churchyard.

g) Peter is 50 and unmarried and his friends call him 'an eligible <u>bachelor/independent/single</u>'.

h) The bridegroom was handed the ring by the <u>assistant groom/best man/godfather</u>.

i) When I was a <u>bloke/chap/lad</u> I used to walk ten miles to school.

j) We call her 'Auntie Flo', though she is not really any <u>family/relation/relative</u> to us.

3
Complete each sentence with one of the words given. Do not use a word more than once.

| aggressive | attentive | devoted | insensitive | solitary |
| apathetic | conscientious | extrovert | mature | prejudiced |

a) Sharon works very hard and is extremely ....

b) David does everything alone. He is a rather .... person.

c) What a lovely couple! They seem absolutely ....

d) Jim has extreme views, and is .... against all immigrants.

e) Very few students wanted to join in the activities. They seemed rather ....

f) Simon is always getting into fights, he's so ....

g) Jane may look rather young, but she has a very .... attitude.

h) Pauline is a good teacher, and very .... to the needs of the students.

i) Bill is shy but his brother Mike is more ....

j) Mary doesn't realise how she hurts people. She is really ....

4

Rewrite each sentence so that it contains the word in capitals, and has the same meaning. Do not change the word in any way.

a) Jenny and Kate grew up happily.   UPBRINGING

b) When he was small Jim used to collect stamps.   AS

....

c) If children don't get affection, it is harmful.   LACK

....

d) I can't understand the way football hooligans think.   MENTALITY

e) Was she offended by what I said?   TAKE

....

f) Sue very closely resembles her mother.   ALIKE

....

g) Everybody in the office likes Harry.   POPULAR

h) Janet hasn't got married yet.   SINGLE

....

i) Graham spends all his time working.   DEVOTED

....

j) Michael and Elaine are very friendly.   CLOSE

....

5

Choose the most suitable word or phrase.

a) From an early age, Wolfgang had a/an .... for music.
    A) interest   B) passion   C) involvement   D) tendency

b) Larry never spoke to anyone, and kept himself ....
    A) outside   B) withdrawn   C) superior   D) aloof

c) Sarah delivered a/an .... appeal to the court and asked for mercy.
    A) sensational   B) sentimental   C) emotional   D) affectionate

d) When I gave her the present, my mother .... with satisfaction.
    A) beamed   B) grinned   C) giggled   D) guffawed

e) In answer to my question, my sister .... in agreement.
    A) shook   B) grimaced   C) wriggled   D) nodded

f) After my uncle's death, my aunt remained a/an .... for only a few months before remarrying.
    A) in-law   B) widow   C) single   D) bride

g) I can't tell Peter and Paul apart; they are .... twins.
    A) similar   B) alike   C) resemblance   D) identical

h) Many people consider that the .... of marriage is under threat.
    A) institution   B) constitution   C) attribution   D) restitution

i) After the accident, the police informed the victim's next of ....
    A) relation   B) blood   C) kin   D) generation

j) I'm sorry I snapped at you like that, but I'm in a bad ....
    A) mind   B) mood   C) mentality   D) manner

6

Complete each sentence with one of the words given.

| abandoned criticised neglected quarrelled separated |
| adopted humiliated offended retired scolded |

a) Keith's parents .... him badly when he was a baby.
b) The small child was being .... by its mother for getting dirty.
c) Tom deeply .... Ann by ignoring her at the party.
d) David is not my real father, I was .... by him when I was small.
e) Ian and Fiona are .... and they may get divorced.
f) I .... with my boyfriend but we made it up in the end.
g) Jack .... on his 65th birthday and received his pension.
h) My parents .... me for having a ring in my nose.
i) Julie's mother .... her when she was a few months old and she grew up in an orphanage.
j) My boss utterly .... me in front of important clients so I resigned.

7

Replace the words underlined with one of the phrases given. Do not use any phrase more than once.

| fell out   turned him down   moved in with   got on well with   kept in touch with |
| ran away from   got to know   let him down   grew up   went out together |

a) When Brian asked her to marry him, Ann <u>said no</u>.
b) I <u>communicated regularly with</u> most of my old friends.
c) Ann <u>spent her childhood years</u> in London.
d) David and Jean <u>dated</u> for three months before they got engaged.
e) Kate <u>quarrelled</u> with her boyfriend and they stopped seeing each other.
f) Helen <u>had a good relationship with</u> her in-laws.
g) Harry <u>left</u> home <u>without his parents' permission</u>.
h) Sophia promised to meet Michael after work but <u>disappointed him</u>.
i) After a few weeks I <u>went to live in the house of</u> some friends.
j) I <u>grew friendly with</u> Pam when we worked together.

8

Match each expression a) to j) with one of the explanations 1) to 10).

a) nearest and dearest
b) newlyweds
c) the nuclear family
d) adults
e) a community

f) a generation
g) contemporaries
h) the extended family
i) a household
j) outcasts

1) people who are alive at the same time or eg attend the same school
2) people who have only recently been (or are still) on their honeymoon
3) all the people of approximately the same age
4) the people in a family who live together under the same roof
5) the entire range of relatives in one family
6) all the people living together in the same area
7) a person (or people) from your immediate family
8) people who are no longer teenagers
9) people abandoned by their families or by society in general
10) parents and their children

10 Social Problems

1

Choose the most
suitable word for
each space.

Ask most people for their list of Top Ten fears, and you'll be sure to find (1).............. burgled fairly high on the list. An informal survey I carried out among friends at a party last week revealed that eight of them had had their homes (2) .... into more than twice, and two had been burgled five times. To put the record straight, (3) .... of my friends owns valuable paintings or a sideboard full of family silverware. Three of them are students, in fact. The most typical (4) .... , it seems, involves the (5) .... of easily transportable items – the television, the video, even food from the freezer. This may have something to do with the (6) .... that the average burglar is in his (or her) late teens, and probably wouldn't know (7) .... to do with a Picasso, whereas selling a Walkman or a vacuum cleaner is a much easier (8) .... They are perhaps not so (9) .... professional criminals, as hard-up young people who need a few pounds and some excitement. (10) .... that this makes having your house turned upside down and your favourite things stolen any easier to (11) .... In most cases, the police have no luck (12) .... any of the stolen goods. Unless there is any definite (13)............. , they are probably unable to do anything at all. And alarms or special locks don't seem to help either. The only advice my friends could (14) .... was 'Never live on the ground floor' and 'Keep two or three very fierce dogs', which reminded me of a case I read about, where the burglars' (15) .... included the family's pet poodle.

1) A) been	B) having	C) being	D) out
2) A) robbed	B) broken	C) taken	D) entered
3) A) none	B) some	C) all	D) few
4) A) burglary	B) item	C) one	D) invariably
5) A) carrying	B) robbing	C) example	D) theft
6) A) information	B) fact	C) idea	D) knowledge
7) A) where	B) how	C) what	D) whatever
8) A) matter	B) price	C) event	D) one
9) A) many	B) much	C) that	D) rarely
10) A) Given	B) So	C) Not	D) Despite
11) A) believe	B) accept	C) do	D) attempt
12) A) taking	B) about	C) tracking	D) recovering
13) A) case	B) burglary	C) investigation	D) evidence
14) A) come up with	B) get by with	C) bring up with	D) put in with
15) A) takings	B) profit	C) loot	D) receipts

2

Choose the most
appropriate word
underlined.

a) The police arrested Jack and took him into <u>custody/detention/prison</u>.
b) In most countries, the <u>capital/death/execution</u> penalty has been abolished.
c) A man is said to be helping the police with their <u>arrests/detection/inquiries</u>.
d) The judge in the court was wearing a <u>hairpiece/head-dress/wig</u>.
e) Two football fans were later charged with <u>aggression/assault/attack</u>.

f) Less serious cases are dealt with in the <u>criminal/juvenile/magistrate's</u> court.

g) I was given a light sentence because it was my first <u>case/charge/offence</u>.

h) A patrol car stopped me because I was <u>racing/running/speeding</u> in a built-up area.

i) The case was dismissed for lack of <u>evidence/a jury/witnesses</u>.

j) 'Members of the jury, what is your <u>answer/summary/verdict</u>?'

3

Complete each sentence with one of the words given.

| blocked failed held skidded sustained |
| evacuated fired met spread tripped |

a) She suffered the injury after she .... over a toy left on the stairs.

b) Throughout the flooded area, villages are being .... by helicopter.

c) The terrorists threatened to kill their hostages if their demands were not ....

d) Several buildings .... damage from the earthquake.

e) Trees were uprooted and many roads were ....

f) The two trains collided after one .... to stop at signals.

g) Rescue teams .... out little hope of finding other survivors.

h) The blaze rapidly .... to neighbouring buildings.

i) Police .... tear-gas in an attempt to disperse the mob.

j) The coach .... on an icy patch and overturned.

4

Complete each sentence with a word or compound word formed from the word in capitals.

a) Many .... people sleep on the streets of the capital.   HOME

b) Drug .... is a problem causing great concern.   ADDICT

c) .... creates hardship for all members of the family.   EMPLOY

d) We feel that the laws against begging should not be ....   FORCE

e) Police arrested well-known .... before the match.   TROUBLE

f) It seems unjust to arrest a poor old person for ....   SHOP

g) Dr Smith, a .... , has published two books about murder.   CRIME

h) The inquiry was set up after the .... of a train near Leeds, the third accident on the line this year.   RAIL

i) Some MPs are calling for the introduction of .... without trial to combat terrorism.   DETAIN

j) The judge described Jones as a '............... criminal' who was a danger to members of the public.   HARD

5

Choose the most suitable word or phrase.

a) All the classroom windows were broken, but nobody knew who the .... was.
   A) victim   B) culprit   C) guilty   D) responsible

b) Seven vehicles were involved in a .... in thick fog on the M2.
   A) jam   B) congestion   C) stoppage   D) pile-up

c) Mr Baxwell threatened to .... the newspaper for libel.
   A) sue   B) arrest   C) blackmail   D) enforce

d) Police have .... off the town centre and are searching for the bomb.
   A) withdrawn   B) surrounded   C) sealed   D) assembled

e) The death .... in the weekend's traffic exodus has risen to sixteen.
   A) score   B) rate   C) toll   D) mark

f) After the collision, two seamen were slightly injured in the.............. explosion.
   A) following   B) ensuing   C) aftermath   D) consequential
g) The police are concentrating on arresting drug.............. rather than casual users.
   A) traffickers   B) agents   C) merchants   D) entrepreneurs
h) The railway station was full of .... asking passengers for money.
   A) wanderers   B) beggars   C) penniless   D) petitioners
i) More than £100 000 went up in .... in a fire at Bingley's Bank.
   A) burns   B) ashes   C) soot   D) smoke
j) The whole building collapsed, but fortunately there were no ....
   A) wounded   B) hurt   C) casualties   D) victims

6
Complete each sentence by putting *one* or *two* suitable prepositions in each space.

a) The new law on dropping litter comes .... force next month.
b) Ann was released from prison and now she is .... probation.
c) Local students have been banned .... taking part in the demonstration.
d) The police have charged her .... driving without due care and attention.
e) Local people have called for an investigation .... the causes of the fire.
f) Football fans went .... the rampage in the centre of Norwich last night.
g) She claimed that the selling of habit-forming drugs was getting .... control.
h) The car left the road and crashed .... a tree.
i) Several guests at the hotel were robbed .... jewellery and money.
j) David, 19, has been sleeping .... a park bench for the past six months.

7
Replace the words underlined in each sentence with one of the words given.

| abolished deported neglected rioted swerved |
| cheated dispersed pardoned squatted swindled |

a) At the end of the demonstration, the crowd <u>went off in different directions</u> peacefully.
b) The problem is that the government has <u>not done anything about</u> this problem.
c) It turned out that the employees had been <u>cheated</u> out of their pensions by their employer.
d) Hundreds of young people <u>ran out of control</u> in the streets, looting shops.
e) Dave was <u>officially released from his punishment</u> after the police discovered new evidence.
f) Brian was an illegal alien, and when the police caught him he was <u>made to leave the country.</u>
g) Jim and Sue <u>lived illegally without paying rent</u> in a house in East London for two years.
h) Jane was asked to leave the examination after she <u>acted dishonestly</u> and was caught.
i) Capital punishment was <u>brought to an end</u> several years ago in this country.
j) The bus <u>turned suddenly</u> to avoid a pedestrian, and crashed into a wall.

8
Beside each problem a) to j), write the best solution from 1) to 10).

Problems	The authorities should:
a) high unemployment	1) introduce tougher measures to control crowds.
b) homelessness	2) reduce speed limits.
c) drug addiction	3) retrain anyone made redundant.
d) football hooliganism	4) encourage retailers to use closed-circuit television.
e) road accidents	5) clamp down on traffickers and dealers.
f) deaths from smoking	6) increase the number of local foot patrols.
g) petty crime	7) provide more hostels and cheap accommodation.
h) accidents in the home	8) mount a campaign to educate parents and children.
i) shoplifting	9) raise taxes to discourage people from doing this.
j) vandalism of public property	10) make the culprits repair the damage they cause.

11 Arts and Entertainment

1
Choose the most suitable word for each space.

Until the early part of this century there was certainly a distinction between popular music, the songs and dance (1) .... of the masses, and what we have come to call (2) .... music. Up to that point, however, there were at least some points of contact (3) .... the two, and perhaps general recognition of what made a good voice, or a good song. With the development of (4) .... entertainment, popular music split away and and has gradually (5) .... a stronger life of its (6) .... , to the point where it has become incompatible with (7) .... classics. In some respects, it is now dominated by the (8) .... of youth culture, so that a concert by Elton John is just as much a fashion (9) ...., and other artists may be promoting dance styles, or social (10) .... For this reason, it is impossible to talk about popular music as if it were a unified art. The kind of music you like may (11) .... on what kind of person you are. Curiously, there are now classical musicians and operatic singers who have (12) .... the status of rock stars, and have been marketed in the same way. This seems to suggest that many young people enjoy classical music but do not wish to be associated with the (13) .... of those who are traditionally supposed to enjoy it. Or it may simply be that recording companies have discovered that there is an insatiable (14) .... for 'sounds', and that classical music is beginning to sound exciting to a generation (15) .... on rock but now settling into affluent middle-age.

1) A) halls   B) tunes   C) musicians   D) artists
2) A) rock   B) modern   C) underground   D) classical
3) A) with   B) between   C) by   D) of

	A)	B)	C)	D)
4)	mass	live	recorded	the
5)	founded	lived	developed	suggested
6)	supporters	self	fans	own
7)	other	the	some	further
8)	promotion	discovery	tendency	survival
9)	as	however	event	design
10)	service	grace	protest	science
11)	depend	identify	suppose	be
12)	lost	admired	penetrated	achieved
13)	number	dislike	lifestyle	meaning
14)	desire	sale	interest	outlet
15)	raised	carrying	dependent	listening

2

Choose the most appropriate word underlined.

a) Everyone clapped enthusiastically when the actors came on screen/stage.

b) Most critics agree that Celia gave the best acting/performance.

c) It was a very long play so there were three interludes/intervals.

d) Jean has decided to join an amateur dramatic/theatrical society.

e) It was a good film, and I thought Nick Nolte acted/played really well.

f) There was so much suspense that I was kept on the edge of my place/seat.

g) The leading lady unfortunately lost her voice during the dress/stage rehearsal.

h) Most modern plays don't need a lot of complicated scenery/scenes.

i) I thought it was a good film but it got terrible critics/reviews.

j) Quite honestly, I haven't much time for horror/horrific films.

3

Match each person with one of the descriptions.

acrobat	cast	conductor	juggler	understudy
ballerina	clown	director	stuntman	vocalist

a) someone who makes people laugh at the circus

b) someone who tells actors what to do

c) someone who sings

d) someone who is a member of this is an actor

e) someone who entertains others by throwing and catching things

f) someone who entertains others by performing gymnastics

g) someone who takes an actor's place in an emergency

h) someone who tells an orchestra what to do

i) someone who performs dangerous actions in place of an actor

j) someone who dances gracefully in a leading role

4

Complete each sentence with one of the words given.

brass	chorus	lyrics	organ	string	choir
concert	opera	percussion	woodwind		

a) I went to a rock .... held in a large football stadium.

b) The .... section of the orchestra needs a new violinist.

c) Marianne had a good voice and joined the school ....

d) Keith wanted to learn a .... instrument so took up the clarinet.

e) Their music is really great, but I can't understand the ....

f) As we entered the church, the .... began playing a solemn tune.

g) I used to play the trumpet in the local .... band.

h) You need a good voice and acting ability to perform in a/an ....

i) I'll sing the first verse, and everyone will join in for the ....

j) Nowadays it is possible to simulate most .... instruments electronically, so drums are not always needed.

5

Choose the most suitable word or phrase.

a) The play is full of very .... remarks made by the main character.
   A) hilarious   B) witty   C) comic   D) jolly

b) I bought a new stereo but I didn't have enough money for new ....
   A) echoes   B) announcers   C) speakers   D) megaphones

c) Pauline's play has been .... in the West End for the past year.
   A) playing   B) acting   C) producing   D) running

d) Reggae used to be popular but it's a bit .... fashion at the moment.
   A) out of   B) away from   C) beyond   D) outside

e) I watched the match on television but the .... got on my nerves.
   A) commentator   B) announcer   C) director   D) describer

f) Diane is going to the studio to .... one of her old songs.
   A) write   B) transcribe   C) preserve   D) record

g) I can't understand this song. It doesn't make any ....
   A) meaning   B) effort   C) sense   D) realisation

h) The star of the circus was a/an .... seal, which did incredible tricks.
   A) acting   B) performing   C) playing   D) dramatic

i) The play was put on in the .... air, in one of the London parks.
   A) natural   B) open   C) country   D) fresh

j) Nigel Kennedy, the .... violinist, will perform at the concert.
   A) known   B) recognised   C) defamed   D) celebrated

6

Match each activity given with one of the sentences a) to j).

billiards	cards	darts	jigsaw puzzle	television
board game	chess	draughts	table tennis	video

a) If you look at the picture on the box it's easier to decide where the pieces go.

b) Whenever you deal you seem to get at least three aces.

c) The white ball hit the red ball and went into the corner pocket.

d) I managed to take all of his pieces in one move! I swept the board!

e) The picture keeps flickering. It must be the vertical hold.

f) Throw the dice twice and then pick up a card from the middle.

g) The bulls-eye is worth fifty, but it's a bit hard to hit.

h) If the ball hits the net when you serve, it doesn't count.

i) You can easily put her in check next move with your queen.

j) Don't forget to wind it back when it finishes and put it back in the box.

7

Complete each sentence with a preposition.

a) The clowns walked into the ring .... stilts, looking about three metres tall!

b) The stadium was packed .... people for the athletics meeting.

c) Janet holds the world record .... long distance cycling.

d) During the match, a message came .... the loudspeakers.

e) There is a craze .... skateboarding at the moment.

f) Harry last appeared .... the role of King Lear at the National Theatre.

g) Have you got any tickets left .... the front stalls, please?

h) Alex accompanied Helen's singing .... the piano.

i) The play was so bad that the actors were booed .... the stage.

j) David challenged Cathy .... a game of chess.

8

Choose the most suitable word underlined.

a) The audience enjoyed the play so much that they clapped aloud/heavily/loudly.

b) Our team won, but the match was not very amusing/enjoyed/entertaining.

c) At the end of the concert the audience gave the conductor a/an applauding/cheering/standing ovation.

d) The orchestra tried hard, but several members were quite out of breath/music/tune.

e) Everyone watching the trapeze-artist was clapping/crying/gasping with admiration.

f) The clown was so funny that he had everyone in applause/in laughter/in stitches.

g) The group's performance was really dreadful and the audience clucked/hissed/screamed and booed at the end.

h) Nick Turton, as Iago, gave a particularly illegible/inept/unable performance.

i) Some of the sketches were amusing, but I am afraid that most of the jokes fell flat/foul/short.

j) At the end of the musical, the entire audience boomed/broke/burst into applause.

12 Government and Society

1

Choose the most suitable word for each space.

Viewed from the outside at least, the Houses of Parliament give a firm impression of all those (1) .... which we are supposed to value in the British form of government. The architecture gives the place a (2) .... look, and the buildings are sandwiched between a busy square and the river, with Westminster Abbey not far away, making them a (3) .... between the country house of an eccentric duke and a Victorian railway station. You have only to learn that the (4) .... refer to each other as 'The Honourable Member for So and So' to complete the picture of a dignified gentlemen's club, with of course a few ladies to (5) .... the numbers. Sadly, over the past few years first radio, and now television, have shown the general (6) ...., who are after all the electorate, what in fact goes on when bills are (7) .... and questions are asked. The first obvious fact is that the chamber is very rarely full, and there may be only a (8) .... of members present, some of (9) .... are quite clearly asleep, telling jokes to their neighbour, or engaged in shouting like badly-behaved schoolchildren. There is not enough (10) .... for them all in the chamber in any case, which is a second worrying point. Of course, television does not follow the work of (11) .... which are the small discussion groups that do most of the real work of the House. But the (12)........... impression that we as (13) .... receive of the workings of government is not a good one. To put it bluntly, parliament looks disorganised, is clearly behind the times and seems to be (14) .... with bores and comedians. This is presumably why members resisted for so long the efforts of the BBC to broadcast parliamentary (15) .... on television.

1) A) views	B) appearances	C) identities	D) features
2) A) fashionable	B) traditional	C) close-up	D) notorious
3) A) mixture	B) combination	C) cross	D) match
4) A) members	B) candidates	C) delegates	D) senators
5) A) take away	B) bring about	C) make up	D) set in
6) A) situation	B) public	C) interest	D) rule
7) A) paid	B) determined	C) voted	D) discussed
8) A) handful	B) majority	C) few	D) number
9) A) these	B) whom	C) them	D) others
10) A) seats	B) places	C) room	D) around
11) A) elections	B) those	C) everyone	D) committees
12) A) overall	B) visual	C) positive	D) striking
13) A) audience	B) often	C) voters	D) well
14) A) working	B) inevitably	C) filled	D) much
15) A) matters	B) committees	C) speeches	D) debates

2

Choose the most appropriate word underlined.

a) By the early evening, most people had administered/cast/selected their votes.

b) The government has decided to hold/introduce/organise an early election.

c) Voting for strike action must be done by secret ballot/electorate/poll.

d) Each member of parliament represents a specific candidate/constituency/convention.

e) Before the election, each party published its election brochure/manifesto/synopsis.

f) Mark Brown has been delegated/nominated/represented for the post of honorary treasurer.

g) It's impossible to predict which way the election will go because there are so many indefinite/undecided/unknowing voters.

h) My sister has decided to candidate/put in/stand for parliament in the next election.

i) The party's election campaign/movement/struggle proved to be successful.

j) The National Party won the election with an increased majority/percentage/score.

3

Complete each sentence with one of the words given. Do not use a word more than once.

| administration bill council motion power |
| authorities cabinet mayor poll reign |

a) Mr Bill Bradford has been elected .... of Greenswold for the third time.
b) The government has introduced a .... outlining its plans for the coal industry.
c) Mrs Fletcher has wide experience of .... , having previously been head of a large school in Bristol.
d) According to the latest opinion .... , the National Party are well ahead of their nearest rivals, the Cooperative Party.
e) Although there is an elected assembly, it is generally recognised that General Domenico wields the real ....
f) There is a locally elected .... which has responsibility for roads, street lighting, and other facilities.
g) The king enjoyed a long .... , and was eventually succeeded by his son, George.
h) The .... were slow to take control of the situation after the earthquake.
i) The Leader of the Opposition proposed a .... of no confidence in the government.
j) Members of the .... have a meeting with the Prime Minister each week.

4

Replace the word or words underlined with one of the words given. Do not use a word more than once.

| abolished binding illegal permitted restricted |
| barred compulsory licensed required voluntary |

a) The proprietor is <u>officially allowed</u> to sell alcohol.
b) The sale of drugs is <u>controlled by law</u> in most countries.
c) Education from the age of five is <u>obligatory</u> in Britain.
d) Students have been <u>banned</u> from using local pubs since the incident.
e) The law prohibiting the sale of fruit in the street has been <u>done away with</u>.
f) For both parties to the agreement, the terms of this contract are <u>to be obeyed</u>.
g) With the application, a passport-sized photograph is <u>necessary</u>.
h) Smoking is not <u>allowed</u> in the classroom.
i) You don't have to stay after school to help; it's <u>your own decision</u>.
j) Parking in this street is <u>not allowed</u> on weekdays at certain times.

5

Choose the most suitable word or phrase.

a) The minister has .... new proposals for discussion with the union.
A) made out B) set down C) drawn up D) worked in
b) The Prime Minister stated that law and order must be .... at all costs.
A) maintained B) imposed C) suppressed D) conveyed
c) Mr Jackson challenged the government as to who exactly was .... the country.
A) reigning B) ministering C) administrating D) running
d) Union leaders called for .... between themselves and the government.
A) speeches B) elections C) debates D) consultations
e) The chairman asked the secretary to take the .... of the meeting.
A) minutes B) discussions C) rulings D) notes

f) The generals .... the country in a lightning coup d'état.
   A) overwhelmed   B) took over   C) ran over   D) overruled

g) The minister has a talent for talking to ordinary people as if they were her ....
   A) level   B) fellows   C) counterparts   D) equals

h) There are so many rules and .... about importing food that you need to consult a good lawyer.
   A) laws   B) regulations   C) licences   D) orders

i) A politician always needs to protect his or her ....
   A) notoriety   B) publicity   C) reputation   D) rumour

j) Parliament has now .... a law making skateboarding illegal on Sundays.
   A) passed   B) legislated   C) voted   D) billed

6
Match the words and phrases in a) to j) with the explanations in 1) to 10).

a) civil disobedience   f) a radical
b) a conformist   g) self-determination
c) a dictatorship   h) the establishment
d) the head of state   i) a licence
e) middle of the road   j) the civil service

1) If you are this, then technically you rule the country.
2) If you are one of these, you believe in complete political change.
3) If you are this, you like to behave in the same way as everyone else.
4) This consists of powerful people and organisations who support the social order.
5) This is an organised campaign involving breaking the law.
6) You might need one of these to get married, to drive, or to ... a gun.
7) This is the right for people to decide about their future for themselves, rather than let a colonial power do it for them.
8) If you live under one of these, then you live in a state controlled by one powerful person.
9) If you are this, you have no strong political opinions.
10) the various departments of the government

7
Complete each sentence with one of the words given.

> conventional   diplomatic   oppressed   progressive   rebellious
> courteous   formal   privileged   reactionary   respectable

a) If you are .... , you are tactful when dealing with people.
b) If you are .... , you have a good reputation in your community.
c) If you are .... , you are polite.
d) If you are .... , you are strongly against any kind of change.
e) If you are .... , you are being ruled unjustly or cruelly.
f) If you are .... , you behave just like everyone else, perhaps too much so.
g) If you are .... , you are against authority and hard to control.
h) If you are .... , you have more advantages than other people.
i) If you are .... , you like to follow social rules and customs on certain occasions.
j) If you are .... , you are in favour of new ideas.

8

Match the words given to the explanations.

ambassador	delegate	patriot	ringleader	terrorist
chairperson	minister	president	sovereign	traitor

a) This person may be the elected head of state.
b) This person is responsible for a government department.
c) This person leads others to make trouble.
d) This person represents their country abroad.
e) This person loves their country.
f) This person represents others at a meeting or conference.
g) This person betrays their country.
h) This person may be the head of state by birth.
i) This person uses violence rather than the political system for political ends.
j) This person is the head of a formal meeting.

13 Health and the Body

1

Choose the most suitable word for each space.

Keeping fit and staying healthy have, not surprisingly, become a growth industry. (1) .... apart from the amount of money spent each year on doctors' (2) .... and approved medical treatment, huge sums are now spent on health foods and (3) .... of various kinds, from vitamin pills to mineral water, not to mention health clubs and keep-fit (4) .... and videos. We are more concerned than ever, it seems, (5) .... the water we drink and the air we breathe, and are smoking less, though not yet drinking less alcohol. This does not appear to mean that (6) .... and sneezes have been banished, or that we can all expect to live to a hundred. To give a personal example, one of my friends, who is a keep-fit (7) .... , a non-smoker and teetotaller, and who is very (8) .... about what he eats, is at present languishing in bed with a wrist in (9) .... and a badly sprained ankle. Part of his healthy (10) .... is to play squash every day after work, and that (11) .... for the ankle. He also cycles everywhere, and if you have ever tried to cycle through the rush-hour traffic with a sprained ankle, you will understand (12) .... he acquired the broken wrist. For (13) .... , it seems, is not just a matter of a good (14) .... and plenty of exercise. Too much exercise can be harmful, as many joggers have discovered. Eating the right food can easily become an obsession, as can overworking, which you might have to do so as to be able to afford your (15) .... of the squash club, your mountain bike, your health food, and a few holidays in peaceful and healthy places.

1) A) Poles   B) Far   C) Quite   D) So
2) A) prescriptions B) surgeries   C) hospitals D) payments
3) A) medications B) cures   C) drugs   D) remedies
4) A) books   B) television   C) advice   D) enthusiasts
5) A) than   B) about   C) for   D) hence
6) A) colds   B) coughs   C) flu   D) fevers

7) A) fanatic	B) follower	C) fad	D) person
8) A) interested	B) varied	C) detailed	D) particular
9) A) crutches	B) plaster	C) treatment	D) danger
10) A) living	B) lifetime	C) lifestyle	D) liveliness
11) A) is	B) caters	C) depends	D) accounts
12) A) how	B) that	C) whenever	D) thus
13) A) fit	B) this	C) health	D) all
14) A) diet	B) eating	C) menu	D) recipe
15) A) share	B) visit	C) membership	D) subscription

2

Choose the most appropriate word underlined.

a) These tablets may make you feel <u>dazed/dozy/drowsy</u> so don't drive.

b) I've been working for twelve hours and I feel <u>exhausting/tiresome/worn out</u>.

c) After I drank a cup of black coffee I felt wide <u>awake/awoken/woken</u>.

d) The doctor said I was <u>all in/run down/stale</u> and gave me some vitamins.

e) Bill's father is a/an <u>disabled/handicapped/invalid</u> and doesn't go out much.

f) After walking for miles over the mountains, my feet were <u>limp/sore/sprained</u>.

g) Ann needs a holiday. She has been under a lot of <u>depression/pain/stress</u> lately.

h) The authorities are worried about the increase in drug <u>abuse/disuse/misuse</u>.

i) I told the doctor that climbing the stairs left me <u>catching/gasping/panting</u> for breath.

j) Mary spent a week in bed with a/an <u>attack/case/outbreak</u> of rheumatism.

3

Complete each sentence with one of the words given. Do not use a word more than once.

chin	heel	knuckles	shoulder	throat
elbow	knee	neck	thigh	wrist

a) My left shoe is too tight and I've got a blister on my ....

b) I can't give my speech today because I've got a bad sore ....

c) Jean can't move her leg after twisting her .... when she went skiing.

d) My arm is in a sling and I can't bend my ....

e) I can't use my right hand because I have sprained my ....

f) Barry bruised his .... when he punched someone in a fight.

g) I pulled a .... muscle while running, and now I can hardly walk.

h) I can't use a tennis racket properly since I injured my ....

i) Peter cut himself badly on the .... while shaving.

j) I've got a really painful boil on my .... What should I do?

4

Match the words in a) to j) with the explanations in 1) to 10)

a) ambulance	1) This is a large room with beds in a hospital.
b) bandage	2) This is where you visit a doctor.
c) emergency	3) This is dangerous and unexpected and requires immediate action.
d) casualty	4) This supports a person who has difficulty in walking.
e) plaster	5) This is a vehicle used for transporting the sick.
f) operating theatre	6) This is put around broken limbs to immobilise them.
g) stretcher	7) This is used for carrying people who are unable to walk.
h) surgery	8) This is where a surgeon works.

i) crutch   9) This is used for wrapping wounds.

j) ward   10) This is someone injured in an accident.

5

Choose the most suitable word or phrase.

a) I don't want to be rude, so I'll just say he is a bit ....
    A) flabby   B) plump   C) overweight D) obese

b) Keith was .... ill during the wedding reception.
    A) taken   B) fallen   C) diagnosed   D) considered

c) Can we visit her in hospital, or is what she's got ....?
    A) unhygienic B) catching   C) influential D) contaminating

d) Ouch! I've just been .... by a bee!
    A) bitten   B) poisoned   C) hit   D) stung

e) Don't .... your head, Jimmy. You'll make it sore!
    A) itch   B) tear   C) scratch   D) grate

f) The old man .... and died while watching the football match.
    A) tripped   B) collapsed C) fell   D) tumbled

g) Helen spoke for so long at the conference that she became ....
    A) hoarse   B) speechless C) dumb   D) inarticulate

h) After the dentist extracted my tooth I was in ....
    A) peril   B) suffering C) agony   D) aches

i) I do admire Karen's figure. She's so lovely and ....
    A) thin   B) skinny   C) shapeless   D) slim

j) I am being .... for my bad back by a physiotherapist.
    A) cured   B) healed   C) tend   D) treated

6

Match each sentence a) to j) with an explanation from 1) to 10).

a) I nodded.	1) I moved my eyebrows together to show disapproval.
b) I chuckled.	2) I laughed uncontrollably, in a silly way.
c) I grinned.	3) I looked with wide-open eyes at the same place for several moments.
d) I shook my head.	4) I laughed quietly under my breath.
e) I scowled.	5) I opened my mouth uncontrollably to show boredom or tiredness.
f) I giggled.	6) I gave a large smile.
g) I yawned.	7) I moved my head from side to side meaning 'no'.
h) I frowned.	8) I made a threatening expression with my lips.
i) I choked.	9) I moved my head up and down meaning 'yes'.
j) I stared.	10) I had trouble breathing because my throat was blocked.

7

Replace the words underlined in each sentence with one of the words given.

> crawling hobbling marching staggering tiptoeing
> dashing limping rambling strolling wandering

a) I really enjoy <u>walking for pleasure in the countryside</u>.

b) After about six months babies start <u>moving about on their hands and knees</u>.

c) My sister was <u>walking on the front part of her foot so as to make no noise</u> along the corridor.

d) The injured player began <u>walking with one leg more easily than the other</u> off the pitch.

e) The drunken man was <u>moving unsteadily</u> from one side of the street to the other.

f) Nowadays soldiers have motorised transport and do little <u>moving on foot</u>.

g) There is nothing more pleasant than <u>walking in a leisurely manner</u> along the sea front.

h) I've been <u>moving very rapidly</u> backwards and forwards all day, and I'm exhausted.

i) When I visit a new town I like <u>walking with no particular purpose</u> around looking at the sights.

j) I wasn't used to so much walking, and ended up <u>moving with difficulty</u> home, with blisters on both feet.

8

Match the formal sentences a) to j) with an everyday explanation from 1) to 10).

a) She fractured her arm.	1) She was resting to recover from being ill.
b) She vomited.	2) She felt a bit funny.
c) Her condition deteriorated.	3) She passed out.
d) She was convalescing.	4) She was drunk.
e) She suffered from insomnia.	5) She broke it.
f) She fainted.	6) She got worse.
g) She was pregnant.	7) She was feeling low.
h) She was depressed.	8) She was sick.
i) She was intoxicated.	9) She was expecting a baby.
j) She was unwell.	10) She couldn't sleep.

14 World Issues

1

Choose the most suitable word for each space.

Over the past thirty years or so, the methods used for collecting money from the public to (1) .... the developing world have changed out of all recognition, along with the gravity of the problems faced, and the increasing (2) .... among the population that something must be done. At the beginning of this period, it would have been common to put (3) .... in a collecting box, perhaps on the street or at church, or to receive a small 'flag' to wear in the lapel. The 1960s saw the development of shops which sold secondhand goods, (4) .... by the public, and which also began to sell articles manufactured in the developing world in projects set up by the parent (5) ...., to guarantee a fair income to local people. The next development was probably the charity 'event', in which participants were (6) .... to run, cycle, swim or what have you, and collected money from friends and relatives according to how far or long they managed to keep going. The first hint of what was to become the most successful means of (7) .... money was the charity record, where the artists donated their time and talent, and the (8) .... from sales went to a good cause. This was perhaps a reflection of the fact that young people felt (9) .... concerned about the obvious differences between (10) .... in Europe and the United States, and that in most of Africa and Asia, and this concern was reflected in songs, besides being clearly shown on television. The problems were becoming hard to (11) ...., but a feeling of frustration was building up. Why was so little being done? The huge success of Band Aid, and subsequent televised concerts, reflected the (12) .... of the media, and of music in particular, but also differed in style from other events. People phoned up in their thousands on the day and (13) .... money by quoting their credit card numbers. After all, if you have enough money to buy CDs and a stereo player, you can (14) .... something for the world's (15) .... children.

1) A) finance	B) aid	C) pay	D) loan
2) A) habit	B) wish	C) clamour	D) awareness
3) A) this	B) money	C) them	D) funds
4) A) donated	B) freed	C) offered	D) awarded
5) A) government	B) concerned	C) charity	D) company
6) A) sponsored	B) invited	C) required	D) used
7) A) borrowing	B) such	C) further	D) raising
8) A) change	B) means	C) proceeds	D) rest
9) A) it	B) increasingly	C) less	D) this
10) A) being	B) life	C) them	D) lifestyles
11) A) avoid	B) understand	C) define	D) implement
12) A) mass	B) ability	C) style	D) power
13) A) loaned	B) handed in	C) pledged	D) raised
14) A) waste	B) add	C) deposit	D) afford
15) A) famine	B) underdeveloped	C) starving	D) own

2
Choose the most appropriate word underlined.

a) Many small houses and huts were flooded away/pushed away/washed away when the river burst its banks.

b) Poor farming methods are responsible for soil devaluation/erosion/migration in many areas of sub-Saharan Africa.

c) During the earthquake, many people were buried/collapsed/covered alive.

d) The forest fire left a wide area of the mountainside blackened and ablaze/crackling/smouldering.

e) Villagers are hoping for rain this month after nearly a year of draft/draught/drought.

f) Before the hurricane struck, many people were abducted/evacuated/shifted to higher ground.

g) Thousands of children in the famine-stricken area are suffering from malnutrition/starvation/undernourishment.

h) Heavy snow has fallen in the mountains and many villages have been blocked out/cut off/swept away for the past two days.

i) The Aids epidemic/outbreak/plague has begun to have serious effects in many African countries.

j) Many small islands in the Indian Ocean are threatened by rising sea beds/levels/shores.

3

Complete each sentence a) to j) with one of the part sentences 1) to 10).

a) After a month of fighting, the United Nations managed to arrange ....

b) The President complained bitterly about ....

c) The World Bank has finally agreed to ....

d) Neighbouring countries have strongly protested about ....

e) Aid agencies are at present involved in setting up camps for ....

f) Most third world economies have been hit badly by ....

g) Many poor countries still spend a disproportionate amount on ....

h) The general warned outside countries not to interfere in ....

i) Rising prices and unemployment have contributed to ....

j) In an attempt to stabilise the economy, the government has resorted to ....

1) .... the cancellation of more than £300 million of foreign debt.

2) .... the rising scale of ethnic conflict in the area.

3) .... the thousands of refugees made homeless by the fighting.

4) .... the supplying and equipping of large armies.

5) .... the exploitation of his people by foreign mining companies.

6) .... the devaluation of the currency by fifty per cent from today.

7) .... the fall in commodity prices, and their burden of foreign debt.

8) .... a ceasefire between the government and the guerrillas.

9) .... the civil war, or send arms to what he called the 'rebel forces'.

10).............. the invasion and occupation of the small kingdom.

4

Complete each sentence with one of the words given. Do not use a word more than once.

| balance fuels gas lead species chemicals |
| fumes greenhouse pesticide waste |

a) Factories often dispose of .... products in rivers and the sea.

b) The chimpanzee is one of many ....which will soon be found only in zoos.

c) The earth's atmosphere is growing warmer partly because of the so-called '.............. effect'.

d) Many scientists believe that the natural .... of the world's ecology is threatened.

e) Over-exploitation of fossil .... such as coal and oil will lead to an energy crisis.

f) Many people prefer to eat fruit and vegetables which have not been sprayed with ....

g) Within a few years, ...-free petrol will be used throughout Europe.

h) Many household products actually contain .... which are harmful to the environment.

i) In some cities a poisonous smog is created from car exhaust ....

j) Another cause of global warming is emission of carbon dioxide .... from power stations and factories.

5

Choose the most suitable word or phrase.

a) A large area of Southern California has been .... by a major earthquake.

    A) trembled   B) shaken   C) upset   D) vibrated

b) At the traffic lights there were poor people .... for money.

    A) urging   B) requesting   C) pleading   D) begging

c) There is a steady .... of young people from villages to the cities.
   A) drift   B) stampede   C) current   D) motion

d) Many countries have sent medicines for .... of the latest fighting.
   A) injured   B) wounded   C) victims   D) culprits

e) In many countries poor children face a grim .... for existence.
   A) struggle   B) attempt   C) effort   D) toil

f) .... is still common in many countries, even though it is illegal.
   A) Enslavement   B) Slavery   C) Servility   D) Slavering

g) The government has decided to send more .... to Saharan countries.
   A) charity   B) aid   C) collections   D) donations

h) Some of the people had little to wear and were literally dressed in ....
   A) strips   B) cloths   C) rags   D) patches

i) As soon as the supplies arrive, they will be .... to the starving people.
   A) dispersed   B) assigned   C) dealt   D) distributed

j) The books you see here are the .... of four fully grown trees.
   A) equivalent   B) match   C) parallel   D) counterpart

6

Complete each sentence with a word beginning as shown, formed from one of the words or part words given. Do not use a word more than once.

| burdened | estimated | lying | populated | rated |
| crowded | joyed | nourished | privileged | simplified |

a) Many countries with high birth rates are seriously over............... .

b) The usefulness of traditional farming methods in poor countries should not be under............... .

c) When the United Nations relief supplies arrived, the people were over ....

d) The government has seriously under.............. the gravity of the situation in drought-stricken areas.

e) Those who say that developing countries simply need more money have over.............. the problem.

f) Most of the children in the camp were seriously unde............... .

g) Most third world economies are already over.............. with foreign debt.

h) Those of us who live in prosperous countries should try and help the under.............. peoples of the developing world.

i) The refugee camps are now seriously over.............. and more blankets and food are needed.

j) Sending aid to countries may help in the short term, but the under.............. causes of the problem must also be tackled.

7

Replace the words underlined in each sentence with one of the words given.

| densely | illiterate | inadequate | sparsely | urban |
| essential | impoverished | rural | traditional | wealthy |

a) In many countries, there is a drift of population from <u>country</u> areas to the cities.

b) Education is desperately needed in many countries where a high percentage of the population is <u>unable to read and write</u>.

c) Remote villages usually lack <u>basic</u> services such as piped water and electricity.

d) When villages move to the city, they usually lose touch with their <u>time-honoured</u> ways of life.

e) <u>Rich</u> people often find it hard to understand how the poor become poor.

f) The mountain region of the country is <u>thinly</u> populated.

g) Many <u>poor</u> nations can no longer afford to run schools and hospitals.

h) Poor immigrants often end up living in shanty towns in <u>city</u> areas.

i) In <u>thickly</u> populated areas, unemployment may be a cause of poverty.

j) The diet of most children in this area is <u>poor</u>.

8

Match the words and phrases a) to j) with the explanations 1) to 10).

a) recycling
b) a charity
c) reforestation
d) organic
e) irrigation
f) conservation
g) negotiation
h) self-sufficiency
i) a subsidy
j) immunisation

1) the settling of a dispute through discussion
2) the ability of a country or person to support themselves without outside help
3) a means of protecting people against some diseases
4) food of this kind is grown without the use of chemical fertilisers
5) the collection of raw materials so that they can be used again
6) money used by a government to lower the prices of eg basic foods
7) a system of distributing water to places which need it for agriculture
8) an organisation which collects money from the public and uses it to help people in need
9) an organised means of saving resources, buildings, or animal and plant life
10) a programme for planting trees to replace those which have been destroyed

15 Thinking and feeling

1

Choose the most suitable word for each space.

Interpreting the feelings of other people is not always easy, as we all know, and we (1) .... as much on what they seem to be telling us, as on the (2) .... words they say. Facial (3) .... and tone of voice are obvious ways of showing our (4) .... to something, and it may well be that we (5) .... express views that we are trying to hide. The art of being (6) .... lies in picking up these signals, realising what the other person is trying to say, and acting so that they are not embarrassed in any way. For example, we may understand that they are in fact (7) .... to answer our question, and so we stop pressing them. Body movements in general may also (8) .... feelings, and interviewers often (9) .... particular attention to the way a candidate for a job walks into the room and sits down. However, it is not difficult to present the right kind of (10) .... , while what many employers want to know relates to the candidate's character traits, and (11) .... stability. This raises the awkward question of whether job candidates should be asked to complete psychological tests, and the further problem of whether such tests actually produce (12) .... results. For many people, being asked to take part in such a test would be an objectionable (13) .... into their private lives. After all, a prospective employer would hardly ask a candidate to run a hundred metres, or expect his or her family doctor to provide (14) .... medical information. Quite apart from this problem, can such tests predict whether a person is likely to be a (15) .... employee or a valued colleague?

1) A) estimate	B) rely	C) reckon	D) trust
2) A) other	B) real	C) identical	D) actual
3) A) looks	B) expression	C) image	D) manner
4) A) view	B) feeling	C) notion	D) reaction
5) A) unconsciously	B) rarely	C) unaware	D) cannot
6) A) good at	B) humble	C) tactful	D) successful
7) A) reluctant	B) used	C) tending	D) hesitant
8) A) have	B) indicate	C) contain	D) infer
9) A) set	B) gain	C) in	D) pay
10) A) appearance	B) candidate	C) manners	D) introduction
11) A) similar	B) physical	C) psychological	D) relevant
12) A) faithful	B) regular	C) reliable	D) predictable
13) A) invasion	B) intrusion	C) infringement	D) interference
14) A) classified	B) secretive	C) reticent	D) confidential
15) A) thorough	B) particular	C) laborious	D) conscientious

2

Choose the most suitable word underlined.

a) As there is little hope of being rescued, I have abandoned/decided/resigned myself to the worst.

b) Tom didn't believe us, and it took a long time to convince/establish/persuade him.

c) I define/regard/suppose this project as the most important in my career.

d) In my point of view/viewpoint/view, this plan will not work.

e) Are you aware/conscious/knowledgeable that £10 000 has gone missing?

f) I haven't really the faintest sense/notion/opinion of what you are talking about.

g) Mr Smith has appointed his best friend as the new director! It's a clear case of favouritism/prejudice/subjectivity.

h) Your new boyfriend recollects/remembers/reminds me of a cousin of mine.

i) Sue just can't stop thinking about football! She is biased/concerned/obsessed with her local team!

j) I just can't understand the attitude/manners/mentality of people who are cruel to animals.

3

Complete each sentence with one of the words given. Do not use a word more than once.

> conceited considerate lenient naughty sentimental
> conscientious envious loyal rash unscrupulous

a) John's children used to be well-behaved but now they are quite ....

b) When my brother managed to buy a sports car, I was really ....

c) Steve thinks too much of himself. He's very .... in fact.

d) Helen now realises that suddenly giving up her job was rather ....

e) My new assistant couldn't care less about his work. I need someone who is much more ....

f) Thank you for all your help. You have been very ....

g) Mary talks about the past all the time, as if everything in her life was better then. She does tend to be rather ....

h) I suppose I should punish you, but instead I'm going to be ....

i) Janet doesn't care about right and wrong when she wants to make a sale. She is totally ....

j) Thank you all for standing by the company during this difficult time. You have all been very ....

4

Replace the words underlined with one of the words or phrases given. Do not use a word or phrase more than once.

cherished	dreaded	mourned	regretted	resented
deplored	loathed	offended	reproached	stressed

a) Peter <u>was very sorry about</u> leaving his old job.

b) The Prime Minister <u>strongly disapproved of</u> the behaviour of the demonstrators.

c) Lily <u>felt bitter about</u> the fact that everyone had been promoted except her.

d) David <u>felt extremely worried about</u> visiting the dentist.

e) Sally <u>held very dear</u> the memory of her childhood in the country.

f) Neil <u>grieved for</u> the death of his mother and father for many weeks.

g) I am sorry if I <u>hurt the feelings of</u> your sister.

h) Brenda really <u>felt a strong dislike for</u> her new boss.

i) Our teacher <u>laid emphasis on</u> the importance of regular study.

j) Jim <u>strongly criticised</u> me for not doing my fair share of the work.

5

Choose the most suitable word or phrase.

a) I'm sorry that I giggled so much. I was in rather a silly ....
A) temper   B) mood   C) feeling   D) outlook

b) When our teacher saw what we had done he was absolutely ....
A) angry   B) upset   C) furious   D) annoyed

c) In a/an .... moment, I decided to climb the cliff on my own.
A) rash   B) impulsive   C) sudden   D) risky

d) Stop looking at yourself in the mirror! You're so .... !
A) conceited   B) self-centred   C) vain   D) proud

e) Jean has been the subject of much .... gossip in the village.
A) evil   B) vicious   C) abusive   D) malicious

f) Tom is quite a/an .... character and easy to understand.
A) frank   B) straightforward C) candid   D) undemanding

g) I am a/an .... reader of science fiction novels.
A) avid   B) ardent   C) zealous   D) fervent

h) Do stop banging that drum, Billy. You're being rather ....
A) nuisance   B) wearying   C) disturbing   D) tiresome

i) We found the dance performed by the small children really ....
A) compelling   B) enchanting   C) gripping   D) enticing

j) The film didn't really .... our expectations, unfortunately.
A) meet with   B) fall short of   C) put in for   D) come up to

6

Match each comment in 1) to 10) with one of the character descriptions a) to j).

a) You are so tense.
b) I find you rather aloof.
c) Your trouble is, you're too impulsive.
d) You're very touchy, aren't you!
e) Stop being so stubborn.
f) You're really spiteful, you are!
g) What a sly person you are!
h) Don't be so nosey.
i) I think you are a bit inhibited.
j) Why are you so pessimistic?

1) You don't have to bite my head off, you know!
2) Try saying something nice about everyone for a change!
3) If I were you, I'd mind my own business.
4) Just take the time to think things over before you do something.
5) Why don't you relax for a change!
6) You need to come out of your shell more often.
7) Look on the bright side for once in your life!
8) You pretend to do one thing, and then go behind my back!
9) Try to mix more with the others, you'll enjoy it.
10) Why don't you consider making a small compromise?

7

Replace the words underlined with one of the more formal words given. Do not use a word more than once.

abuse attachment distress indifference revenge animosity
consolation expectation preoccupation sympathy

a) My main <u>worry</u> at the moment is whether the delivery will be on time.
b) The other driver shouted <u>swear-words</u> at me as I drove away.
c) I feel a considerable <u>liking</u> for this part of the city.
d) There is strong <u>hatred</u> between the two communities.
e) After the team were badly defeated, they wanted <u>to get their own back</u>.
f) When I was ill, listening to music was my one <u>comfort</u>.
g) I told Jack about my problem, but he didn't show much <u>understanding</u>.
h) The war has caused a lot of <u>suffering</u> among the population.
i) The police showed complete <u>lack of interest</u> when we explained our problem.
j) My <u>prediction</u> is that you will pass the examination.

8

Complete each sentence with one of the words given. Do not use a word more than once.

appreciate follow mislead put utter
express imply plead spot wonder

a) I don't quite know how to .... this, but I'm afraid the money has gone!
b) Could you say that again? I didn't quite .... you.
c) I would .... it if you could help me with this job.
d) I was so flabbergasted that I couldn't .... a single word.
e) I simply said we had lost the order. I didn't .... that it was your fault.
f) I was so overwhelmed that I just couldn't .... my feelings.
g) Whenever I ask you about damage to the car, you always .... ignorance.
h) I .... that you can get up at 6.00 after what you were doing last night!
i) Most of the clues in a detective story are there to .... the reader.
j) Did you .... the deliberate mistake on page two?

16 Technology

1
Choose the most suitable word for each space.

When faced with some new and possibly bewildering technological change, most people react in one of two (1) .... They either recoil from anything new, claiming that it is unnecessary, or too (2) .... or that it somehow makes life less than (3) .... Or they learn to (4) .... to the new invention, and eventually (5) .... how they could possibly have existed without it. (6) .... computers as an example. For many of us, they still represent a (7) .... to our freedom, and give us a frightening sense of a future in which all (8) .... will be taken by machines. This may be because they seem mysterious, and difficult to understand. Ask most people what you can (9) .... a home computer for, and you usually get (10) .... answers about how 'they give you information'. In fact, even those of us who are familiar with computers, and use them in our daily work, have very little idea of how they (11) .... But it does not take long to learn how to operate a business programme, even if things occasionally go wrong for no apparent reason. Presumably much the same happened when the telephone and the television became (12) .... What seems to alarm most people is the speed of (13) .... change, rather than change itself. And the (14) .... that are made to new technology may well have a point to them, since change is not always an improvement. As we discover during power cuts, there is a lot to be said for the oil lamp, the coal fire, and forms of entertainment, such as books or board games, that don't have to be (15) .... in to work.

1) A) moments	B) kinds	C) ways	D) types
2) A) complicated	B) much	C) obscure	D) tiresome
3) A) formerly	B) lively	C) personal	D) human
4) A) adapt	B) react	C) conform	D) use
5) A) decide	B) wonder	C) suppose	D) admit
6) A) Discuss	B) Propose	C) Take	D) Thus
7) A) hazard	B) risk	C) control	D) threat
8) A) measures	B) decisions	C) chances	D) instructions
9) A) run	B) apply	C) learn	D) use
10) A) vague	B) such	C) up with	D) hundreds
11) A) are	B) work	C) manage	D) consist
12) A) in existence	B) widespread	C) through	D) extensive
13) A) future	B) machinery	C) physical	D) technological
14) A) objections	B) appliances	C) criticisms	D) fears
15) A) wired	B) batteries	C) plugged	D) connected

2
Choose the most appropriate word underlined.

a) I can't undo this nut. I need a larger screwdriver/spanner.
b) You won't be able to open the wine without a bottle-opener/corkscrew.
c) For extra security, I've fitted a bolt/padlock on the front door.
d) Could you hand me that hammer so I can bang in this nail/screw?
e) I do all my own car repairs since I bought this tool gear/kit.

f) You can't make a hole in the wall without a <u>drill/file</u>.

g) I buy coffee beans and put them in a <u>grinder/mixer</u>.

h) We had to hire a <u>crane/lift</u> to put our piano in our top-floor flat.

i) The electrician twisted the wires together using a pair of <u>chisels/pliers</u>.

j) The good thing about this knife is that the <u>blade/edge</u> can be replaced.

3

Complete each sentence a) to j) with one of the phrases 1) to 10). Do not use a phrase more than once.

a) This chair wobbles a lot.

b) Take the car to the garage every six months.

c) There is nothing wrong with the TV remote control.

d) The car won't start because the battery is flat.

e) No wonder the air conditioning makes you feel ill.

f) The pipes are leaking because this joint is loose.

g) I'm not surprised your television picture is so bad.

h) This axe won't cut anything.

i) You can't just tie this broken railing together.

j) The video won't work like that.

1) Only the battery needs replacing.

2) It just needs tightening.

3) It needs connecting properly.

4) The leg needs fixing.

5) The aerial needs adjusting.

6) The filter needs changing.

7) It needs sharpening.

8) It needs regular servicing.

9) The parts need welding.

10) It needs charging.

4

Match the objects a) to j) with the activities 1) to 10).

a) desk lamp

b) car engine

c) hinge

d) radiator

e) washer

f) wristwatch

g) binoculars

h) calculator

i) fan

j) bicycle

1) It may need winding up.

2) You may need to change this to stop a tap dripping.

3) Some adjustment may be necessary if you want to see well.

4) You will have to change the bulb occasionally.

5) It is useful for doing difficult sums.

6) It turns and keeps you cool.

7) The chain might come off this.

8) This warms a room and is part of a central heating system.

9) It needs tuning occasionally.

10) You may need to oil it if the door squeaks.

5

Choose the most suitable word or phrase.

a) The .... on the town-hall clock showed it was nearly midnight.

A) pointers   B) hands   C) fingers   D) indicators

b) The builders put up .... so they could clean the outside of the tower.

A) scaffolding   B) framework   C) poles   D) woodwork

c) I've decided to start wearing contact ....

A) glasses   B) spectacles   C) lenses   D) faces

d) Pauline works in a local garage as a/an ....

   A) engineer   B) technician   C) mechanic   D) operative

e) Metal pipes .... if you heat them.

   A) enlarge   B) expand   C) extend   D) encroach

f) The old bus slowly .... to a halt outside the school.

   A) clanked   B) squeaked   C) whizzed   D) ground

g) It is easy in some regions to............... electricity in hydro-electric power stations.

   A) generate   B) create   C) fabricate   D) propagate

h) My car was so old that I could only sell it for ....

   A) rubbish   B) debris   C) scrap   D) waste

i) The word processor .... of a keyboard, a monitor and a printer.

   A) composes   B) consists   C) comprises   D) constitutes

j) We'll come and .... your new central heating system on Monday.

   A) set up   B) lay   C) establish   D) install

6

Complete each sentence a) to j) with one of the comments 1) to 10). Do not use a comment more than once.

a) I don't know what's the matter with my watch.

b) This knife is no good.

c) It's no use trying the lift.

d) Don't use that old screw.

e) I've got to ring the garage about the car.

f) This pipe is going to leak a lot.

g) I can't get a good picture on this set.

h) I'd like to change the calculator I bought here yesterday.

i) There's something wrong with the lock. My key won't fit.

j) This bolt is too small for this nut.

1) It's rusty.   6) It's been tampered with.

2) It's flickering.   7) It won't go.

3) It's blunt.   8) It's faulty.

4) It won't fit.   9) It's coming loose.

5) It's broken down.   10) It's out of order.

7

Complete each sentence with one of the words given.

appliance	component	equipment	gadget	manual
automation	contraption	experiment	machinery	overhaul

a) What a peculiar ....! What on earth is it for?

b) A washing-machine is probably the most useful household ....

c) We will have to order a new .... to replace the damaged one.

d) The noise of .... filled the factory and nearly deafened me.

e) I can't make this computer work. Let's read the .... again.

f) Scientists in this laboratory are conducting an interesting ....

g) When .... is introduced, the number of workers will be reduced.

h) Do you like this new .... I bought for peeling potatoes?

i) Every six months the nuclear reactor needs a complete ....

j) My brother has a shop selling photographic ....

8

Choose the most appropriate word in each sentence.

a) The hair-drier is fitted with a three point <u>cable/plug/socket</u>.
b) Don't touch that wire! It's <u>live/lively/living</u>.
c) This small vacuum cleaner is <u>motivated/powered/run</u> by batteries.
d) The set wouldn't work because there was a faulty <u>connection/joint/link</u>.
e) I can't use my drill here. The <u>lead/plug/wire</u> isn't long enough.
f) Turn off the mains first in case you get a/an <u>impact/jolt/shock</u>.
g) Oh dear the lights have gone off! The <u>cable/fuse/safety</u> must have gone.
h) Can you lend me that cassette? I want to <u>record/transcribe/write</u> it.
i) The appliance is powered by a small electric <u>engine/machine/motor</u>.
j) Jim has just started work as an <u>electric/electrical/electricity</u> engineer.

17 Quality and Quantity

1

Choose the most suitable word for each space.

Ask anyone over forty to make a comparison (1) .... the past and the present and nine (2) .... ten people will tell you that things have been getting (3) .... worse for as long as they can remember. Take the weather for example, which has been behaving rather strangely lately. Everyone remembers that in their childhood the summers were (4) .... hotter, and that winter always included (5) .... falls of snow just when the school holidays had started. Of course, the food in (6) .... days was far superior too, as nothing was imported and everything was fresh. Unemployment was (7) ...., the pound really was worth something, and you could buy a (8) .... house even if your means were (9) .... And above all, people were (10) .... better in those days, far more friendly, not inclined to crime or violence, and spent their free time making model boats and tending their stamp collections (11) .... than gazing at the television screen for hours on end. As we know that this picture of the past (12) .... cannot be true, and there are plenty of statistics dealing with health and prosperity which prove that it is not true, why is it that we all have a (13) .... to idealise the past? Is this simply nostalgia? Or is it rather that we need to believe in an image of the world which is (14) .... the opposite of what we see around us? Whichever it is, at least it leaves us with a nagging feeling that the present could be better, and perhaps (15) .... us to be a little more critical about the way we live.

1) A) with	B) from	C) between	D) in
2) A) out of	B) to	C) or	D) from
3) A) out	B) so	C) virtually	D) steadily
4) A) not only	B) at least	C) rarely	D) considerably
5) A) lavish	B) abundant	C) bulky	D) prolific
6) A) most	B) early	C) those	D) former
7) A) petty	B) negligible	C) miniature	D) trivial
8) A) middling	B) sizeable	C) medium	D) voluminous
9) A) mediocre	B) confined	C) rationed	D) limited
10) A) more	B) as	C) somehow	D) whatsoever

11) A) other   B) rather   C) usually   D) different
12) A) simply   B) hardly   C) especially D) specifically
13) A) habit   B) custom   C) tendency   D) practice
14) A) quite   B) widely   C) utterly   D) rather
15) A) reassures   B) supports   C) makes   D) encourages

2
Choose the most appropriate word underlined.

a) We advertised the house widely but only a handful/minority of people have shown any interest.

b) The surgeon told Sam that the operation had been only a minor/partial success.

c) The amount of parking space available here is no longer adequate/passable.

d) Sue has already written the bulk/mass of her third novel.

e) You have to use a magnifying glass to see some of the miniature/minute details.

f) I am glad to report that the company has made a large-scale/sizeable profit.

g) There has been quite a dearth/want of good biographies this year.

h) I suppose I have had a fair/good amount of experience in making speeches.

i) We can't afford such a lavish party with the limited/narrow means available.

j) There is really a/an extensive/vast difference between the two plans.

3
Complete each sentence with one of the words given. Do not use a word more than once.

| augmented declined dwindled extended reduced |
| contracted diminished enlarged faded spread |

a) The old railway line has been .... as far as the new airport.

b) In an effort to increase sales, prices will be .... for a short period.

c) Hope has now .... for the two climbers missing since last Friday.

d) Helen .... her small salary by making shrewd share dealings.

e) The school playground has been .... by the addition of the old garden.

f) Unfortunately the fire has now .... to neighbouring buildings.

g) The team's enthusiasm was not at all .... by their early setbacks.

h) As a seaside resort, Mudford has .... a lot since its heyday in the 1920s.

i) The company has .... in size recently, and now employs only 300 people.

j) The number of students attending the class .... until only two remained.

4
Replace the words underlined in each sentence with one of the words or phrases given. Do not use a phrase more than once.

| are not alike   more or less the same as   completely different   similar |
| nothing exactly the same as   is not as good as we had hoped |
| opposite number   calculated in relation to   mixture   wide variety |

a) There is no equivalent to this word in any other language.

b) I am afraid that your sales performance has fallen short of expectations.

c) These two cars are almost alike.

d) The problem can be divided into two distinct parts.

e) Although they are based on the same novel, the two films differ.

f) The salary given will be commensurate with experience.

g) The class I teach contains a strange assortment of people.

h) Any such agreement with the enemy is tantamount to surrender!

i) Mr Smith will have talks with his counterpart in the Spanish government.

j) The island contains a great diversity of plant and animal life.

5
Choose the most
suitable word or
phrase.

a) The attendance at last Saturday's league match was a/an .... low.
  A) disappointing   B) eternal   C) record   D) all-day

b) This is a .... position, and must not be captured by the enemy.
  A) key   B) momentous   C) weighty   D) notable

c) I was shocked by her appearance, but .... more so by her language!
  A) not   B) yet   C) so   D) how

d) It is by no .... certain that Margaret Jones will win the election.
  A) less   B) respect   C) sense   D) means

e) Social status .... for little if you are marooned on a desert island.
  A) applies   B) signifies   C) counts   D) makes

f) The missing plane has apparently disappeared without ....
  A) trace   B) sign   C) word   D) news

g) Can you save me some food from the party, if there is anything ....?
  A) surplus   B) over   C) apart   D) rare

h) Wild rabbits used to be common here but now they are ....
  A) deficient   B) scarce   C) insufficient   D) wanting

i) We only get the .... tourist here in winter. But in summer there are plenty.
  A) infrequent   B) random   C) miscellaneous   D) odd

j) My .... reaction was one of surprise, but then I got used to the idea.
  A) inaugural   B) introductory   C) initial   D) incipient

6
Replace the
word or words
underlined in
each sentence
with one of the
words given. Do
not use a word
more than once.

| altogether considerably especially practically specifically |
| barely effectively moderately respectively thoroughly |

a) United are <u>virtually</u> certain of a place in the final after this result.
b) I'm <u>particularly</u> proud of Jan's contribution to the play.
c) Peter says he is <u>utterly</u> fed up with the government.
d) Be careful! I can <u>hardly</u> walk!
e) After finishing the decorating I felt <u>completely</u> exhausted.
f) Classes 3 and 4 scored 10 points and 15 points <u>each in that order</u>.
g) I am <u>fairly</u> satisfied with the results so far.
h) Since the revolution, the army has <u>to all intents and purposes</u> run the country.
i) We have been <u>greatly</u> heartened by the news from the surgeon in charge.
j) I told you <u>clearly and definitely</u> not to write your answers in pencil, Smith!

7
Complete each
sentence with
one of the words
given. Do not use
a word more than
once.

| abundant excessive lavish middling potential |
| ample inferior major negligible superior |

a) The guests were impressed by the .... scale of the banquet.
b) Water is .... in this part of the country, owing to the heavy rainfall.
c) Make a list of .... clients, and then send them our brochure.
d) Response to our sales campaign was only .... , which was a little bit disappointing.
e) The government was accused of making .... demands on the taxpayers.

f) There is no need to rush. We have .... time before the meeting.

g) Since winning the pools, Helen and Joe have moved to a ....
neighbourhood.

h) There's no need to take the car to a garage. The damage is ....

i) The signing of the peace treaty was an event of .... importance.

j) Just because you don't have your own desk in the office, you needn't
feel ....

8

Add a suitable
comment from 1)
to 10) to each
sentence a) to j).
Do not use a
comment more
than once.

a) United are much better than City.

b) You threw the ball before I was ready.

c) These wines taste just the same to me.

d) Why don't I pick you up at your house?

e) Why bother waiting here when we've missed the last bus?

f) Congratulations on your promotion!

g) The hotel we are staying in is a bit disappointing.

h) There's no food in this cupboard.

i) Pauline has got a new Benson 500.

j) Our product is without doubt the best on the market.

1) Personally, I don't think much of it.   6) I can't tell the difference.
2) It would be less bother.   7) It has no equal.
3) It doesn't count.   8) It doesn't come up to expectations.
4) There's no comparison.   9) It's pointless.
5) None whatsoever.   10) You deserve it.

18 Word Formation 1

1

Complete each
sentence with
one of the words
given.

| bank | book | foot | head | match | blow | chair | hand | key | table |

a) I've got to .... it to you! You really know what you are doing!

b) Don't worry, it's a safe bet. You can .... on it.

c) I'm trying to find some shoes that .... this dress.

d) Everyone voted that Jane should .... the meeting.

e) Mary has one of the .... positions in the company.

f) We've decided to .... in the direction of Rome and stop on the way.

g) I have set out the results of the survey in this ....

h) Jack received a severe .... on the head and felt very dizzy.

i) Don't forget to .... a table at the restaurant for this evening.

j) What worries me is who is going to .... the bill?

2

Complete each
sentence with a
word made from
the word in capitals.

a) Please .... our letter of the 14th. We have not had a reply.   KNOW

b) Keith's exam results turned out to be ....   DISASTER

c) There will be no pay rises in the .... future.   SEE

d) Jim is one of the most .... members of the committee.   SPEAK

e) What are the entry .... at this university?   REQUIRE

f) Jackie suffered as a child from a very strict ....   BRING

g) I think that your .... about the cost are wrong.   ASSUME

h) This statue .... the soldiers who died in the war.   MEMORY

i) The idea that the sun 'rises' is a popular ....   CONCEIVE

j) Ruth has gone back to college to get a teaching ....   QUALIFY

3
Complete the word in each sentence by adding an appropriate prefix.

a) I didn't pay the bill and now the electricity has been ....connected.

b) There is a law against dropping litter, but it is rarely ....forced.

c) When the cassette finished, don't forget to ....wind it.

d) I thought the effects in the film were rather ....done.

e) The rumours about the minister's death were completely ....founded.

f) Anyone with a ....ability may qualify for a special pension.

g) I am ....debted to you for all the help you have given me.

h) When a currency is ....valued, it is worth less internationally.

i) I found the instructions you gave us very .... leading.

j) John rents the house and I ....let a room from him.

4
Replace the words underlined in each sentence with one word ending in *-ly* and beginning with the letter given.

a) The country imports <u>every year</u> over two million tons of rice.   a ....

b) Harry's work has improved <u>a great deal</u>.   c ....

c) <u>By coincidence</u>, I'm driving there myself tomorrow.   c ....

d) I'll be with you <u>straight away</u>.   d ....

e) The two sisters were dressed <u>in exactly the same way</u>.   i ....

f) I'm afraid that Carol's writing is <u>quite</u> illegible.   a ....

g) Tim only understands <u>in a hazy manner</u> what is going on.   v ....

h) I think that this plan is <u>downright</u> ridiculous!   t ....

i) Diana <u>just</u> wants to know the truth.   m ....

j) The passengers <u>only just</u> escaped with their lives.   b ....

5
Complete the word in each sentence with *over-* or *under-*.

a) The ....lying causes of the problem are widely known.

b) What a terrible film. It's really ....rated in my view.

c) The first time I tried out my new bike I ....balanced and fell off.

d) Don't forget to give the door an ....coat as well as a coat of gloss paint.

e) The bath ....flowed and the water dripped through into the living room.

f) It is not as easy as all that. I think you are ....simplifying the problem.

g) I apologise for the delay in sending your order but we are ....staffed at present.

h) You can get to the other side of the road by going through this ....pass.

i) The garden had been neglected and was ....grown with weeds.

j) You should have turned the meat off before. It's ....done now.

6
Complete each word with either *-able* or *-ible*. Make any necessary spelling changes.

a) Brenda's new book is really remark............... .

b) I don't find your new colleague very like............... .

c) The pie looked very good, but it wasn't very easily digest............... .

d) That was a really contempt............... way of getting the boss on your side!

e) I think that anything is prefer............... to having to tell so many lies.

f) The advantage of these chairs is that they are collapse............... .

g) I do hope that you find your room comfort............... .

h) Why don't you go to the police? It's the sense............... thing to do.

i) John takes good care of the children and is very response............... .

j) I find your aunt a very disagree............... person I'm afraid.

7

Make a compound word in each sentence by adding one of the words given. Do not use a word more than once.

| burst   dust   flake   mare   quake   decay   fire   knob   post   shift |

a) We used cushions and blankets as a make............... bed.

b) I woke up screaming after having a terrible night............... .

c) The house was severely damaged by an earth............... .

d) We got soaked to the skin in a sudden cloud............... .

e) The car ran off the road and crashed into a lamp-............... .

f) If you clean your teeth regularly, this will reduce tooth-............... .

g) I gripped the door-............... and turned it but the door wouldn't open.

h) The floor of the workshop was covered in saw............... and shavings of wood.

i) The children made a poster based on the shape of a snow............... .

j) The United Nations tried to arrange a cease............... but without success.

8

Complete each sentence with a word made from the word in capitals.

a) The villages in the mountains are quite ....during winter. ACCESS

b) The inquiry decided that the police were not entirely............... .BLAME

c) Sam was accused of stealing some .... documents from the safe. CONFIDENCE

d) You do not have to go. Your decision must be entirely .... VOLUNTEER

e) How do you like my latest...............for my stamp collection? ACQUIRE

f) The minister gave .... answers to the interviewer's questions. EVADE

g) The two prisoners are to be .... next month. TRIAL

h) Most people agree that Christmas has become too .... COMMERCE

i) The dancer's movements were extremely .... GRACE

j) The cost of .... to the show is quite reasonable. ADMIT

19 Word Formation 2

1

Complete the word in each sentence.

a) One of the draw............... of this car is its high petrol consumption.

b) From the hotel there is a breath............... view across the canyon.

c) Peter's gambling ability gave him a nice little wind............... of £300.

d) We always lock the computer in this cupboard, just as a safe............... .

e) The booklet includes official guide............... for tourists with pets.

f) Michael's playboy life............... was the envy of all his friends.

g) That building has been ear............... for redevelopment by the council.

h) We cannot take off because the run............... is rather icy.

i) From my stand.............. , this would not be a very profitable venture.

j) There is wide............... dissatisfaction with the government's policies.

2

Complete each sentence with a word made from the word in capitals.

a) Bill was given a medal in .... of his services. RECOGNISE

b) All .... must be received before July 20th 1994. APPLY

c) Karen and Catherine are .... twins. IDENTITY

d) You look rather.............. . Are you worried about something? OCCUPY

e) I'm sure that the whole problem is a simple .... UNDERSTAND

f) Going swimming every day would have very............. effects. BENEFIT

g) It's much more .... to buy large size packets. ECONOMY

h) My ankle is really .... and I can't walk easily. SWELL

i) The government's .... approach has brought criticism. COMPROMISE

j) The meeting adopted a .... calling for Smith to resign. RESOLVE

3

Complete the word in each sentence with an appropriate suffix.

a) I object strongly to the commercial............... of sport.

b) Skateboarding is no longer very fashion............... in this country.

c) Don't touch that glass vase! It's absolutely price...............!

d) We decided to go to watch some tradition............... dances in the next village.

e) Helen's uncle turned out to be a really remark............... person.

f) We have not yet received confirm............... of your telephone booking.

g) Driving on these mountain roads in winter is a bit hazard............... .

h) I just couldn't put up with his relent............... nagging.

i) The doctor will be available for a consult............... on Thursday morning.

j) None of this work has been done properly. Don't you think you have been rather neglect...............?

4

Complete each word with either *in-* or *un-*.

a) Why are you so ....sensitive to other people's problems?

b) The garden is divided into two ....equal parts.

c) I think you were ....justified in punishing both boys.

d) I am afraid that the world is full of ....justice.

e) This ticket is ....valid. You haven't stamped it in the machine.

f) Thank you for your help. It was ....valuable.

g) Quite honestly I find that argument ....tenable.

h) The government's ....action can only be explained as sheer neglect.

i) The amount of food aid the country has received is quite ....sufficient.

j) Her remarks were so rude they were frankly ....printable.

5

Complete each sentence with a word ending in *-er* or *-or*.

a) After his second book Kevin became a famous ....

b) The orchestra enjoyed working with the new ....

c) The football team and the coach disagreed with their ....

d) The ticket-............... told me I was on the wrong train and had to pay extra.

e) After my bathroom pipes burst I had to call the ....

f) The course .... is responsible for the quality of the lessons.

g) You get served quickly in this restaurant if you tip the ....

h) I don't do any housework; a .... comes in twice a week.

i) Helen studied law and now works as a .... dealing with house contracts.

j) Jim is a .... and has over a thousand sheep.

6

Complete each sentence with a word formed from *think* or *thought*.

a) Russell was one of the greatest .... of the century.

b) How kind of you. That was very ....

c) We cannot possibly surrender. The idea is ....

d) I don't like that idea. It doesn't bear .... about.

e) You might have phoned to say you'd be late. It was a bit ....

f) This plan won't work. We'll have to .... the whole idea.

g) Thanks for sending a card. It was a very kind ....

h) You look very serious. A penny for your ....!

i) Jack is very generous, and very .... brought us some champagne.

j) I wasn't paying attention and .... I threw the receipt in the dustbin.

7

Make a compound word in each sentence by adding one of the words given. Do not use a word more than once.

> addressed   called   going   laid   priced   advised
> fashioned   hearted   legged   taught

a) What I'd really like for breakfast is a nice new-............... egg.

b) We say that the so-............... 'leader' of the group is just a petty tyrant.

c) I have never had any painting lessons. I am entirely self-............... .

d) Our teacher isn't strict at all. She is very easy-............... .

e) To be honest, I enjoy eating in high-............... restaurants.

f) Please enclose a self-............... envelope.

g) Everyone began the holiday in a light-............... mood.

h) This particular kind of long-............... sheep can run quite fast.

i) I think you would be ill-............... to sell the house at the present time.

j) I much prefer having a drink in an old-............... country pub.

8

Complete each sentence with a word made from the word in capitals.

a) When Jean made up for the play she was ....   RECOGNISE

b) Dave isn't really a friend, only an ....   ACQUAINT

c) I thought the test was .... easy, actually.   COMPARE

d) There was a .... between a lorry and two cars.   COLLIDE

e) The pain became .... during the night so I called the doctor.   ENDURE

f) Professor Smith has joined the company in an .... capacity.   ADVICE

g) I can't put up with your .... complaining!   CEASE

h) Visitors complained about the .... in the old museum.   ORGANISE

i) The government has taken a .... decision to ban motorcycles.   CONTROVERSY

j) Mr Maxdell stated that the .... against him were unfounded.   ALLEGE

20 Word Formation 3

1
Choose the most appropriate word underlined.

a) We feel that you have been <u>negligent/negligible</u> and that you are to blame.
b) Can you tell me what the charge is for <u>excess/excessive</u> baggage?
c) The team gave a totally <u>inapt/inept</u> performance and lost heavily.
d) The government's <u>economic/economical</u> policy has come in for criticism.
e) Paul works hard but he lacks <u>experience/an experience</u> in selling.
f) Children over 10 are <u>illegible/ineligible</u> for the competition.
g) The <u>sensible/sensitive</u> thing to do would be to invest the money.
h) Could you please <u>remember/remind</u> me to your brother.
i) There are times when everyone needs to be <u>alone/lonely.</u>
j) The escaped prisoner managed to <u>evade/avoid</u> his pursuers and vanished.

2
Complete each sentence with a word made from the word in capitals.

a) Little Jimmy has been a bit .... today.   TROUBLE
b) You cannot enter the country without the .... documents.   REQUIRE
c) The evidence in this case is entirely ....   CIRCUMSTANCE
d) The failure of this scheme would have serious ....   IMPLY
e) There is a .... living-room, with french windows.   SPACE
f) Have you read the latest .... about Madonna's private life?   REVEAL
g) The fuel .... of this car is rather high.   CONSUME
h) I was so angry I was absolutely ....   SPEECH
i) A list of .... events will be posted on the noticeboard.   COME
j) Janet had to .... from the team because of injury.   DRAW

3
Complete the word in each sentence with an appropriate suffix.

a) Why bother to write another letter to him? It seems point............... to me.
b) If you threat............... me, I shall simply inform the police.
c) One of the Duke's descend............... is well-known racing driver.
d) I'm afraid that the play didn't quite come up to my expect............... .
e) There is intense rival............... between the two brothers.
f) My father paid me a small allow............... while I was at college.
g) The inquiry will report its find............... early next month.
h) I've been looking on the appoint............... page for a new job.
i) Lillian is consider............... taller than when we saw her last.
j) You have to make a distinction between convention............... weapons and nuclear ones.

4
Replace the words underlined in each sentence with one word ending in -*ify*, -*ise* or -*en*. The first letter of the word is given.

a) Jim failed to q............... for the final stage of the competition.
b) This road is so jammed with traffic that the council is going to w............... it.
c) That was rotten luck! I really s............... with you.
d) This book is so difficult. Someone should s............... it.
e) Customers won't know about your products unless you a............... .
f) Turn that music down! It's so loud it will d............... you!
g) The Board will n............... candidates of their results within two weeks.
h) Read this note once, m............... it, and then destroy it.

i) I feel hot in this suit and tie. I'm going to l............... my collar.

j) That is a totally unreasonable decision! How on earth can you j............... it?

5

Complete each word so that it ends in *-hood*, *-ship* or *-dom*.

a) After ten years in prison Paul was given his free............... .

b) A true friend............... lasts throughout life.

c) There is not much like............... that I will get the job.

d) Good sales............... is a partly about getting on well with the customers.

e) Many young musicians find it hard to cope with the demands of star............... .

f) I spent most of my child............... reading horror comics.

g) What you say happened bears little relation............... to the facts.

h) The final cost will be in the neighbour............... of £10 000.

i) If I lose my driving licence, I will lose my live............... .

j) Sheila received considerable sponsor............... for her cross-Channel swim.

6

Complete the word in each sentence.

a) The Concorde was the world's first super............... airliner.

b) Most of the poor children were suffering from mal............... .

c) You can cross the road if you go through this sub............... .

d) Mr Minor will be having talks with his Australian counter............... .

e) After such a terrifying opening scene, the rest of the film was an anti............... .

f) These plugs can go in either socket; they are inter............... .

g) The decorator has done a great job! This room has been trans............... .

h) The caves contain pre............... paintings thousands of years old.

i) Norman made a long and very mono............... speech which bored everyone to tears.

j) What an extra............... person she is! Really weird!

7

Make a compound word in each sentence by adding one of the words given. Do not use a word more than once.

back	card	goer	sick	script
bite	exchange	hand	signal	washer

a) Don't forget to tell everyone about the meeting before............... .

b) There was a long post............... at the end of the letter.

c) Don't worry if you don't have enough cash on you. We can use my credit-............... .

d) The average theatre............... will find this play completely incomprehensible.

e) If I were you, I'd spend a bit more and buy the hard............... version.

f) After six months abroad, Angela was beginning to feel home............... .

g) Put all the dirty knives and forks in the dish-............... .

h) I've got a painful mosquito-............... right on the tip of my nose.

i) I gave my old car as part-............... for this new model, though I didn't get much for it.

j) Gordon forgot to give a traffic-............... and two other cars crashed into his.

8

Complete each
sentence with a
word made from
the word in
capitals.

a) British Rail apologise for the .... of the 4.20 to Bath.   CANCEL
b) I didn't believe him. His story was very ....   CONVINCE
c) The police said that they were awaiting further ....   DEVELOP
d) I'm afraid that your report is full of ....   ACCURATE
e) The company was hit by a .... of crises.   SUCCESS
f) Bill assured us that the .... against him were untrue.   ACCUSE
g) I have told you on .... occasions not to leave the
   safe unlocked.   NUMBER
h) There was a/an .... rise in the cost of living this year.   PRECEDENT
i) Deirdre is a .... on football matches for local radio.   COMMENT
j) Although we were in danger, Ann seemed quite ....   CONCERN

Words and Phrases 1

These units also revise items from earlier units.

1

Come

Complete each sentence with one of the words or phrases given. Use each word or phrase once only.

| expectation fortune pressure strike useful |
| force light realise undone world |

a) I'm afraid that Jim's new play didn't come up to ....

b) The building workers have voted to come out on ....

c) The government is coming under .... to change the law.

d) When her uncle died, Susan came into a ....

e) The truth of the matter came to .... during the investigation.

f) Oh bother! My shoelaces have come ....

g) Bring the torch with you. It might come in ....

h) Ted used to be quite wealthy, but he has come down in the ....

i) Recently I have come to .... that you were right all the time.

j) The new traffic regulations come into .... tomorrow.

2

Hand

Match each sentence a) to j) with one of the explanatory examples 1) to 10).

a) She did it single-handed.

b) You have to hand it to her.

c) She can turn her hand to just about anything.

d) Her behaviour was rather high-handed.

e) She played right into their hands.

f) She's an old hand at this kind of thing.

g) At the end they gave her a big hand.

h) I think her behaviour is getting out of hand.

i) She has managed to keep her hand in.

j) She was given a free hand.

1) She unsuspectingly gave them an advantage.

2) She took advantage of her position to use her power wrongly.

3) She was allowed to do whatever she wanted.

4) She is becoming uncontrollable.

5) She was applauded loudly.

6) She has practised so as not to lose her skill.

7) She did it on her own.

8) She can learn any skill very easily.

9) She has to be congratulated.

10) She has a lot of past experience.

3

Wood and Metal

Complete each sentence with the most suitable word from the list. Use each word once only.

| beam pole plank stick trunk girder post rod twig wand |

a) A small bird was carrying a .... in its beak back to its nest.

b) The wall was supported by a thick metal ....

c) Wasps had made a hole in the .... of the old fruit tree.

d) A workman pushed the wheelbarrow along a ....

e) The magician waved the .... and the rabbit vanished.

f) We have to replace an old oak .... which supports the ceiling.

g) I use a long piece of bamboo as a fishing ....

h) Our neighbour crashed his car into our gate ....

i) After I left hospital I could only walk with a ....

j) We hoisted the flag to the top of the ....

4

Prefix *un-*
Rewrite each sentence beginning as given, so that it contains a form of the word underlined beginning *un-*.

a) I don't <u>envy</u> his position.
His position ....

b) Little Philip flew to New York without his parents' <u>company</u>.
Little Philip flew to New York ....

c) Margaret has no <u>inhibitions</u> at all.
Margaret is completely ....

d) There is no <u>foundation</u> to the rumour that I have been dismissed.
The rumour that I have been dismissed ....

e) I just can't <u>bear</u> this heat!
For me, this heat ....

f) The government will not <u>compromise</u> on this issue.
The government's position on this issue ....

g) The sound of Jenny's voice cannot be <u>mistaken</u>.
The sound of Jenny's voice ....

h) There is no <u>justification</u> for your behaviour.
Your behaviour is quite ....

i) There is no <u>precedent</u> for such action.
Such action ....

j) Ian teaches but has no teaching <u>qualifications</u>.
Ian is an ....

5

Verbs of movement
Choose the most suitable word or phrase.

a) The drunken soldier was .... crazily from one side of the street to the other.
A) marching   B) racing   C) staggering   D) scrambling

b) George suddenly .... into the room waving a telegram.
A) dashed   B) slunk   C) rambled   D) arrived

c) Sue found it very difficult to .... the busy street.
A) pass   B) overtake   C) surpass   D) cross

d) Passengers who wish to .... at the next station should travel in the front four coaches.
A) leave   B) alight   C) get down   D) descend

e) The runner with the injured foot .... across the finishing line.
A) limped   B) trundled   C) scrambled   D) flashed

f) Kate spent the morning .... along the sea-front.
A) hiking   B) rambling   C) strolling   D) crawling

g) Harry .... along the landing, trying not to make any noise.
A) strode   B) tiptoed   C) trudged   D) filed

h) The road was icy, and I .... over.
A) slid   B) skidded   C) skated   D) slipped

i) I managed to .... up behind the burglar before he noticed me.
A) creep   B) slink   C) strut   D) wriggle

j) After the meal we .... over our coffees for an hour or so.
A) loitered   B) staggered   C) lounged   D) lingered

6

In

Complete each sentence with one of the words or phrases given. Use each word or phrase only once.

| advance comparison doubt practice sympathy |
| charge detention earnest response way |

a) All the pupils who misbehaved have been kept in ....

b) I'm not joking. I'm speaking in ....

c) Your rent is, of course, payable in ....

d) The bus drivers are on strike, and the railway workers have come out in ....

e) This city makes London seem quite small in ....

f) It's a depressing book, but I enjoyed it in a ....

g) Everyone else is away, so I am in .... of the office.

h) Theoretically term ends at 4.00 on Friday, but in .... everyone leaves at lunchtime.

i) If in .... , do not hesitate to contact our representative.

j) We have decided to show the film again in .... to public demand.

Words and Phrases 2

1

Get

Rewrite each sentence, replacing the words underlined by using one of the expressions given.

| get you down   get your own back   get the sack   get it straight |
| get hold of   get the idea across   get up speed   get rid of |
| get away with murder   there's no getting away from it |

a) If you're not careful, you're going to be dismissed.

....

b) Doesn't this gloomy winter weather depress you?

....

c) You're going to grow old one day. You can't ignore it.

....

d) Willie treated you really badly. How are you going to take revenge?

....

e) These trains start very slowly but they soon accelerate.

....

f) Ann talks well but she doesn't always communicate what she wants to say.

....

g) The pipes have burst. We must try to find a plumber.

....

h) Let's understand each other. I don't want to go out with you!

....

i) Philip is the teacher's favourite. She lets him do whatever he wants.

....

j) I feel awful. I can't seem to shake off this cold.

....

2

Idioms
Complete each
sentence a) to j)
with an
appropriate
ending from 1) to
10).

a) Gosh, it's incredibly hot today.
b) I'm really terribly sorry about damaging your car.
c) I feel that proof of Smith's guilt has now been established.
d) Well, that's the last item we had to discuss.
e) Why didn't you phone me at all?
f) It's a good plan, I suppose.
g) You may be the office manager.
h) The search has gone on now for three days.
i) Don't worry about the missing money.
j) Haven't you heard about Gordon and Eileen then?

1) But that doesn't give you the right to speak to me like that.
2) Chances are it's just an administrative error.
3) Beyond the shadow of a doubt, in my opinion.
4) For all you know, I might be dead!
5) I thought it was common knowledge.
6) I could really do with a cold drink.
7) As far as it goes, that is.
8) So I think that covers everything.
9) And hope appears to be fading, I'm afraid.
10) All I can say is that it certainly won't happen again.

3

See
Complete each
sentence with
one of the words
or phrases given.
Use each word or
phrase once only.

better days	my way	the last	things	it through
eye to eye	red	the light	a lot	the joke

a) I started this project, and I intend to see ....
b) If you ask me, this restaurant has seen ....
c) Well, so much for Jack. I think we've seen .... of him for a while.
d) I don't think we really see .... over this matter, do we?
e) Come on, laugh! Can't you see ....?
f) When Brenda told me I had been dismissed, I saw ....
g) I don't think I can see .... to lending you the money after all.
h) Mark and Ellen have been seeing .... of each other lately.
i) At last! The director has seen .... and come round to my way of thinking.
j) Ghosts! Don't be silly! You're seeing ....!

4

Colour
Choose the most
suitable word or
phrase.

a) When Bill saw my new car he was .... with envy.
   A) blue   B) green   C) yellow   D) white
b) Tina never comes here now. We only see her once in a .... moon.
   A) white   B) gold   C) yellow   D) blue
c) When the visitors from Japan arrived, the company gave them the ....
   carpet treatment.
   A) blue   B) orange   C) red   D) green
d) I'm fed-up with this job. I feel completely .... off.
   A) browned   B) blued   C) blacked   D) yellowed

e) Julie's letter was unexpected. It arrived completely out of the ....
   A) pink   B) green   C) blue   D) red

f) The ....-collar workers received a rise, but the workers on the shop-floor were told they had to wait.
   A) blue   B) black   C) white   D) grey

g) We decided to celebrate by going out and painting the town ....
   A) red   B) purple   C) gold   d) brown

h) Tony can't be trusted yet with too much responsibility, he's still ....
   A) green   B) pink   C) yellow   D) orange

i) You can talk to him until you're .... in the face, but he still won't understand.
   A) white   B) blue   C) black   D) pink

j) The company fell deeper and deeper into the .... and then went bankrupt.
   A) black   B) green   C) yellow   D) red

5

Suffix -*ful*
Rewrite each sentence beginning as shown, so that it contains a form of the word underlined ending in -*ful*.

a) Martin did his <u>duty</u> as a son.
   ....

b) You didn't show much <u>tact</u>, did you?
   ....

c) I think the whole idea is a flight of <u>fancy</u>.
   ....

d) We have a relationship which <u>means</u> something.
   ....

e) I have my <u>doubts</u> about this plan.
   ....

f) I can only <u>pity</u> his performance, I'm afraid.
   ....

g) Smoking definitely <u>harms</u> the health.
   ....

h) It would be of some <u>use</u> to know what they intend to do.
   ....

i) Jim doesn't show any <u>respect</u> to his teachers.
   ....

j) I'm afraid your directions weren't much <u>help</u>.
   ....

6

Out
Complete each sentence with one of the words or phrases given. Use each word or phrase once only.

| of the way   on strike   of range   of my control   of breath |
| of order   and about   of all proportion   of character   of doors |

a) I don't spend all my time in the office, I get out .... quite a lot.
b) She doesn't usually behave like that. It's completely out ....
c) I wish you'd get out ....! I can't get past.
d) After running up the stairs I was quite out ....
e) The gunners couldn't fire at the castle because it was still out ....
f) This was a small problem which has been exaggerated out ....

g) The children spend a lot of time out .... in the garden.
h) Don't bother trying the lift, it's out .... again.
i) The railway workers are out .... again.
j) I can't do anything, I'm afraid, it's out ....

Words and Phrases 3

1
On
Complete each sentence with one of the words or phrases given. Use each word or phrase only once.

| loan average my retirement the market a regular basis |
| good terms purpose the premises the verge of its own merits |

a) Each of the five peace plans will be judged on ....
b) The company gave me a gold watch on ....
c) We have decided to employ Diana on .... from now on.
d) This is easily the best type of outboard motor on ....
e) The Rembrandt is on .... to the National Gallery at present.
f) There should be at least five fire extinguishers on ....
g) Mary has remained on .... with her ex-husband.
h) Paul's doctor says he is on .... a nervous breakdown.
i) We serve ten thousand customers on .... every week.
j) I don't think that was an accident. I think you did that on ....

2
One
Choose the most suitable word or phrase.

| one at a time for one one another one-time one-way |
| one by one all one one-off one-sided one in three |

a) You may disagree, but I .... think the play is a ghastly failure.
b) The match was a .... affair, with United dominating throughout.
c) Irene Woods, the .... singing star, has written her third musical.
d) According to a survey, ... of all students is unable to pay tuition fees.
e) We are willing to make you a .... payment of £1000 as compensation.
f) Not all together please! Can you come out to the front ....
g) We can eat here now, or later at home. It's .... to me.
h) .... the weary soldiers fell exhausted along the side of the road.
i) We can't turn left here. It's a .... street.
j) I wish you kids would stop pushing .... and start behaving yourselves.

3
Break
Match each sentence a) to j) with one of the explanatory sentences 1) to 10).

a) They have broken down several miles from home.
b) They worked on without a break.
c) They took the corner at breakneck speed.
d) They got on well as soon as they broke the ice.
e) Their marriage is about to break up.

1) They have made an important discovery.
2) They have been burgled.
3) They got over their initial shyness.
4) Their message was interrupted.
5) They went on without stopping.

f) They have made a breakthrough at last.   6) They made her very unhappy.

g) They broke off at that point.   7) They are on the verge of separating.

h) There has been a break-in at their house.   8) They revealed what had happened.

i) They broke the news to Pauline gently.   9) They have had trouble with their car.

j) They broke her heart in the end.   10) They were going extremely fast.

4
Sounds
Choose the most
suitable word or
phrase.

a) A bee was .... angrily against the window pane, unable to get out.

    A) humming   B) buzzing   C) crashing   D) howling

b) The crowd .... in disagreement as the politician left the platform.

    A) rustled   B) banged   C) neighed   D) booed

c) The bus stopped at the traffic lights with a .... of brakes.

    A) screech   B) howl   C) crash   D) grind

d) I had to put some oil on the hinges to stop the door ....

    A) crying   B) whimpering   C) squeaking   D) mooing

e) The sack of potatoes fell from the lorry with a heavy ....

    A) splash   B) crunch   C) rattle   D) thud

f) The helicopter passed overhead with a .... sound, like a giant insect.

    A) grinding   B) crashing   C) chirping   D) whirring

g) The mirror fell from the wall with a ....

    A) whoosh   B) crash   C) ping   d) screech

h) Air was escaping from the punctured tyre with a .... sound.

    A) hissing   B) bubbling   C) blowing   D) puffing

i) The tiny bells on the Christmas tree were .... in the draught.

    A) clanging   B) ringing   C) tinkling   D) gurgling

j) The saucepans fell onto the floor with a great ....

    A) clatter   B) whoosh   C) crunch   D) squeak

5
**Words with more
than one meaning**
Complete each
sentence with
one of the words
given, in a
suitable form.
A word may be
used more than
once.

| application   appreciation   degree   file   lead |
| board   cast   engagement   position   palm |

a) The soldiers took up .... at the edge of the wood.

b) I regret I cannot accept your invitation as I have a previous ....

c) It was a tiny tropical island with some bushes and a few .... trees.

d) Once Lucky Number was in the .... , the race was more or less over.

e) You will not succeed in this job without a great deal more ....

f) Two members of the .... were unable to attend the dress rehearsal.

g) The cases are both serious, but not both to the same ....

h) The .... of directors will be meeting at ten tomorrow morning.

i) The gypsy offered to read my .... if I gave her £5.

j) The prisoner managed to cut through the metal bars with a ....

k) Peter was awarded his .... after retaking his final exams.

l) There has been a rapid .... in the value of these shares over the past week.

m) I am afraid that the .... advertised has already been filled.

n) I can't plug the stereo in here, the .... isn't long enough.

o) Sophia is wearing a plaster .... after breaking her arm while skiing.

244

6
Memory
Rewrite each sentence so that it contains the word or words in capitals.

a) This house makes me think of the place where I grew up. REMINDS

....

b) You are always forgetting things! MEMORY

....

c) Please say hello to your mother for me. REMEMBER ME

....

d) Edward couldn't remember anything about the crash. MEMORY

....

e) I'm sorry, but I've forgotten your name. RECALL

....

f) Don't let me forget to put the rubbish out. REMIND

....

g) That makes me think of something that happened to me. BRINGS

....

h) I can never remember anything. AM VERY

....

i) No one can forget Nureyev's brilliant dancing. IS

....

j) Brenda is very good at memorizing phone numbers. BY

....

Words and Phrases 4

1
Formality
Replace each word or phrase underlined with one of the more formal words given.

| abandoned scrutinised dismissed beneficial investigated |
| commensurate discrepancy rudimentary inopportune lucrative |

a) George was <u>given the sack</u> yesterday.
b) I am afraid I have only a/an <u>basic</u> knowledge of physics.
c) The whole matter is being <u>looked into</u> by the police.
d) I'm looking for a job <u>on a level</u> with my abilities.
e) The actual voting is carefully <u>watched over</u> by special officers.
f) Terry was <u>left somewhere by her parents</u> when she was a baby.
g) I must apologize if I have arrived at a/an <u>bad</u> moment.
h) There is a/an <u>difference</u> between the sum of money sent, and the sum received.
i) Carol's new catering business turned out to be very <u>profitable</u>.
j) I am sure that a month's holiday would be <u>good for you</u>.

2
Compound words
Rewrite each sentence so that it contains a compound word formed from two or more words in the sentence. Some changes can be made to the words. They may be formed into one new word, and may or may not be hyphenated.

a) A girl with fair hair answered the door.

....

b) Their style of life is extremely modern.

....

c) When we set out on this project, you knew the risks.

....

d) Jack loses his temper after just a short time.

....

e) I am not sure which point of view you are taking on this problem.

....

f) You have to serve yourself in this restaurant.

....

g) We have certainly had some trouble from our neighbours.

....

h) The people upstairs have a child who is five years old.

....

i) I stood on the step outside the door at the back of the house.

....

j) The sight of the waterfall took my breath away.

....

3
No
Complete each sentence with one of the phrases given.

| concern   trace   likelihood   means   choice |
| matter   wonder   point   knowing   use |

a) It's unfortunate, but I'm afraid you give me no ....
b) By the time the police arrived, there was no .... of the burglars.
c) It's no .... asking me the way, I'm only a visitor here.
d) If you will smoke so much, it's no .... you have a bad cough.
e) You go home, there's no .... in both of us waiting.
f) Mind your own business, it is no .... of yours.
g) As far as we know, the old man has no .... of support.
h) There is really no .... what Eric will do next.
i) I couldn't solve the puzzle, no .... how hard I tried.
j) At the moment there is no .... of the Prime Minister resigning.

4
People
Choose the most suitable word or phrase.

a) I thought that Wendy's action was rather out of ....
   A) personality   B) character   C) being   D) role
b) Paul was easy to manage when he was crawling, but now he is a/an .... , it's a little more difficult.
   A) infant   B) youngster   C) brat   D) toddler
c) Tim has been been visiting some distant .... in the country.
   A) relatives   B) parents   C) family   D) relationships
d) She's not a teenager any more. She looks quite .... now.
   A) overgrown   B) outgrown   C) grown-up   D) grown through

e) I can't understand Keith, he's a funny sort of ....
   A) individual   B) figure   C) human   D) one

f) Good heaven, it's you, Tom. You are the last .... I expected to see here.
   A) person   B) personality   C) personage   D) persona

g) Mary later became a/an .... of some importance in the academic world.
   A) figure   B) adult   C) being   D) character

h) With the end of childhood, and the onset of .... , young people experience profound changes.
   A) teenage   B) childhood   C) middle age   D) adolescence

i) Do you think that .... will ever be able to live on other planets?
   A) population   B) human beings   C) masses   D) human races

j) Jean has a very easy-going .... , which is why she is so popular.
   A) role   B) characteristic   C) personality   D) reputation

5

Make

Complete each sentence with one of the phrases given.

> point   effort   impression   provision   sense
> offer   time   way   inquiries   difference

a) Don't be silly. What you are saying just doesn't make ....

b) It's getting late. What do you make the .... , as a matter of interest?

c) If you made more .... , you would succeed.

d) Although the police made .... about the missing car, it was never found.

e) I don't know how much I want. Why don't you make me a/an ....?

f) What .... are you trying to make, exactly?

g) You may not care one way or the other, but it makes a .... to me.

h) Jack made ample .... for his family in his will.

i) Well, it's time we started making our .... home, I think.

j) I'm afraid the play didn't make much .... on me.

6

Head

Match each sentence a) to j) with one of the explanatory examples 1) to 10).

a) I never even thought of it.

b) It's far too difficult for someone like me to understand.

c) I made sure that something had to be decided.

d) I'm not a practically minded person.

e) I'm involved so far that it's out of my control.

f) I don't understand it at all.

g) I've gone mad.

h) I've let my feelings get out of control.

i) I never lose control of my emotions.

j) I find it really easy.

1) I always keep my head.

2) It never entered my head.

3) I brought matters to a head.

4) My head is in the clouds.

5) I can't make head or tail of it.

6) I'm in way over my head.

7) I could do it standing on my head.
8) It's completely gone to my head.
9) I'm off my head.
10) It's above my head.

Words and Phrases 5

1

Size - adjectives
Complete each
sentence with
one of the words
or phrases given.
Use each word or
phrase once only.

mere	bare	minor	considerable	substantial
slight	sheer	good	well over	widespread

a) The soldiers held out for a while, but in the end were overwhelmed by .... numbers.

b) There were .... ten thousand people shouting outside the parliament building.

c) Jack was given a/an .... part in the play. He only had one line.

d) There was a/an .... thousand people at last week's hockey match.

e) A .... number of people have reported sighting a UFO over Exmoor.

f) Wendy had a/an .... cold, but thought that it wouldn't get any worse.

g) The company suffered .... losses after the stock market crash.

h) I'm not hurt, it's a/an .... scratch, nothing serious.

i) We expected a good turn-out for the meeting, but a .... handful of people turned up.

j) There is a/an .... belief that the economic situation is about to improve.

2

Headlines
The headlines
a) to j) contain
special 'headline
words'. Each
'headline word' has
a more common
equivalent in
1) to 25). Match
'headline words'
with their common
equivalents.

a) ARMS SWOOP: TWO HELD
b) TORIES BACK PITS AXE
c) PEACE TALKS HEAD FOR SPLIT
d) NUCLEAR SCARE RIDDLE
e) GO-AHEAD FOR SCHOOLS PROBE
f) PRINCESS TO RE-WED PUZZLE
g) PM HITS OUT IN JOBLESS ROW
h) DEATH TOLL RISES IN DISCO BLAZE
i) PRESIDENT OUSTED IN COUP DRAMA
j) SMOKING BAN STAYS: OFFICIAL

1) disagreement	10) Conservatives	19) the Prime Minister
2) discussions	11) coalmines	20) remains
3) raid	12) criticises	21) public alarm
4) confusing news	13) arrested	22) cuts
5) approval	14) number killed	23) dispute
6) revolution	15) removed by force	24) armaments
7) prohibition	16) mystery	25) with legal authority
8) the unemployed	17) marry again	
9) investigation	18) fire	

Rewrite the headlines a)- j) in everyday language.

3
Body Movements
Choose the most suitable word or phrase.

a) I .... the bag of money tightly so no one could steal it.
  A) clutched   B) grabbed   C) cuddled   D) surrounded

b) Several people came forward to congratulate me and .... me by the hand.
  A) held   B) grasped   C) shook   D) picked

c) Pauline was only wearing a thin coat and began .... in the cold wind.
  A) trembling   B) agitating   C) vibrating   D) shivering

d) I can't control this movement, doctor. My arm keeps .... like this.
  A) twitching   B) revolving   C) ticking   D) wandering

e) With a violent movement, the boy .... the purse from Jane's hand.
  A) eased   B) launched   C) snatched   D) dashed

f) Could you .... me that file on your desk, please?
  A) extend   B) past   C) catch   D) hand

g) The barman began to .... his fists in a threatening manner so I left.
  A) gather   B) fold   C) bundle   D) clench

h) If you really .... can you reach that book on the top shelf?
  A) lengthen   B) stretch   C) expand   D) sprawl

i) Please don't .... against that wall. It dirties the new paint.
  A) itch   B) lean   C) curl   D) tumble

j) Harry .... down behind the desk, trying to hide.
  A) hopped   B) crept   C) crouched   D) reclined

4
Suffixes
Complete the word in each sentence with a suitable suffix.

a) The customs official was accused of bribe............... and corruption.
b) This painting has a certain charming child............... quality.
c) Long leather boots were extremely fashion............... at one time.
d) A shelf fell on Jim's head and knocked him sense............... .
e) Helen served her apprentice............... as a reporter on a small local paper.
f) The prime minister handed in his resign............... yesterday.
g) The film didn't live up to my expect............... at all.
h) The government has a commit............... to helping the elderly.
i) Paul doesn't just like to be clean, he is obsessed with clean............... .
j) We have no plans to move house for the foresee............... future.

5
Once
Complete each sentence with one of the words or phrases given. Two items are used twice, the others must be used once only.

| once upon a time   once (2)   once more   for this once |
| once and for all   once in a while   at once (2)   once or twice |

a) This is a very important letter. Please see it is typed ....
b) I don't really play golf, but .... I go round the course with a friend.
c) All right, ... you can park here, but not again.
d) After you've used the mixer .... , you'll see how it works.
e) Four people were trying to get through the door .... , and were stuck.
f) .... there were three bears, who lived in the forest.
g) .... you get used to the weather, you'll enjoy living in Siberia.
h) There was .... an old man, who was very rich, and who had one daughter.
i) If you ask me what the time is .... , I'll scream!
j) Don't ask me again! .... , you can't buy a pony and keep it in the garden!

6

At
Rewrite each sentence so that the underlined words are replaced by an expression beginning with *at*.

a) <u>Suddenly</u> there was a knock at the door.

b) I could see just <u>from looking quickly</u> that Sam was ill.

c) The captain is <u>on the ship</u> at the moment, in the middle of the Atlantic.

d) Harry is <u>a very skilful tennis player</u>.

e) <u>Originally</u> I thought this book was rather dull, but I've changed my mind.

f) A new carpet will cost <u>not less than</u> £500.

g) <u>Anyway</u>, whatever happens the government will have to resign.

h) Paul shot <u>in the direction of</u> the duck, but missed it.

i) Brenda ran up the stairs <u>taking three stairs in one step</u>.

j) Tim won the 100 metres gold medal <u>when he tried for the second time</u>.

Words and Phrases 6

1

Set
Match each sentence a) to j) with one of the explanatory sentences 1) to 10).

a) I don't set much store by it.
b) I've set my mind on it.
c) I've had a set-back.
d) I'm dead set against her marriage.
e) I've set up the meeting for next week.
f) I've set the table in the living-room.
g) I've got the whole set.
h) I have set you two exercises for today.
i) It sets my teeth on edge.
j) I've set it to turn on at seven.

1) I've arranged the meal.
2) I am strongly opposed.
3) I have operated the timer.
4) I've decided for certain.
5) I have had a reversal of fortune.
6) I've made the arrangements.
7) I don't consider it very important.
8) I don't like the bitter taste.
9) I have a complete collection.
10) I have given you some homework.

2

Places
Complete each sentence with one of the words given. Use each word once only.

post	location	site	venue	haunt	spot
whereabouts	point	plot	position		

a) The missing girl's exact .... are still uncertain.
b) The sculpture cannot be appreciated unless you stand in the right ....
c) Don't go to that part of town. It is a well-known .... of muggers.
d) The film was made on .... in West Africa.
e) There is an empty .... opposite the church where a school could be built.

f) The precise .... of the ancient temple is a matter of scholarly dispute.

g) We had our picnic at a local beauty ....

h) The .... where these two lines meet gives us our position on the map.

i) The .... for our next concert has been changed to Wembley Stadium.

j) Helen was the first past the winning ....

3
Words with more than one meaning
In each sentence replace the words underlined by one of the words given.

sound	dead	fast	bare	high
rare	live	clean	even	late

a) We tied the boat <u>securely</u> to the tree, and went for a walk.

b) I only take the <u>absolute</u> essentials with me when I go camping.

c) The sales campaign is <u>exactly</u> on target so far.

d) I wouldn't eat that meat if I were you, it smells a bit <u>off</u>.

e) The robbers got <u>completely</u> away from the police in a sports car.

f) I'd like my steak <u>underdone</u>, please.

g) Mr Jones erected a memorial to his <u>recently dead</u> wife.

h) Don't touch that wire. It is <u>carrying an electric current</u>.

i) He dropped my drink and I dropped his, so now we are <u>equal</u>.

j) I think that the idea of investing the money is very <u>reliable</u> advice.

4
Speaking
Choose the most suitable word or phrase.

a) The accused sat silently throughout the proceedings and did not .... a word.
   A) emit   B) communicate   C) pronounce   D) utter

b) I forgot to .... earlier that I'll be home late this evening.
   A) announce   B) mention   C) relate   D) narrate

c) We were just having a friendly .... about football.
   A) chat   B) whisper   C) gossip   D) report

d) I'm sorry to .... , but did you happen to mention the name 'Fiona'?
   A) butt in   B) cut you   C) intercede   D) jump

e) The police officer .... the children for ten minutes about the dangers of cycling, but then let them off with a warning.
   A) argued   B) spoke   C) lectured   D) addressed

f) John was .... something under his breath, but I didn't catch what he said.
   A) whispering   B) muttering   C) growling   D) swallowing

g) It is difficult for me to .... exactly what I mean in a foreign language.
   A) speak   B) express   C) pronounce   D) address

h) The two people involved in the accident were both .... dead on arrival at Kingham Hospital.
   A) pronounced   B) called   C) defined   D) stated

i) My boss didn't say it in so many words, but she .... that I would get a promotion before the end of the year.
   A) asserted   B) clarified   C) declared   D) implied

j) After we saw the film, we stayed up half the night ....
   A) disputing   B) arguing   C) criticising   D) discussing

5

Within
Complete each
sentence with
one of the
phrases given.

> the law   a reasonable time   means   power   sight
> reason   competence   the hour   reach   enquire

a) The police promised to do everything within their .... to help us.

b) The notice on the door said '.............. Within.'

c) You will be expected to complete your work within ....

d) I'm sorry, but this matter is not within my .... You will have to refer to a higher authority.

e) Provided you live within your ...., you won't get into debt.

f) As long as we stay within .... , we won't have any legal problems.

g) There are several shops within easy .... of the house.

h) The ship sank when it was within .... of land.

i) You can have anything you want for your birthday, within ....!

j) Hurry up! The president will be here within ....

6

Suffix -ing
Rewrite each
sentence so that it
contains a word
ending -ing
formed from the
word given in
capitals.

a) There was a very strong smell coming from the chemistry lab.   POWER
....

b) Oh dear, we don't seem to have understood each other.   UNDERSTAND
....

c) I was really frightened by that horror film.   TERROR
....

d) The root cause of the problem is an economic one.   LIE
....

e) Building the hydro-electric dam is of supreme importance.   RIDE
....

f) The plane appears to be breaking up in mid-air.   INTEGRATE
....

g) The operation will not leave you with an ugly scar.   FIGURE
....

h) The government is intent on basing the country's economy on industry.   INDUSTRY
....

i) They will be cutting off the electricity in the morning.   CONNECT
....

j) I think you are making this problem seem simpler than it is.   SIMPLE
....

Words and Phrases 7

1
By
Complete each sentence with one of the words or phrases given. Use each word or phrase once only.

> the way   and large   the time   far   all means
> no means   and by   chance   myself   rights

a) This type of video-recorder is by .... the best available at this price.
b) By .... , I should give you a parking-ticket, but I'll let you off this time.
c) Please wait out here, and the doctor will be with you by ....
d) It is by .... certain that the bill will become law.
e) We met the other day at the supermarket by ....
f) By .... , the members more or less agreed that the new rules were necessary.
g) I don't really like going to the cinema all by ....
h) By .... , are you coming to the office party next week?
i) By .... wait here if you have got nowhere else to wait.
j) By .... I got back to the bus-stop, the bus had already passed.

2
Adjective-noun collocations
Complete each sentence with one of the adjectives given.

> high   significant   blunt   calculated   sound
> sole   common   scattered   heavy   standing

a) Jenny was the .... survivor of the air crash in the Brazilian jungle.
b) The island has only a .... population of less than a thousand.
c) Terry's old car is a .... joke among the people at her office.
d) It is .... knowledge that the director has applied for another job.
e) The management bears a .... responsibility for this strike.
f) The college expects a .... standard of behaviour from its students.
g) Janet has a .... grasp of theoretical nuclear physics.
h) The victim was hit on the head from behind with a .... instrument.
i) Buying the shares was a .... risk, but luckily it came off.
j) There has been a .... increase in the number of unemployed.

3
Have
Rewrite each sentence so that it contains an expression which includes the verb *have*.

a) A few days of our holiday still remain.
....

b) Old Mrs Jones can't climb stairs very easily.
....

c) I don't want to hear you complaining any more!
....

d) I do not intend to call the police.
....

e) I don't want to be a nuisance.
....

f) I really don't know where we are.
....

g) I am pleased to inform you that you have won first prize.
....

h) I can't remember posting the letter.

....

i) I went to the hairdresser's this afternoon.

....

j) Last Monday was a holiday for me.

....

4
Verbs of seeing
Choose the most suitable word or phrase.

a) Jack .... the map for several minutes, unable to believe his eyes.
A) watched   B) glanced   C) stared at   D) glimpsed

b) Would you like to .... the house that is for sale this afternoon?
A) view   B) regard   C) observe   D) overlook

c) Police .... the wanted man in the crowd outside a football ground.
A) gazed at   B) noted   C) faced   D) spotted

d) She .... her daughter's boyfriend up and down, and then asked him in.
A) watched   B) observed   C) noticed   D) eyed

e) I .... at my watch. It was already well after three.
A) glanced   B) faced   C) viewed   D) checked

f) The burglar turned to .... me and said, 'Don't you recognise me?'
A) view   B) regard   C) face   D) watch

g) I only .... we were running low on petrol after we had passed the last filling station.
A) observed   B) witnessed   C) beheld   D) noticed

h) Tony was .... the page, looking for his name in print.
A) scanning   B) viewing   C) noticing   D) gazing

i) I only .... the Queen from a distance before her car drove away.
A) watched   B) viewed   C) glimpsed   D) looked

j) Sally was sitting by the sea, ... at the shape of the distant island.
A) glancing   B) gazing   C) facing   D) gaping

5
Other uses for names of parts of the body
Complete each sentence with one of the words or phrases given. Use each word or phrase once only.

foot   head   arm   cheek   neck   chest   hand   leg   heart   spine

a) My football team won the first .... of the two-match tie.

b) You can't fool me, I'm an old .... at this game!

c) The hotel lies in the .... of the English countryside.

d) Absolutely right! You have hit the nail right on the ....

e) The trouble with paperback books is that the .... often breaks.

f) I sat on the .... of the chair because there was nowhere else to sit.

g) The village lay at the .... of the mountain beside the lake.

h) You have got a lot of .... to speak to me like that!

i) We didn't have a corkscrew so we broke the .... of the bottle.

j) We packed all our clothes into a strong .... and sent it by rail.

6

Do

Match each sentence a) to j) with one of the explanatory sentences 1) to 10).

a) He'll do you a favour
b) It does him credit.
c) He's having a do.
d) He just won't do.
e) He was doing over a hundred.
f) He does go on.
g) He'll make do.
h) He likes do-it-yourself.
i) He won't do you any harm.
j) He could do with one.

1) He is unsatisfactory for the job.
2) The dog is quite safe.
3) He will help you.
4) He can manage, don't worry.
5) He talks all the time.
6) He needs one of those.
7) It's his party on Saturday.
8) His hobby is fixing his own house.
9) It shows how good he is.
10) He was driving extremely fast.

Words and Phrases 8

1

Collocations: nouns linked by *of*

Complete each sentence with one of the words given. Use each word once only.

matter slip offer waste right
difference lapse price evasion term

a) As people get older they often suffer from this kind of .... of memory.
b) The opposition accused the government of a/an .... of responsibility.
c) The two leaders had a/an .... of opinion over the right course of action.
d) She said that her use of the word 'Baldy' was a/an .... of endearment.
e) The .... of failure in this case will be the loss of 2000 jobs.
f) The authorities have had to turn down our .... of help.
g) As far as I'm concerned, the meeting was a/an .... of time.
h) I feel that we should treat this as a/an .... of importance.
i) Our neighbours claim that this footpath is a public .... of way.
j) I'm sorry I said that, it was just a/an .... of the tongue.

2

From

Complete each sentence with one of the words given. Use each word once only.

memory home appearance heart today
scratch another life head exhaustion

a) What I am saying to you now comes truly from the ....
b) George can repeat whole pages of books from ....
c) The houses are so much alike that we couldn't tell one from ....
d) We decided to abandon all the work we had done and start again from ....
e) Two members of the expedition died from ....
f) She was dressed completely in white from .... to foot.
g) His paintings of the islanders were all done from ....
h) From .... on the price of petrol is rising by ten per cent.
i) I think he will feel much more relaxed once he is away from ....
j) From Carol's .... you wouldn't guess that she was over fifty.

3

Bring

Match each
sentence a) to j)
with one of the
explanatory
sentences
1) to 10).

a) She couldn't bring himself to do it.
b) This brought her quite a lot.
c) She brought all her powers to bear on it.
d) It brought her to her knees.
e) It brought it home to her.
f) Eventually she was brought to book.
g) It brought it all back to her.
h) She brought the house down.
i) She brought him into the world.
j) She brought it about.

1) It nearly defeated her.
2) She was punished.
3) She did everything she could to find a solution.
4) She gave birth to him.
5) She remembered.
6) She couldn't bear the idea.
7) She made it happen.
8) She was applauded enthusiastically.
9) It fetched a good price.
10) It made her realise.

4

Feelings

Choose the most
suitable word or
phrase.

a) I didn't go to the party as I felt a bit under ....
   A) the weather   B) the water   C) the clouds   D) the blankets
b) When he called me those names I just .... red and hit him.
   A) went   B) imagined   C) saw   D) simply
c) Peter agreed reluctantly to sign the form but looked extremely
   ill-at-............... .
   A) agreement   B) ease   C) heart   D) soul
d) When I saw the door begin to open I was scared out of my ....
   A) wits   B) teeth   C) blood   D) bones
e) I asked Ted to be frank so he gave it to me straight from the ....
   A) head   B) stomach   C) spine   D) shoulder
f) You look rather out of .... Why don't you see a doctor?
   A) order   B) shape   C) tune   D) sorts
g) When Diane told me I was going to become manager I was pleased as
   ....
   A) punch   B) a piglet   C) powder   D) a parson
h) Hearing about people who mistreat animals makes me go hot under the
   ....
   A) sleeves   B) collar   C) vest   D) chin
i) When Sally told me she was my lost sister I was completely taken ....
   A) to task   B) by shock   C) aback   D) with surprise
j) Sam is a happy-............... kind of person, and worried about nothing.
   A) go-lucky   B) over-heels   C) tempered   D) may-care

5
Well-
Complete each sentence with one of the words or phrases given. Use each word or phrase once only.

nigh   meaning   informed   advised   founded
to-do   chosen   done   worn   groomed

a) Carol reads a lot and is extremely well-............... .
b) Her attempts to help were well-............... but rather ineffective.
c) You would be well-............... to take out travel insurance before you leave.
d) 'Let's go for it' is becoming a rather well-............... expression.
e) Ann doesn't spend much on clothes but is always well-............... .
f) Peter brought the meeting to an end with a few well-............... words.
g) The rumour about Sarah's engagement turned out to be well-............... .
h) We found the climb up the cliff to the castle well-............... impossible.
i) I prefer my steak well-..............., please. I can't stand the sight of blood.
j) Harry lives in a large house in a well-............... neighbourhood.

6
Size
Complete each sentence with one of the words given. Use each word once only.

minute   miniature   massive   astronomic   reasonable
insignificant   medium   substantial   vast   sizeable

a) The town was defended in medieval times by a/an .... wall.
b) The two calculations varied in their results by a/an .... amount.
c) You can travel from one end of the park to the other on a/an .... railway.
d) It's a smallish town, but has a/an .... park in the centre.
e) Jean's handwriting is so .... that you can hardly read it.
f) The cost of building a tunnel under the Atlantic would be ....
g) Chorton is a/an .... sized city in the west of the country.
h) Travel to other planets involves covering .... distances.
i) It's a small flat, but the rooms are all of a/an .... size considering.
j) We have already made .... progress towards solving the problem.

Words and Phrases 9

1
Adverbs
Complete each sentence with one of the words given. Use each word once only.

extensively   broadly   largely   practically   invariably
widely   considerably   effectively   literally   relatively

a) The music from the four loudspeakers was .... deafening.
b) The factory is now .... given over to the manufacture of spare parts.
c) It has been .... rumoured that Mr Murwell is about to be arrested.
d) The weather .... changes for the worse whenever we go on holiday.
e) .... speaking, I would agree with Jane Bowling, though not entirely.
f) The decorating is ...., finished, and we should have everything ready soon.
g) The theatre was .... damaged in the explosion and will have to close.
h) We thought that this year's exam paper was .... easy.
i) Her career .... ended after her knee injury, although she did play again.
j) The government will be .... encouraged by these latest figures.

2

Time expressions

Complete each sentence with one of the words or phrases given. Use each word or phrase once only.

> | the time being | before long | this minute | while | shortly |
> | any minute now | by then | now and again | as of now | not long |

a) I see Sophia .... , but I wouldn't say it was very often.

b) Hurry up! They'll be arriving .... and we're not ready yet!

c) .... parking outside the main entrance has been banned.

d) We're supposed to finish at 8.00, but we won't be ready ....

e) The government is due to announce its economic proposals ....

f) I'm willing to put you up for .... , but you'll have to move out soon.

g) Come and clear away this mess .... , or there'll be trouble!

h) Fancy seeing you again! It's .... since we met at the Browns' house.

i) You mark my words; .... Helen will take over this company.

j) I'll be a little .... longer, so would you mind waiting?

3

Give

Rewrite each sentence so that it contains an expression including the verb *give*.

a) Why don't you phone me tomorrow?

....

b) Can you assure me that the money will be paid?

....

c) What makes you think you can just come in here like that?

....

d) You really make my neck hurt!

....

e) All right, officer, I'll come quietly.

....

f) How much did that car cost you?

....

g) The old wooden floor collapsed under their weight.

....

h) If you want to leave this job, you have to tell us two weeks in advance.

....

i) I'd rather have old-fashioned dance music any day.

....

j) Julia had a baby last week.

....

4

Modifiers

Choose the most suitable word or phrase.

a) It is .... certain whether the plan will go ahead.

   A) altogether   B) by no means   C) rather   D) doubtfully

b) To all intents and .... , the matter has been settled.

   A) purposes   B) reasons   C) statements   D) proposals

c) The minister has, in a .... of speaking, resigned.

   A) form   B) means   C) kind   D) manner

d) There has .... been no sighting of the ship for a week or more.

   A) constantly   B) hardly   C) indistinctly   D) apparently

e) As a matter of .... , I bought my fridge at the same shop.

   A) concern   B) fact   C) truth   D) coincidence

f) Some people .... still believe that the Earth is flat.
   A) surely   B) realistically   C) actually   D) truthfully

g) The plan is a very good one, as far as it ....
   A) goes   B) lasts   C) operates   D) seems

h) The police are .... certain who the culprit is.
   A) in some ways   B) more or less   C) here and there D) by and by

i) In some ...., it was one of the cleverest crimes of the century.
   A) aspects   B) prospects   C) respects   D) suspects

j) The work is beyond the shadow of a .... one of the best she has written.
   A) doubt   B) contradiction   C) criticism   D) suspicion

5
Words with more than one meaning
Complete each sentence with one of the words or phrases given. Use each word or phrase once only.

> blow drop bay deal plain
> burst hand minutes post set

a) We have been seeing a good .... of each other lately.
b) I don't want too much milk in my tea, just a .... will do.
c) I managed to keep the cold at .... by drinking lemon juice.
d) We decided to buy them a .... of cutlery as a wedding present.
e) The victim was killed by a .... to the back of the head
f) More than a hundred people applied for this ....
g) I have to take my watch to be repaired. The hour .... has fallen off.
h) After you cross the mountains you come to a wide ....
i) Fifty metres from the end Carol put on a .... of speed and took first place.
j) Sam was secretary and so he took down the .... of the meeting.

6
But
Match each sentence a) to j) with one of the explanatory sentences 1) to 10).

a) We couldn't help but lose our way.
b) But for you we would have lost our way.
c) Everyone but us lost their way.
d) We tried, but we lost our way.
e) You have but to ask, and you won't lose your way.
f) But for losing our way, we would have found you.
g) We had nothing but trouble and lost our way.
h) We've done everything but lose our way.
i) We all but lost our way.
j) Nothing but losing our way would have stopped us.

1) We had a lot of problems.
2) We managed not to.
3) That is the only thing which would have prevented us coming.
4) It happened despite our efforts.
5) We haven't lost our way yet, though we have had other problems.
6) It was bound to happen.
7) If it hadn't happened, that is.

8) It nearly happened.
9) Thanks for your help.
10) If you get some advice everything will be all right.

Words and Phrases 10

1

Put
Complete each
sentence with
one of the words
or phrases given.
Use each word or
phrase once only.

vote ease stop foot test flight blame expense bed market

a) The real culprits managed to put the .... on us.
b) When I asked her if she was Phil's mother, I realised I had put my .... in it.
c) In Saturday's violent storm, the new sea defences were put to the ....
d) When policeman saw the boys fighting, he soon put a .... to it.
e) After the second attack, the troops were easily put to ....
f) We've found a new house and so we have put this one on the ....
g) Having to repair the car put us to considerable ....
h) When the proposal was put to the .... , it was passed easily.
i) The sick man was examined by the nurse and then put to ....
j) Carol soon put the candidate at .... by chatting about the weather.

2

Run
Complete each
sentence with
one of the words
or phrases given.
Use each word or
phrase once only.

| luck pound police feeling riot |
| play money family eye house |

a) Peter has been on the run from the .... for three months.
b) In the second half the team ran .... and scored five goals.
c) During the recent financial crisis there was a run on the ....
d) Do you think you could just run your .... over this for me?
e) Having a good singing voice runs in the ....
f) I would have won easily but I had a run of bad ....
g) They gave us the complete run of the .... while they were away.
h) You can't really complain, you've had a good run for your ....
i) After recent pay cuts and redundancies, ... among the work force is running high.
j) The .... had an extremely long run in the West End.

3

Prefix *under-*
Rewrite each
sentence so that it
contains a word
beginning *under-*

a) We thought our opponents were worse than they actually were.

....

b) Fiona is having treatment for a back condition.

....

c) There are not enough people working in this hotel.

....

d) Harry's father arranges funerals.

....

e) The shop didn't ask me for enough money.

....

f) I managed to hide in the grass and bushes.

....

g) Edward got his promotion in a rather dishonest fashion.

....

h) The children had clearly not been fed properly.

....

i) The wheels of the plane fell off as it was about to land.

....

j) We have not yet discovered the cause which explains the accident.

....

4

Names
Choose the most suitable word or phrase.

a) What does your middle .... stand for?
   A) name　　　　　B) letter　　　　　C) initial　　　　　D) abbreviation

b) I'd rather not be called Miss or Mrs, please call me ....
   A) Mas　　　　　B) Ms　　　　　C) M　　　　　D) Missis

c) Her first book was published under a/an ....
   A) pseudonym　　B) acronym　　　C) homonym　　　D) synonym

d) Many people think that .... such as Lord or Sir, are out of date.
   A) prefixes　　　B) addresses　　　C) pronouns　　　D) titles

e) People are often surprised that the British do not carry ....
   A) identity cards　B) identity　　　C) identifications　D) identities

f) Her married name is Dawson, but Graham is her .... name.
   A) maiden　　　　B) childish　　　　C) girlish　　　　D) virgin

g) At school we gave all our teachers .... We called the maths teacher 'Fido'.
   A) namesakes　　B) pen-names　　　C) name-tags　　　D) nicknames

h) William Bonney, ... Billy The Kid, was a famous Wild West gunman.
   A) bogus　　　　B) versus　　　　C) alias　　　　D) ergo

i) It's a small black dog and .... to the name of 'Emily'.
   A) belongs　　　B) answers　　　C) obeys　　　D) responds

j) I .... this ship 'Titanic'. May God bless all who sail in her.
   A) name　　　　B) entitle　　　　C) christen　　　D) register

5

Call
Complete each sentence with one of the words or phrases given. Use each word or phrase only once.

question	halt	names	bar	box
mind	duty	attention	blame	close

a) The children were calling each other .... in the playground.

b) The police called a .... to the investigation after they found the letter.

c) I found a call .... , but I didn't have the right change.

d) David studied the law for ten years before being called to the ....

e) After the loss of our supplies, the whole expedition was called into ....

f) That was a .... call! We nearly hit that lamp-post!

g) Well, I must be going. .... calls, I'm afraid.

h) This kind of weather calls to .... the severe winter of 1946-47.

i) Don't feel guilty. You have no call to .... yourself.

j) I would like to call your .... to something you may have overlooked.

6

Verbs with *up*
Complete each
sentence with
one of the words
or phrases given.
Use each word or
phrase only once.

dream sell slip wind hang dig take cheer tot link

a) I didn't really expect anyone to .... up such an unsatisfactory offer.

b) Whoever it was on the phone decided to .... up when I answered.

c) A journalist managed to .... up some interesting facts about Charles.

d) If you're not careful, you'll .... up paying twice as much.

e) When they find out who has managed to .... up, there will be trouble!

f) The Russian expedition is hoping to .... up with the Americans.

g) Of course it's not true! He managed to .... up the whole thing

h) If you .... up the figures again, I think you'll find I'm right.

i) Why don't you .... up! Things could be worse!

j) The company was not doing well so we decided to .... up.

Index